PLANNING
IN THE FACE
OF POWER

PLANNING
IN THE FACE
OF POWER

JOHN FORESTER

University of California Press
Berkeley   Los Angeles   London

University of California Press
Berkeley and Los Angeles, California

University of California Press, Ltd.
London, England

© 1989 by
The Regents of the University of California

Library of Congress Cataloging-in-Publication Data

Forester, John, 1948–
    Planning in the face of power.

    Bibliography: p.
    Includes index.
    1. Policy sciences.   2. Social policy.   3. Planning.
I. Title.
H97.F67   1989   361.6'1   88–40241
ISBN 0–520–06310–4 (alk. paper)
ISBN 0–520–06413–5 (pbk. : alk. paper)

Printed in the United States of America
1   2   3   4   5   6   7   8   9

For my parents
and the memory of their parents

Contents

List of Tables

Preface

A book may be written by one person, but it is inevitably the product of many others. Among the varied sources of this book I find that one, one I seldom thought directly about as I wrote these chapters, lies at the foundation of all the others: my parents' emigration from fascism in 1939. I doubt that the word "fascism" even appears in the chapters that follow. Yet this whole book is about the vulnerabilities of democracy, about power and professional responsibility, about political action and ideology, inequality, domination and resistance, illegitimate authority and democratizing practices. These issues arise as subtle matters of everyday practice for planners of all kinds, for planners routinely work to assess future choices, to think practically about who we shall become—in our neighborhoods, in our schools, in our health-care system, and so on. Citizens and public servants can presume the legitimacy of established power only at great risk. But if legitimacy cannot be presumed, and concentrations of economic power seem to threaten classical democratic political processes, what then? What are planners to do?

This is no simple question. It is one of the classical problems that motivate the study of political philosophy, and it is one form of the more pressing political question faced every day by every political actor: "What is to be done?" This book draws from social and political theory to illuminate ordinary practical problems of professional, bureaucratic, and, more generally, political action. Thus, a second source of the chapters that follow is scholarly. Here my debts are many. Faculty at my alma mater, the University of

California at Berkeley, realized, as Stephen Blum quipped, that nature was not organized the way universities were. Mel Webber encouraged a group of graduate students and faculty to explore practical-ethical aspects of planning. Where disciplinary doors seemed closed, Martin Krieger blew them open. Jack Dyckman brought an authority and brilliance to the study of planning that remains an unsurpassed inspiration. C. West Churchman transformed philosophical arguments into practical strategies—and vice versa. In their different ways too, Michael Teitz and Richard Meier always found the heart of matters at hand, the one by probing, the other by changing the subject without doing so. Neil Smelser and Hanna Pitkin helped me to understand that social and political theory were all about planning, though they remained a bit puzzled about what went on in Wurster Hall, home of the Department of City and Regional Planning. They were not alone in their puzzlement. Fellow students taught as much as the faculty. Where issues of philosophy and social science seemed chaotic, Jan Dekema brought passion, insight, order, and humor. In the face of a diffuse planning literature, Dudley Burton was always thoughtful, careful, systematic. We worked to keep each other honest: Howell Baum, Stephen Blum, Dudley Burton, Bayard Catron, Janet Corpus, Jan Dekema, Richard Dodson, Chip Downs, Ira Kurzban, Meta Mendel, Leland and Donna Neuberg, and Gary Tobin—and of course we had our work cut out for us.

Back then, and in all the years since, Simon Neustein was editing, probing, refuting, clarifying, and editing again even before anything was written. I should have known what to expect from him later. More than anyone else, he is responsible for whatever clarity, grace, and power this book achieves.

Yet if one source of this book is scholarly, another source is empirical, based on lengthy observations of environmental review planners, several years of participant-observation in local and regional health planning processes, and, more recently, fieldwork observing and interviewing urban and suburban planners and planning directors. In San Francisco I had been lucky enough to meet Dr. Selina Bendix, then environmental review officer in the San Francisco City Planning Department. One spring day Selina listened to me describe my interests in the ways planners did their day-to-day work, and she invited me to the following Tuesday's

8 A.M. environmental review meeting. There I found a fascinating world in which building project proposals were reviewed, negotiated, investigated, delayed, improved, sped along, or sent back to the drawing boards; in which judgments of aesthetics, politics, law, and technique were often merged; in which the most simple conversations routinely raised questions of political and bureaucratic strategy. As the following chapters indicate, I have spent years trying to understand and point to the more general political and moral significance of what Selina's staff did each week.

Sometimes explicitly and other times implicitly, this book also draws from and seeks to clarify a somewhat mystified and inaccessible literature referred to by sociologists and political scientists as critical social theory. If I have been even half-successful, readers who are familiar with this literature will come to see its applications still more clearly; readers who are unfamiliar with it, though, should not find these chapters any less clear as a result. To avoid confusion for readers unfamiliar with this body of work, the "theory chapter" has been placed at the end of the book as a synthetic conclusion (Chapter Nine). Nevertheless, this book is directly concerned with planning practice. It therefore uses and reformulates, but is *not* for the most part "about," planning theory.

This book grew slowly over several years. Individual chapters have been widely circulated along the way and published. I have benefited from generous comments, suggestions, and criticisms from more colleagues and students than I might faithfully be able to acknowledge here. I am grateful to Simon Neustein for his persistent friendship, his ruthless editing, his criticisms of arguments matched only by his encouragement and hope. Without Howell Baum's encouragement and invitations to present material on planning practice with him at various conferences, several of these chapters might never have been written. Ralph Hummel, Ray Kemp, and Stephen Blum struggled with many similar issues, and their suggestions and questions were continually helpful. Jim Mayo and Sy Adler had a sense of the forest even as I saw only the trees; they asked for the whole when I saw only its parts, while I worked on earlier versions of the following chapters. The Planners Network was a continual source of solidarity. With an essential mixture of confidence and patience, Elizabeth Falcao also watched and helped this book grow.

Detailed critical comments have come over many years from Guy Adams, Ernest Alexander, Ricard Bolan, John Bryson, Dudley Burton, Bayard Catron, Barry Checkoway, Robert Denhardt, Jack Dyckman, Susan Fainstein, John Friedmann, Meric Gertler, Harvey Goldstein, Patsy Healey, Charles Hoch, Jerome Kaufman, James Killingsworth, Joochul Kim, Richard Klosterman, Robert Kraushaar, Martin Krieger, Jacqueline Leavitt, Seymour Mandelbaum, Lawrence Susskind, John Whiteman, and Michael Zisser. At key points Robb Burlage spoke to the connections, the concreteness, and the vision that any real critical social theory—and analysis of planning—must provide.

I am grateful, too, for specific suggestions from Johann Albrecht, David Allor, Michael Basseches, Robert Beauregard, Michael Breheny, Gordon Clark, Pierre Clavel, Janet Corpus, Dana Cuff, Judith DeNeufville, Richard Diehl, Charles Downs, Leonard Duhl, Louise Dunlap, William Dunn, Charles Ellison, Steve Ferris, William Goldsmith, Chester Hartman, Barclay Jones, Deborah Kolb, Norman Krumholz, Alan Mandell, Peter Marcuse, Peter Marris, Richard Meier, Kenneth Pearlman, David Prosperi, Lloyd Rodwin, Victor Rodwin, Shoukry Roweis, Donald Schön, Ann Shepardson, Bruce Stiftel, Michael Teitz, Michael Tomlan, William Torbert, Melvin Webber, Michael Wheeler, and Jay White. At Cornell I have been fortunate to work with Cathy Campbell, John Davis, Kieran Donaghy, Linda Gondim, Pierre LaRamée, Bruce Pietrykowski, Charles Rock, Annette Sassi, and Francie Viggiani, students who were natural teachers. Thanks go, too, to Lynn Coffey, Nancy Leonhardt, Jan Rutledge, and Dianne Wiegand for preparing earlier versions of these chapters, and, for editorial diligence, to Mary Renaud.

I am indebted also to a number of colleagues and scholars who work in disciplines other than planning and public administration. Helping me particularly to clarify a variety of methodological, institutional, and normative questions were Richard Bernstein, Fred Dallmayr, Michael Dear, Brian Fay, Frank Fischer, Tom McCarthy, Dieter Misgeld, Donald Moon, James O'Connor, Claus Offe, John O'Neill, Trent Schroyer, Peter Watkins, and Stephen White.

I have been very fortunate to have had such instructive criticism, and I hope that as a result this book will stimulate further and better work on the politics and possibilities of planning practice.

Part One

Recognize Problems, Seize Opportunities

Chapter One

The Challenges of Planning Practice

Planning is the guidance of future action. In a world of intensely conflicting interests and great inequalities of status and resources, planning in the face of power is at once a daily necessity and a constant ethical challenge.

This book is about planning for people in a precariously democratic but strongly capitalistic society. As we will see, the structure of the economy organizes autonomy and independence for some people, powerlessness and dependency for others. Planners do not work on a neutral stage, an ideally liberal setting in which all affected interests have voice; they work within political institutions, on political issues, on problems whose most basic technical components (say, a population projection) may be celebrated by some, contested by others. Any account of planning must face these political realities.

Planning can take many forms. An environmental planner may draft regulations to protect air and water quality or public parklands. A land-use planner may work more as a generalist, reviewing a real estate developer's proposal in the morning and drawing up an open-space plan in the afternoon. A health planner may assess community needs for improved prenatal care or for new diagnostic technologies, and then work to meet these needs without encouraging wasteful, however privately lucrative, oversupply. Their labels aside, each of these planners will remind us that they plan for people. This book explores the practice of planning and assesses the practicalities and difficulties, the challenges and opportunities that are presented by the pursuit of the public good in many arenas of modern society.

Notice that planners who seek to meet public needs face even greater challenges than their more romanticized private-sector counterparts, the corporate "strategic" planners. For publicly oriented planners need to worry not only about waste but also about social justice; they need to worry not only about efficiency but also about decent outcomes; they need to worry not only about satisfied customers but also about the food, housing, and jobs the perfect market promises and the actual market fails to provide. Compared to the job that public-sector planners have, the planner with private-sector clients has it easy.

Throughout the book, we refer to "planners" as a shorthand for a broad array of future-oriented actors, including project and program managers, public administrators, program evaluators, and policy analysts, as well as local, regional, state, and federal agency planners, both urban and rural. Thus, this book explores the vocation of planning for public well-being or, to put it more traditionally, for social welfare and social justice.

The vocation of planning has often been misunderstood in two ways, however, and this book attempts to provide an alternative to those views. Planning has sometimes been understood either as a technical problem-solving endeavor or (somewhat the opposite) as purely a matter of the hustle, bustle, and nastiness of politics. These images of planning have aspects of truth to them—there are often *both* technical and political dimensions to planners' work—but such stereotypes poorly capture the realities of planning practice. That practice is both far more complex and far more fascinating than these images suggest.

Planners work on problems, with people. The problem-work is potentially technical, but it may often be more craft-like or routine; the people-work is always political, sometimes explicitly so, at other times not. As the problems planners work on vary, from health-planning cases to natural-resource management to financial planning, the necessary techniques and technical skills required to address those problems vary as well. Likewise, the people-work that planners do will also vary from the local to the federal level, from voluntary organizations to public agencies, from administrative to staff positions, and so on. But nevertheless, a recurrent set of practical, organizational, and political issues confronts planners of all kinds, and this book is about those issues. Consider several briefly.

In a world of poor information and limited time to work on problems, how are careful analyses of alternative futures possible? In a world of conflicting interests—defined along lines of class, place, race, gender, organization, or individuals—how are planners to make their way? In a society structured by a capitalist economy and a nominally democratic political system, how are planners to respond to conflicting demands when private profit and public well-being clash? When planners are mandated to enable "public participation" even as they work in bureaucratic organizations that may be threatened by such participation, what are planners to do? When "solving" problems depends in large part on the interests, perceptions, commitments, and understanding of others, how can planners best convey their ideas, show what is consequential, expose dangers, and open up fruitful opportunities for action?

In planning practice, talk and argument matter. A rigorous analysis that no one can understand can be worse than useless—it can be counterproductive and damaging, just as it might also at other times serve deliberately to obfuscate important issues. The planner's knowledge of the organizational world matters, too, for a good idea presented the week after a crucial meeting (or too late on an agenda, or on the wrong agenda) will no longer do any good. The planner's ability to anticipate conflict matters, for without an appreciation of structured interests, economic motives, and organizational defensiveness, planners may present rational analyses to politicians, developers, citizen groups, and other agencies and then be bewildered when no one seems to listen, at least not to the merits of the case. This book focuses on these problems to explore the ways planners can anticipate obstacles and respond practically, effectively, in ways that nurture rather than neglect—but hardly guarantee—a substantively democratic planning process.

This book is organized in five parts, including a supplement on planning education.[1] Part One asks how we understand and risk significantly misunderstanding what planners and policy analysts really do. Part Two takes on the problems of power and rationality in planning practice: How can planners act politically, anticipating relations of power, and act rationally nonetheless? Part Three turns to the organizational contexts in which planners work: If organizations are not well-ordered mechanisms to achieve goals, if indeed conflicts are rampant and confront planners every day, what are planners to do? Part Four examines two activities that are central to planning but have nevertheless received far less attention than they deserve: the practical and critical work of listening and that of designing. Throughout, of course, the political and practical character of planning remains central. Part Five then presents a synthetic theoretical framework that links the arguments encompassing conceptions of practice and power, rationality and organization, conflict and its mediation, intervention and design. Finally, to explore a sorely neglected area of study, the Supplement on Planning Education provides an analysis of an innovative experiment in the teaching of planning practice. Consider now each of these parts briefly in turn.

Perhaps because I studied planning after receiving a master's degree in mechanical engineering, I was puzzled by claims that planners were "problem-solvers." When I studied environmental planners in the course of my dissertation research, technical problem-solving seemed to be just one small part of the planners' multifaceted work. A few planners did focus primarily on technical problems, as did some consultants' staff, but most of them did not. Although the technical problem-solving image of planning appeals to a sense of scientific legitimacy, it really sells planning practice short.

But if technical problem-solving was not an accurate description or metaphor that fit actual planning practice, what was? What about the essential and perplexing place of value judgment, accountability, the power of information, political bias, the structural political-economic setting, the (symbolic?) promises of public participation? Neither Charles Lindblom's solution (describing planners and administrators as disjointed incrementalists) nor Herbert Simon's formulation (describing decision-makers' lowering of expectations when faced with constraints) began really to face these problems. Beginning to account for the political richness, the practical judgments, and the complexity of planning practice is the task of the first two chapters, Part One, of this book.

Part Two argues that to be rational in practice, planners must be able to think and act politically—not to campaign for candidates, but to anticipate and reshape relations of power and powerlessness. Only if the practical context of power relations, conflicting wants and interests, and political-economic structures are assessed clearly can planners respond to real needs and problems in anything approaching an actually rational, if not textbook-like, way. Even the most factual information, for example, can mean different things in different contexts, in different institutional settings; and the planner who writes or speaks as if these settings do not matter is likely to fail miserably, to be misunderstood, to be seen as unresponsive, self-isolating, insensitive to the needs of others.

Furthermore, as Simon and Lindblom have made vividly clear, the planner or administrator who fails to appreciate institutional constraints will overreach and underachieve—and will be ineffective, if only because time and resources are always scarce, organizationally allocated, forcing bounds upon the practitioner's analysis. Ignoring the opportunities and dangers of an organizational setting is like walking across a busy intersection with one's eyes closed.

How can planners practically anticipate the shifting influences of the institutional and informational environment in which they work? In different situations, different strategies will be required. Chapter Three shows how the control of information is a source of power in the planning process. How might a "progressive planner," concerned with responding to structural sources of power and inequality, handle information any differently from planners less attentive to the biases of the structural settings in which they act every day?

Chapter Four provides a practical, political reformulation of Herbert Simon's seminal notion of bounded rationality. Distinguishing several ways that planning practice may be constrained or bounded, this analysis suggests a corresponding range of planning strategies to be used in differently constrained settings. Thus, this chapter provides a strategic account of what has recently been called "contingency planning." Only when we understand that it is quite rational to plan differently under different conditions can we then avoid the embarrassment of thinking and saying that our planning may be rational in principle (or "in theory"), yet anything but rational in practice.

Part Three examines problems of power and conflict in the organizational settings in which planners work. How do those settings provide the stages on which planners act? What should planners expect from their organizational environments? When faced with conflicts of many sorts, what can planners do? When planners must negotiate to defend particular interests, yet must act in some ways like mediators between conflicting publics as well, what can they do? What possibilities are suggested by current planning experience?

Planning organizations are, of course, constrained, but the planning process also recreates relations of political power: Some people get timely information and others do not; some gain access to informal and formal sources of power and some do not; some voices are organized and may be influential, whereas others are excluded and may remain silent and ineffectual. Whether in the public or private sector, organizations are not egalitarian utopias; differences of status, power and authority, information and expertise, interests and desires abound. Those realities—including the incompetent manager, the arrogant section head, the misinformed staff analyst, the fight between developer and regulator—cannot be wished away. Given such problems of daily work, what can be done? What can planners do? To address these issues, Chapter Five compares three views of the settings in which planners work: an instrumental, a social, and a reproductive view. Only the reproductive perspective begins adequately to account for the messiness of organizational life and for the ways in which planning organizations recreate themselves and broader relations of status, knowledge, and power as well.

Chapter Six explores how planners do what some theorists and practitioners claim cannot be done: simultaneously mediating between conflicting parties while negotiating as an interested party themselves. This chapter discusses the settings in which many local planning disputes arise, strategies that planners can adopt in response, and the problems—emotional, political, and administrative—that must be faced in turn. Issues of power are particularly important to set out clearly: Must planners who adopt mediated negotiation approaches co-opt weaker parties? Can planners at times empower such parties through these negotiation processes?

In a world of severe inequalities, planning strategies that treat all parties "equally" end up ironically reproducing the very inequalities with which they began. Nowhere is this paradox of "equal opportunity" more obvious and poignant than in apparently democratic, participatory planning processes—in which initial inequalities of time, resources, expertise, and information threaten to render the actual democratic character of these processes problematic, if not altogether illusory. Throughout the book we ask what planners, when they are so inclined, might do to foster more genuinely democratic politics in their communities.

Part Four turns more directly to questions of skill and practice. It investigates the central activities of listening and designing. Even though planners may often have little formal authority, they influence decision-making processes in several subtle ways. We have a great deal to learn from the ways planners listen to some concerns but ignore others, call attention to these issues but neglect or de-emphasize those, time what information they give to whom, and so shape other people's expectations, hopes, and fears.

Chapter Seven focuses on a critical but widely neglected aspect of planning practice: the daily challenges of sensitive and critical listening in the face of possibilities for future action. Not only essential to any investigation of "what is to be done," skillful listening is also a particularly practical interpretive activity. It is fundamentally important in those typical planning situations where issues and statements are ambiguous, where social conflict is the order of the day, and where participants' senses of issues and interests are fluid as well. This chapter reaches beyond planning practice to show how our work of listening well or poorly shapes the actual social policy of our everyday lives. Such listening in practice involves not simply having good intentions and hearing words, but also embodying respect, paying attention, employing critical judgment, and building relationships.

Chapter Eight explores the work of designing as a deeply social, communicative process. In this view, designing is not simply a matter of mastery and intuition. It is also a process in which social actors such as planners, architects, and clients seek to "make sense together" quite practically. This common creation of sense lies at the core of the social process of designing: giving meaningful form to a building, a park, a project, a program that is recognizable, coherent, significant, and realizable by a variety of interested parties.

In project-review negotiations in a local planning office, for example, planners and architects come to shared understandings as they review plans, criticize working drawings, and search for alternatives that promise better results—functionally, aesthetically, or politically. The design of the project evolves not only in the architect's or planner's mind, but more so in the shared sketches and drawings and proposals they can review and agree on together. What evolves is not simply an abstract form but a socially constructed offer or proposal that grows from a history of practical, working conversations that link interested parties. This "socially constructivist" notion of planning practice, and design practices more broadly, enables us to respect the intuitive aspects of the creation of form and also to appreciate the thoroughly social and indeed political character of the communicative process through which any working design is achieved.

The first four parts of the book, then, treat an interrelated set of problems. Planners must have not only technical but also political skills—but what does this mean (Part One)? What relations of power must they be able to anticipate? How can planners acknowledge the messy, political character of their work and yet be rational (Part Two)? What must planners know about the organizational environments in which they work? In complex settings, how can planners deal with diverse conflicts while not perpetuating inequalities of information, expertise, and power (Part Three)? How can we understand the political and practical aspects of the careful listening that planners must do? What of the political and practical dimensions of designing in a social world (Part Four)? These first four parts of the book thus argue that planning can be technical and political at once, attuned to power and rationality at the same time, interpretively critical and pitched to counteract needless suffering as well.

Having set out these arguments about planning practice, can we develop a framework to help us connect and clarify these central problems? Part Five attempts to develop such a framework. Chapter Nine builds on recent critical social theory to develop an accessible and politically sensitive account of planning practice that meets three challenges. First, such an account must do justice to the real, messy settings in which planning takes place. Second, it must embrace the everyday experiences of planners and make sense of their perceptions of the complexities, uncertainties, and ambiguities of daily practice. Third, it must explicitly address normative questions of information distortion, manipulated participation, legitimation, and ideological versus legitimate exercises of power. A critical account of planning practice—as the selective, communicative organizing or disorganizing of attention—points immediately to such questions: to the practical contexts of planning and the communicative, contingently meaningful character of planners' actions; to both the political staging and the dimensions of planners' arguments; and to the advantages of the organized and the vulnerabilities of the unorganized.

Chapter Nine argues not only that the day-to-day work of planners is fundamentally communicative, but also that the organizational and structural staging of that work is contingently historical and political-economic. Most previous accounts of planning have focused either at the micro-level, thus diverting attention from social and political structure, or at the macro-level, thus diverting attention from social and political action, daily practice. Chapter Nine argues that critical social theory allows us to integrate these levels of analysis. Furthermore, although previous accounts of planning and administrative behavior dealt poorly, if at all, with normative questions or problems of ideology, the critical-communicative account of planning advanced here makes such issues central: At stake in such a theory of planning is our recognition not only of planners' potential efficacy and influence but of their possible political functions and problematic legitimacy as well. Any theory that helps us to recognize these problems should also suggest what is to be done, and Chapter Nine seeks to work in that direction, though inevitably without providing recipes or guarantees.

How, one might wonder, can such a complex political and ethical practice be taught? The Supplement on Planning Education (Chapter Ten) explores a seriously neglected area of research: the practical difficulties of teaching practitioners, and the lessons to be learned from this experience. The supplement accordingly provides an in-depth look at an innovative and experimental course taught at the Massachusetts Institute of Technology (M.I.T.) on "Planning and Institutional Processes." Because this course drew together leading faculty-practitioners to assess and evaluate their professional practice in the classroom—as students explored various facets of that practice—this supplement affords a rare glimpse at the intersection of research, teaching, and practice.

The supplement begins by reviewing four case studies that challenged students and faculty alike to think through issues of growth controls and public participation, racism and community development, organizational learning and politics, and environmental mediation and associated problems of power. This supplement reviews the four case studies critically and also assesses pressing issues that promise to confront planning faculty, students, and practitioners in the future.

In sum, a critical theory of planning is no panacea. It is neither dogma, doctrine, nor a quick conceptual fix for timeless problems, a cookbook recipe for planning practice that truly serves the public. The critical theory of planning practice formulated here must be further tested: Can it help students of planning, in schools or in agencies, to recognize more clearly and act on the precarious possibilities of effective, ethically sensitive, politically astute planning practice?

It is true, of course, that theories do not solve problems in the world; people do. Nevertheless, good theory is what we need when we get stuck. Theories can help alert us to problems, point us toward strategies of response, remind us of what we care about, or prompt our practical insights into the particular cases we confront. In that spirit, Chapter Nine in particular seeks to capture the essential aspects of a critical understanding of planning practice. If this book goes even halfway toward such ends and stimulates others to carry out critical work that goes still further, perhaps both theory and practice will improve.

Finally, this book makes no foolish claim to completeness. It claims neither the presumptuous truth of having offered the last word on its subject nor the illusory, detached objectivity that so often leads not to freedom from bias but to misunderstanding and irrelevance. Instead, these chapters claim strong plausibility: that in broad realms of planning and administrative practice, these arguments about roles, power, rationality, organizational context, and practical strategies of intervention *fit*, that these arguments can enrich both our understanding and our practice of planning, policy analysis, and administration.

These arguments complement, rather than substitute for, other important analyses that must be done. Planning in the face of power is work by real people in real situations, but people vary and so do the contexts of their actions. The psychological dimensions of planning practice are not extensively treated here, and they demand attention. Likewise, structural political-economic forces that stage day-to-day practice are often referred to, but they are not systematically assessed in the chapters that follow; these forces also demand more attention. Thus, while this book provides an analysis of practice that is both general in its reach and practical in its focus, it does not present comparative analyses of different domains of planning and administrative practice.

Nevertheless, psychological, structural, and comparative analyses depend in turn on fundamental notions not only of what planning and administrative practitioners now do, but also of what they may yet do, may better do, in the messy and conflictual, the constrained, promising, and painful situations in which they work. As one stimulus to further work, then, this book attempts to present a pragmatic but political account of planning practice. Criticisms of these arguments must carry further the psychological, structural, and comparative analyses that will teach us about the possibilities of planning in the face of power.

What, finally, is new here? By developing an argumentative account of planning practice in which planners play a variety of roles, this book argues against several of the old oppositions and dichotomies in the field. Rationality and politics, incrementalism and radicalism, individual action and structural constraints, planners' discretion and established power: These may be distinguished in theory, but they must be integrated in any progressive planning practice. Many analyses suggest the various roles that practitioners may play, or the limits to citizens' participation, or the political-economic stacking of the democratic deck. This book seeks to integrate and build upon these lines of argument and show just what public-serving planning practitioners can do nevertheless—not in theory but in practice, in an organizationally messy world of political inequality and economic exploitation, and in response to Paul Goodman's continually nagging practical question, "Now what?"

Chapter Two

What Do Planning Analysts Do? Planning and Policy Analysis as Organizing

We know that planning analysts are not simply problem-solvers, but we do not know what they really do. We still need an account of what the practice of planning analysis is all about. By "planning analysts" I refer to a family of roles that involve deliberation about proper courses of action: evaluators, policy analysts, planners, administrators, and managers. To understand these practitioners as technical problem-solvers or information-processors would be misleading at best. We would do better, this chapter argues, to understand planning analysts as selective organizers of attention to real possibilities of action. This attention-organizing view can describe what analysts do as well as suggest the distinctive ethical responsibilities and opportunities analysts face in their daily work. Before we turn directly to this argument, let us consider the limits of two common accounts of what planning analysts do.

Two Conventional Theories

One widely held cultural view treats planning as technical problem-solving: Given goals or ends, planners are to figure out the best means to achieve them. A second view borrows from varieties of systems theory and treats planning as a means of processing information and feedback. Both views are appealing, but neither may be true to the realities of practice, as many students of planning have noted.[1]

When we look at the day-to-day work of putting out brushfires, dealing with "random" telephone calls, debating with other staff, juggling priorities, bargaining here and organizing there, trying to understand what in the world someone else (or some document) means, the first, means-ends, view quickly comes to be a tempting but inadequate reconstruction of what actually goes on. We might like to think that a straightforward rationale or goal justifies every action, but justifications are so diverse, so varying and wide-ranging, that no simple (and certainly no formal) overall end helps us explain what planning analysts do. Saying that environmental analysts or planners are working to "preserve environmental quality" does not tell us much about what they really do. Do they protect neighborhoods from disruptive development? Do they "preserve environmental quality" at the cost of slowing housing construction for those who need it? Do they enhance or thwart widespread public participation? To say with hindsight that planners and evaluators "assess or shape reasonable means to organizational or legislated goals" gives us more ambiguity than insight.

In contrast, the second, information-processing, view does bring us closer to day-to-day work in settings where problems are well defined, where goals and measures of success are clear, where co-operation between participants is extensive, and where we know clearly what an "error signal" is. But the opposite situation is more typical: Problems, outcomes, and even programs and outputs are usually not well defined; goals and outcome measures are ambiguous and conflicting; participants are often in conflict and may withhold cooperation; and "error" or "success" is not so obvious—what to settle for is half the problem.

Clearly, planning analysts do much more than "process feedback" to decision-makers. As they formulate problems, analysts preempt decision-makers; they define and select the feedback as well as process it. They watch for new opportunities. They face uncertainties that are anything but well defined and that cannot be routinely monitored. The "systems" and networks within the analysts' organization are fluid, as are those connecting analysts to outsiders. Problems shift, new people are contacted, goal statements change, program strategies shift. Planning analysts are more than navigators who keep their ships on course: They are necessarily involved with formulating that course.[2] Analysts do more than inform the players and orchestrate; they are inevitably involved politically in writing the score as well. The information-processing image of practice abstractly models systems behaviors as "self-regulating," but it does not help us understand or explain everyday practice and action. As one student of politics commented pointedly, social systems—the systems in and on which planners and policy analysts work—are no more politically self-regulating than the Bastille was self-storming (Winner 1977).

Neglected Dimensions of Practice

In complex political situations, planning analysts need to pose and create problems as much as to analyze them. They resolve problems less by calculation ("solving" them) and more by creating them anew, reformulating them so action and strategy are possible, sensible, and agreeable in the case at hand. Given complex problems, analysts often cannot provide either formal analyses or "all the facts." In addition to presenting any "facts," they also practice the art of the possible: They work to create new program possibilities, and they shape attention selectively to *these* program-design options and inevitably neglect others.

In a political world analysts often need to marshal not only information and data but also support. They are coalition builders as well as information accumulators. Because they have to shape the expectations of elected officials, neighbors, developers, and others, planning analysts cannot just render detached, distant analyses. The analysts need to be close to these people, close enough to understand them and to communicate effectively with them. Such contact need not lead to biased analyses. *Criticism is requisite to objectivity; detachment is not.* Objective and solid analysis may help persuade potential coalition members; detachment may simply produce irrelevance.[3]

To get information they need, analysts may require not computer access as much as a network of trusted contacts and self-interested cooperation, even if such cooperation is not always benign. If planning analysis were mechanical and not deeply political, information technology alone might be the top priority. As it stands, though, communications networks, formal and informal, are often more important, for without them information itself would be meaningless.

In addition, a set of questions may be far more effective in shaping action than a report, especially in day-to-day practice. What "flows" in the analyst-other interaction is not simply information, but responsibility—and the ability to respond—as well. When goals are vague, the environment unstable and uncertain, opportunities yet to be clearly recognized, and significant facts still obscure in conflicting stories, spreading questions can be as important for planning analysts as marshaling facts or processing information about a case.

Why Are Analysts Effective at All?

The planner's sources of influence include specialized knowledge or technical expertise, a monopoly on organizationally and politically relevant information, and the role of "gatekeeper" of information and access. Specialization may indeed inform the choice of means, once ends are given; information is both a political and a technical resource. Yet many other sources of analysts' effectiveness and power exist: widespread contacts; formal or informal bureaucratic and political pressure; bargaining with bureaucratic cooperation or possible delays; managing uncertainty and shaping images of the future; preempting definitions of problems and thus approaches to solutions; alerting, warning, or working with outsiders (or insiders); coalition building; and selectively calling attention to particular opportunities or threats.[4] We explore such sources of influence further in Chapters Three and Four. To assess these avenues or strategies of analysts' power and influence, however, we need another image and understanding of what planning analysts do.

Organizing Attention to Possibilities

Consider the planner or the public administrator who provides information to a neighborhood (or constituency) organization about a proposed project. A public works administrator may inform a local merchants' association about a street-widening project likely to disrupt traffic and pedestrian access to local businesses. A local planner may inform community residents about an apartment complex proposed for their neighborhood. In either case the planner or administrator is unlikely to telephone interested parties and simply say, "Hello. A street widening (or an apartment building) is being proposed near you. Hear? Goodbye."

Instead, the planner or administrator is likely to *describe* the proposed project; *indicate* the possible timing; *designate* sources of further information; *explain* the project review process; *alert* the neighborhood residents to their possible participation; *point out* possible alternatives that are being or might be considered; *specify* requirements for citizen participation, such as submitting written comments or paying appeal fees; *suggest* other interested parties who might be contacted; *notify* residents of particular meetings to discuss the proposed project; and *ask* for comments and responses to the proposals as they now stand. In these ways, planners and administrators shape not only facts but attention. Doing more than listing data, they deliberately call attention to both "the facts" ("The proposal just came in yesterday: I contacted you as soon as I could") and to future possibilities ("You might raise those questions at the meeting next week").

Simply to say that analysts provide information is correct, but not terribly helpful. *How* do they provide information, and what practical, political, and ethical difference can they make? The analysts' talk matters. When they speak, analysts act: they notify, inform, alert, point out, designate, ask, warn, and so on.[5] In asking for citizens' responses to proposals, analysts also shift responsibility to others and shape their participation, thus organizing (or disorganizing) attention both to project alternatives and to possibilities of action.[6] So analysts are not apolitical problem-solvers or social engineers. Instead, they are actually pragmatic critics who must make selective arguments and therefore influence what other people learn about, not by technically calculating means to ends or error signals, but by *organizing attention* carefully to project possibilities, organizing for practical political purposes and organizational ends.[7]

When analysts trust the reports and warnings of other staff

members, citizens, or friends, they subtly shift responsibility to those others and come to depend on them. Thus analysts protect good working relationships with other agencies, not just to get accurate information but also to cultivate trusted networks of contacts who can be counted on to respond sensitively, appropriately, and quickly. Planning analysts transmit facts, but they also shape relationships, political ties, and others' attention, thus shaping not only others' thinking but their concerns and participation, too.[8]

Practice and Politics

Once we recognize the organizing and attention-shaping strategies of planning analysts, we can make sense of much of the apparent noise of daily work: the endless meetings that socialize and co-opt no less than disseminate information, the persistent ring of the telephone, and—instead of others' willingness to reason together—the staff member's worry, the supervisor's pressure, the neighborhood resident's disgruntlement, the client's anger or confusion heard on the other end of the telephone, if not face-to-face. An attention-organizing view clarifies the politics of planning analysis as the means-ends and information-processing views do not.[9]

Goals and information are important, but they are not givens to work with or toward. They are practical and political problems to be formulated, reinterpreted, continually reevaluated and reconstructed. How analysts organize attention is the central political problem of their practice. They must stress some issues and downplay others. They clarify some opportunities but obscure others. They encourage the participation of some citizens, but not that of others. They open up particular practical questions, but they close off the discussion of others. Inescapably and subtly, then, planning analysts focus citizens' attention selectively. They organize attention to some possibilities while disorganizing attention to still other options. To ask how analysts organize or disorganize others' attention leads not only to questions about the adequacy, legitimacy, and openness of their practice but also to the same questions about the organizations in which they work—issues the conventional views seem to ignore, as if feedback flows and goals were unambiguous, clearly defined targets. The conventional views promise security at the price of denying the reality of politics.[10] The organizing, attention-shaping view provides both sources of practical strategy and political vision as well.

Implications for Daily Practice

Consider several implications of this general account of planning practice.[11] First, note that the planning analysts' daily actions are practically communicative—creating, reconstituting, reformulating problems as well as simply reporting on them. An analyst's question put to a building developer, the drafting of a section of an evaluation or impact report, even alerting a neighborhood organization to a forthcoming meeting—these are not only means to ends, but they are also communicative actions that build relationships, open possibilities, and shape others' interpretations of meaning and opportunity, of "I can" or "I can't." Revealing the deepest but nevertheless ordinary possibilities here, Stephen Blum has often characterized the work of planning as "the organization of hope."[12]

As analysts shape arguments, they can broaden rather than preempt the bases of policy formulation. Their ability to speak and write effectively—to argue cogently in a political world—is crucial. Rhetoric, the classical art of speech and persuasion, not sophistry, counts.

Second, planning analysts' organizations are not problem-solving machines with simple inputs and outputs. They are structures of power and thus of distorted communication—they selectively channel information and attention, systematically shape participation, services, and (often problematic) promises. Every organization reproduces a world of promise, hope, expectation, frustration, dependence, and trust, just as it may shape the natural or material world.

Third, the ethical and political responsibilities of planning analysts now appear in a new light. Because their actions are not only instrumental, the implicit responsibility of planning analysts can no longer simply be to "be efficient," to function smoothly as neutral means to given and presumably well defined ends. Analysts work in complex, conflict-ridden political worlds. So they must speak and listen, ask and answer, act practically and communicatively within multilayered structures of variously distorted communications, claims and counterclaims, promises and predictions. Under these constrained conditions, the responsibility of planning analysts is *not* to work toward the impossible perfection of "fully open communications." It is to work instead toward the correction of the *needless* distortions, some systematic and some not, that disable, mystify, distract, and mislead others: to work toward a political democratization of daily communications.[13] For example, seen as organizers or disorganizers, analysts become responsible for the parts they can play to prevent and correct false promises; to correct misleading expectations; to eliminate clients' unnecessary dependency; to create and nurture hope; to spread policy and design questions to those affected; to nurture dialogue about options and about the "values" and "interests" by which those options for policy and design may be evaluated; and, thus, to communicate genuine social and political possibilities, to say not only "Hey, that's the way it is," but also "Here's what could be done" and "Here's what we could do."

As any planner or public administrator knows, practical work is full of unnecessarily distorted communication. The very language analysts use in many bureaucracies creates such problems. Analysts often speak in a shorthand few others can understand. Public notices are often incomprehensible to anyone except agency staff. Ralph Hummel recently characterized bureaucratic communication with clients (what there is of it) as predominantly one-way.[14] After all, who tells whom how things are and what is possible? Benjamin Singer speaks of the "form work" demanded of clients before further interaction is possible. In many planning encounters, defensive behaviors include withholding information, suppressing feelings, and the strategic pursuit of unilateral control or dominance.[15] In so-called public hearings, exaggeration, fear, and intransigence often displace any public exploration of the issues involved in the proposals at hand. But Paulo Freire put it most powerfully: To deny other people's ability to communicate, to make sense, to understand and inquire both about what is and about what can yet be is tantamount to doing violence to them.[16]

The crucial point for practice is not that the claims of planners and policy advisors can be distorted. Of course they can be. Yet much distortion is avoidable, contingent and subject to change, and thus unnecessarily harmful to the relatively poor, the unorganized, the powerless in particular. Such practically alterable distortions occur in the simplest of settings. The neighbor of the building site calls, or the community group stews, and the planner is slow to return the call, much less to set up a meeting—editing the text of another report may seem more rewarding. Or developers have money tied up in projects and need to move them along quickly; they can afford to work more intimately, cooperatively, and co-optatively with the planning staff than can the various community organizations or affected groups. The control of capital by the relatively few in society means more than the possession of wealth (Gaventa 1980). It means access, time, and expert ability to press positions and arguments in both formal-bureaucratic and informal settings; it spells a systematic distortion of the possibilities of all affected people coming to terms with events shaping their lives. In their daily work, then, planning analysts face a recurrent political choice: to anticipate and partially counteract such distorted claims, or to acquiesce in the face of them, to be complicit in obscuring them from public view.[17]

Here lies a crucial practical and ethical issue for planning analysts. In a democratic society citizens should be able not only to find out about issues affecting their lives but also to communicate meaningfully with other citizens about problems, social needs, and alternative policy options. If the very work of planners and policy analysts is to shape the communications—the warnings, reports, promises, assurances, justifications, and so on—that influence citizens' action, then should not planning analysts be responsible to anticipate and counteract alterable, misleading, and disabling claims and learn to nurture well-informed, genuinely democratic politics and discourse instead?

Communicative Ethics:
Practical Action and Political Vision

How should analysts do such work? As analysts speak or act in practice, the ways they organize or disorganize others' attention inevitably link issues of ethics and politics.[18] How are analysts to understand their responsibilities and the possibilities here? We will explore several points in the following chapters.

Analysts should recognize that any organization shapes understandings, expectations, and hopes as well as any material services it may provide. Organizations provide their members with schemes of categories and stereotypes that affect insiders and outsiders alike. Adopting these schemes, we may be patients in our doctors' offices, employees at work, children within families, neighbors in our towns and cities, and citizens within nation-states. With each identity come socially constructed prerogatives, obligations, and relations of power and authority.

Analysts should attend, too, to the false promises of some parties and to the futile attitudes, mistaken expectations, or cynicism of others. Doing that, they can work to overcome both stereotypes of others and stereotypes of what it is desirable and possible to do.[19] They might help affected persons explore project and policy possibilities, consequences, values, and uncertainties. They might organize effective participation, building power both outside and within mediated negotiations, for example, and so explore various processes of participatory design or policy criticism and dialogue.[20]

Planners and analysts should also work to counteract the political noise and flak coming from the very structure of the organizations they work within: the flak intimidating outsiders, the noise confusing insiders, the peremptory, bureaucratic "that's how it is [i.e., must be]." Such work requires planning analysts to pose real possibilities of action, asking citizens for reformulations and new proposals, rather than simply "passing along solutions," so perpetuating "one-way communication," as Hummel puts it.

Analysts must recognize clearly that what gets done depends heavily on what gets said, and how it is said, and to whom. By doing so, they can seize opportunities to counteract a wide range of disabling and distorted claims: exaggerated threats, needlessly obscure and confusing analyses, strategically hidden information, manipulated expectations, and so on. Working in these ways, planning analysts can expose, however subtly and partially, unwarranted exercises of power and the resulting obstacles to citizens' political action. Those analysts can aid citizens' organizing efforts to reestablish legitimate and responsive public policy initiatives. The chapters that follow discuss these possibilities in detail.

In contrast to this organizing view, finally, the means-ends and information-processing accounts of planning analysis are empirically less fitting, functionally and strategically less illuminating, and ethically less instructive. To understand planning analysts' work as a potentially critical argumentative practice, selectively organizing (or disorganizing) others' attention to future possibilities of acting, appears to be a much more powerful account of what planning analysts really do—and can yet do.

Part Two

To Be Rational, Be Political

Chapter Three

Planning in the Face of Power

If planners ignore those in power, they assure their own power-lessness. Alternatively, if planners understand how relations of power shape the planning process, they can improve the quality of their analyses and empower citizen and community action. By focusing on the practical issues of information control, misinformation, and distorted communications more generally, this chapter will elaborate a pragmatic and progressive planning role for all those planning in the face of power.

Whether or not power corrupts, the lack of power surely frustrates. Planners know this only too well. They often feel overwhelmed by the exercise of private economic power, or by politics, or by both.[1] In health planning, for example, as in local land-use planning, planners must often react defensively to the initiatives of established, usually private medical care "providers" or project developers. Those providers have time, money, expertise, information, and control of capital; the countervailing consumers, in contrast, have few such resources. Nevertheless, planners in many areas are legally mandated to make democratic citizen participation in the planning process a reality rather than a romantic promise.

Furthermore, planners often have had little influence on the implementation of their plans. Those painstaking plans have too often ended up on the shelf or have been used to further political purposes they were never intended to serve. Given these conditions of work and the intensely political nature of planning practice, how then can planners work to fulfill their legal mandate to foster

a genuinely democratic planning process? What power can planners have? In a time of retrenchment, these questions become more
important than ever.

Once-and-for-all solutions in planning practice should not be
expected, however, because the object of planning, future action,
routinely involves the unique and novel. Even when planning serves
to rationalize economic decisions, it must be attentive to the special problems presented by the case at hand. Even technical problems that can be solved with standard methods exist amid conflicting interpretations and interests, established power, and excluded
segments of the population—all of which inevitably limit the
efficacy of purely technical solutions. But despite the fact that planners have little influence on the structure of ownership and power
in this society, they can influence the conditions that render citizens able (or unable) to participate, act, and organize effectively
regarding issues that affect their lives.

This chapter seeks to demonstrate that by choosing to address
or ignore the exercise of political power in the planning process,
planners can make that process more democratic or less, more
technocratic or less, still more dominated by the established wield-
ers of power or less so. For instance, planners shape not only documents but also participation: who is contacted, who participates in
informal design-review meetings, who persuades whom of which
options for project development. Planners do so not only by shaping which facts certain citizens may have, but also by shaping the
trust and expectations of those citizens. Planners organize cooperation, or acquiescence, in addition to data and sketches. They are
often not authoritative problem-solvers, as stereotypical engineers
may be, but, instead, they are organizers (or disorganizers) of public attention: selectively shaping attention to options for action,
particular costs and benefits, or particular arguments for and
against proposals.[2] A key source of the planner's power to exert
such influence is the control of information.[3]

This chapter therefore argues that (1) information is a complex
source of power in the planning process; (2) misinformation of several distinct types—some inevitable, some avoidable, some systematic, some ad hoc—can be anticipated and counteracted by astute planners; (3) such misinformation undermines well-informed
planning and citizen action by manipulating citizens' beliefs, con-

sent, trust, and sense of relevant problems, and planners can counteract these influences; (4) planners themselves sometimes participate in distorting communications and, in special cases, may be justified in doing so; and (5) because planners can expect misinformation to influence processes of decision making, agenda setting, and political argument more generally, they can counteract it in several ways to foster a well-informed, democratic planning process, thereby empowering affected citizens as well.

Information as a Source of Power

How can information be a source of power for planners? Four ways of answering this question are rather common, but we will also consider a fifth. These reflect the perspectives of the technician, the incrementalist or pragmatist, the liberal-advocate, the structuralist, and what I will call the progressive.[4] Each perspective suggests a different basis of power that planners may cultivate in their practice. We will discuss below how the different approaches to the control and management of information can make a practical difference in planning and in broader political processes. Although each of these perspectives will be discussed separately, in actual practice planners might combine several of them in any given case. For example, a transportation planner might strategically combine the attitudes of the technician and the progressive,[5] or a health planner might utilize approaches of both the pragmatist and the liberal-advocate.[6]

The technician. The technician supposes that power lies in technical information: knowing where the data can be found, which questions to ask, how to perform the relevant data analysis. Here, because information supplies solutions to technical problems, it is a source of power. This view reflects at once the most traditional problem-solving notion of planning and one of the profession's most criticized ideals—for it avoids, or pretends it need not concern itself directly with, politics. The technician supposes that political judgments can be avoided, that the political context at hand can be ignored. Adopting a benign view of politics, the technician believes that sound technical work will prevail on its own merits. But many planners and critics alike have been skeptical of this technocratic attitude.[7]

The incrementalist. The organizationally pragmatic incrementalist holds that information is a source of power because it responds to organizational needs. People need to know where to get information, how to get a project approved with minimum delay, and what sorts of design problems to avoid. Here, knowing the ropes is a source of power: informal networks, steady contacts, and regular communication keep planners informed. This is a social problem-solving view in which "social" is narrowly construed to mean "organizational." Planners do, of course, work in organizational networks in which different actors depend on one another for key information. Ironically, when others depend on the planners' information, that information is a source of power—despite the fact that incrementalist planners (as Lindblom suggested thirty years ago) may not know what good such power may serve beyond its impact on narrow organizational politics.[8]

The liberal-advocate. The liberal-advocate views information as a source of power because it responds to a need created by a pluralist political system; information can be used by underrepresented or relatively unorganized groups to enable them to participate more effectively in the planning process. This is the traditional advocacy planning perspective.[9] It seeks to redress inequalities of participation and distribution by bringing excluded groups into political processes with an equal chance, equal information, and equal technical resources. Traditional technical-assistance projects also fall within this view, aiming to provide technical skills and expertise so that community groups, among others, can compete on an equal footing with developers. The liberal-advocate focuses on the information needs of a particular client, i.e., the disenfranchised, the underrepresented, the poor, and the powerless.[10]

The structuralist. The structuralist paradoxically supposes that the planner's information is a source of power because it serves necessarily, first, to legitimize the maintenance of existing structures of power and ownership and, second, to perpetuate public inattention to such fundamental issues as the incompatibility of democratic political processes with a capitalist political-economy. The structuralist view, ironically, is reminiscent of the conservative functionalism of several decades ago, but now the argument takes a political-economic turn: The actions of the state, and the planners who work within it, inevitably function to prop up capitalism. The structuralist perspective suggests that planners have power but, despite their best intentions, keep people in their place and protect existing power. The planners' power cannot serve freedom.[11]

The progressive. Finally, the progressive approaches information as a source of power because it can enable the participation of citizens and avoid the legitimizing functions of which the structuralist warns. The planner's information can also call attention to the structural, organizational, and political barriers that needlessly distort the information citizens rely on to act.[12] The progressive perspective thus combines the insights of the liberal and the structuralist views and goes one step further. It recognizes that political-economic power may function systematically to misinform affected publics, by misrepresenting risk or costs and benefits, for instance. The progressive view anticipates such regular, structurally rooted misinformation and organizes information to counteract this "noise" (or "ideologizing," as some would call it).[13]

Each of these planning perspectives points to a different source of the need for information, and thus defines a different basis of power: technical problems, organizational needs, political inequality, system legitimation, or citizen action.

Since the progressive view builds on the other positions, it is particularly important to consider it in more detail. Emphasizing popular participation and planners' organizing practices, the progressive view also recognizes the obstacles to such participation. We will first compare the other views; then we will examine the progressive's position.

Limitations of Common Views

The technician is not wrong so much as intentionally neglectful. Politics is thought to "get in the way" of rigorous work. The political context of planning is understood as a threat, not as an opportunity.[14] Yet it was a political process that created not only the set of problems to be addressed but the technician's job as well. Therefore one cannot choose between being technical or being political. The technician is necessarily a political actor; the crucial questions are: In what way? How covertly? Serving whom? Excluding whom?

Following the publication of Lindblom's classic article "The Science of Muddling Through," the incrementalist view first found great favor for being practical, but then inspired no end of criticism for being unprincipled, apolitical, or, in a phrase, for admonishing us to "make do."[15] In its rejection of the rational-comprehensive call to get all the facts, the incrementalist position serves as an important antidote, but it says little about the improvement of planning practice, about what planners should be doing and how they might do it.

The liberal-advocate's view gained a more explicitly ethical following, in part for addressing issues of inequality, but it has been correctly criticized for failing to address the historical and structural character of these issues.[16] The liberal-advocate has been characterized as a nurse, ministering to the sick yet unable to prevent their illnesses from occurring in the first place.

The structuralist's position is as tragic as the liberal-advocate's: pure in intention, yet frustrating in practice. Finding all planning practice to be a legitimation of the status quo, the structuralist systematically fails to address real opportunities in planning.[17] The structuralist view may fail even to identify and exploit what might be called "internal contradictions" in the structure of the political economy and the planning process in particular. The irony of the liberal-advocates' position is that their best intentions may be betrayed by their ignorance of the structural effects of political-economic organization—for example, private control of investment, or the fact that an increased number of environmental-impact reports will not prevent environmental destruction. The tragedy of the structuralist view is that its apparently comprehensive position may be wholly undialectical in that it supposes the power planners face (or serve) to be monolithic and without internal contradictions.[18]

The Progressive Analysis of Power

The progressives have problems, too. Like the more strictly technical planners, they need good information. Like liberal-advocates, they need to supply information to citizens, communities, and labor groups in order to aid their organizing and democratic efforts. Yet the progressives need to act on the basis of a political analysis that tells them how the political system in which they work will function regularly to misinform both participants in the planning process and affected citizens more generally.[19] The progressive planner needs to anticipate, for example, that developers may withhold information or misrepresent likely project consequences, such as revenues; that consultants may be used less for analysis than for legitimation; that agency meeting schedules may favor private entrepreneurs while excluding affected working people whose business is their own daily employment; that documentation provided by a project's planners for public review is not likely to discuss project flaws or alternatives as candidly as project virtues; and so on.

Unlike the incrementalist or liberal-advocate, the progressive believes that misinformation is often not an accidental problem in planning: It may well be a systemic problem to be addressed and counteracted on that basis.[20] The practical tasks facing the progressive planner, then, are like those that community organizers and political actors have traditionally performed. Health planners, for example, increasingly recognize the need for educative and organizing skills to address the problems of daily planning practice.[21] Still, developing such educative, organizing responses to expectable misinformation requires planners to address several crucial, practical questions of political and organizational analysis.

What types of misinformation can be anticipated? Are some distortions inevitable while others are avoidable? Are some distortions socially systematic while others are not? How does misinformation affect planning and citizen action? What practical responses are possible? Might planners themselves be sources of distortion? Can this be justified? How can planners expect misinformation to flow through the relations of power that structure the planning process? Finally, in the face of expectable misinformation and distortion threatening well-informed planning and citizen action, what can progressive planners do in practice? The remainder of this chapter addresses these questions and the larger question of what this analysis means for an effective, progressive planning practice.

Types of Misinformation

We should distinguish several types of misinformation (see Table 1). Some misinformation will be ad hoc, random, or spontaneous. For example, in a public hearing a developer's consultant may

TABLE I.   *Bounded Rationality Refined:*
Communicative Distortions as Bounds to the Rationality of Action

Contingency of Distortion	Autonomy of the Source of Distortion	
	Socially Ad Hoc	Socially Systematic/ Structural
Inevitable distortions	**1** Idiosyncratic personal traits affecting communication Random noise (cognitive limits)	**2** Information inequalities resulting from legitimate division of labor Transmission/content losses across organizational boundaries (division of labor)
Socially unnecessary distortions	**3** Willful unresponsiveness Interpersonal deception Interpersonal bargaining behavior; e.g., bluffing (interpersonal manipulation)	**4** Monopolistic distortions of exchange Monopolistic creation of needs Ideological rationalization of class or power structure (structural legitimation)

speak too quickly or unwittingly use technical terms that the audience fails to understand. As a result, communication suffers, but hardly as the result of any systematic cause. Other instances of misinformation, though, will reflect actors' political-economic roles. Consider the remarks of James C. Miller III, executive director of a presidential task force on regulatory relief, indicating that industry representatives can be expected to exaggerate likely costs of proposed regulations, while government representatives (i.e., the regulators) can be expected to inflate the benefits of the same proposed regulations.[22] Such misrepresentations are clearly not ad hoc; they are rather structural products of political-economic relationships.

If planners can anticipate both types of misinformation (systematic and ad hoc), they can vary their practical responses accordingly. For example, impromptu and informal measures might suffice in response to nonsystematic distortions of information, because such distortions may merely be matters of blind habit. Clarifications can be requested; time for questions and cross-examination can be allotted in hearings, reviews, or commission meetings; a sensitive chairperson can intervene to suggest that a speaker speak more slowly, more directly into the microphone, less technically, and so forth.

In contrast, responses to systematic misinformation must be more strategic, based on the planner's analysis of the power structure at hand. As Steven Lukes argues, systematic misinformation is rooted in the political-economic structures that define who initiates and who reacts; who invokes authority or expertise and who is mystified or defers; who appeals to trust and who chooses to trust or be skeptical; and who defines agendas of need and who is thus defined.[23]

Some instances of misinformation might be socially necessary (that is, unavoidable), whereas still others are not. That there is some division of expertise and knowledge in society seems to be a socially, if not a biologically, necessary matter, not in the particulars of distribution (that being a political question), but in the fact of any unequal distribution at all. Some people will have developed skills for graphic arts, others for community organization, others for music composition; some might be mechanics, others painters, others farmers, and still others teachers. How the division of labor is structured in a given society is a political question—but that there must be *a* division of labor in capitalist, socialist, or future societies seems to be necessary in social life. Thus, some misinformation will be unavoidable; it will flow from *some* division of labor and thus of knowledge, expertise, and access to information. Other misinformation, such as capricious propaganda, will be socially unnecessary and thus avoidable.

This analysis of misinformation and communicative distortion provides the basis for a powerful reformulation of Herbert Simon's notion of the "boundedness" of the rationality of social action.[24] The rationality of action is bounded, to be sure; but how? How inevitably? How politically? We turn to these questions below, and at greater length in the next chapter.

Some constraints on social action may be necessary, but other bounds may just be social or political artifacts—constraints that are contingent on mere relations of custom, status, or power that are hardly inevitable or immutable. Working to alter the *necessary* boundedness of rational action may be foolishness, but working to alter the *unnecessary* constraints that distort rational action may be liberating.

In addition, some constraints on social action will be the result of random disturbances, but still others will be systematic, rooted in the political-economic structures that provide the context for any action. Treating random distortions as though they were systematic is a sign of paranoia; treating systematic distortions as though they were merely ad hoc phenomena is to be ethically and politically blind, assuring only repeated surprise, disappointment, and, most likely, failure.

How Misinformation Can Manipulate Action

How can information and communication, always potentially distorted, shape the actions of the people with whom planners work?[25] How can a politician's promise, a developer's project proposal, or a planner's report influence the actions of city residents? Informed and unmanipulated citizen action depends on four practical criteria in social interaction.[26] In every interaction, a speaker may speak more or less (1) comprehensibly, (2) sincerely, (3) appropriately or legitimately in the context at hand, and (4) accurately. In every interaction, too, a listener's subsequent action depends in part on how these same four criteria are satisfied. Consider each briefly in turn.

First, depending on the terms in which issues are discussed, citizens may find the issues clear or barely comprehensible, relevant to their own concerns or not, framed in ordinary language or in bureaucratese. Planners may, for example, either pinpoint key issues or bury them in data, verbiage, computer printouts, or irrelevant details—and what citizens understand, their *comprehension,* will grow or suffer as a result.

Second, depending on the intentions with which issues are presented, citizens may find their trust deserved or not. Citizens may be misled by false assurances of self-protecting agency staff, by technicians who claim to be neutral, or by established interests who deceptively claim to serve the greater public good. Thus public *trust*, always precarious, may be honored or manipulated.

Third, depending on what justifications are used as issues are presented, citizens may find their consent manipulated or not. Agency staff may claim legitimacy because the proper procedures have been followed; rivals within the community may claim legitimacy because they are acting in the public interest, acting to right wrongs, or acting as representatives of populations in need. In each case, the claim to legitimacy is an attempt to shape citizens' action through the mobilization of their *consent*.

Fourth, depending on the use of evidence and data, citizens may find issues either misrepresented or reported accurately. Politicians and project proponents and opponents alike may exaggerate or fabricate estimates of costs, benefits, risks, and opportunities. Whether or not the truth sets anyone free, systematic misrepresentation in the planning process is likely to breed cynicism, cripple action, and manipulate citizens' *beliefs* as well.[27]

There is no guarantee against the presence of manipulation in planning. Informed planning and citizen action are vulnerable to the mismanagement (whether ad hoc or systematic) of planners' and citizens' comprehension, trust, consent, and beliefs. Tables 2 and 3 show how such mismanagement can occur as the exercise of power through the processes of decision making, agenda setting, or the shaping of people's felt needs.

Responses to Misinformation

Each of the four criteria suggests how different types of misinformation can influence participation in the planning process.[28] More important, each type of misinformation calls for a different type of response from planners. The progressive planner may counter the manipulation of a neighborhood organization's trust by revealing previous instances of such misinformation presented to other neighborhoods—in the case of a developer's suspicious promise, for example. By weeding jargon out of communications and by calling attention to important planning issues that might otherwise be obscured by the sheer volume of data in consultants' reports or

TABLE 2. *Power, Information, and Misinformation:*
The Management of Comprehension, Trust, Consent, and Knowledge

Forms of Misinformation

Modes Through Which Power May Be Exercised	Managing Comprehension (problem framing)	Managing Trust (false assurance)	Managing Consent (illegitimacy)	Managing Knowledge (misrepresentation)
Decision making	Resolutions passed with deliberate ambiguity; confusing rhetoric, e.g., "the truly needy"	"Symbolic" decisions (false promises)	Decisions reached without legitimate representation of public interests but appealing to public consent as if this were not the case	Decisions that misrepresent actual possibilities to the public (e.g., the effectiveness of insufficiently tested medications)
Agenda setting	Obfuscating issues through jargon or quantity of "information"	Marshaling respectable personages to gain trust (independent of substance)	Arguing, e.g., that a political issue is actually a technical issue best left to experts	Before decisions are made, misrepresenting costs, benefits, risks, true options
Shaping felt needs	Diagnosis, definition of problem or solution through ideological language	Ritualistic appeals to "openness," "public interest," and "responsiveness"; encouraging dependence on benign apolitical others	Appeals to the adequacy and efficacy of formal "participatory" processes or market mechanisms without addressing their systematic failures	Ideological or deceptive presentation of needs, requirements, or sources of satisfaction (false advertising, "analysis for hire")

TABLE 3. *Power and Misinformation in Health Planning:*
An Illustration of the Management of Comprehension, Trust, Consent, and Knowledge

Modes Through Which Power May Be Exercised	Forms of Misinformation			
	Managing Comprehension (problem framing)	Managing Trust (false assurance)	Managing Consent (illegitimacy)	Managing Knowledge (misrepresentation)
Decision making	Mute and suppress disagreements, differences of opinion, and conflicts within the board	Appear "democratic"; claim to be "representative," "objective"	Control committee nominations and official appointments	Focus on task only; ignore process, hide omissions
Agenda setting	Overwhelm the board with data	Ensure that sympathetic professionals chair the board and key committees	Selectively schedule and time announcements; use professional language	Avoid sensitive issues of current relevance to the agency
Shaping felt needs	Claim that the best kind of training program is one where the information flows one way, from an expert to the board members	Avoid group-process type training and training in conflict and negotiation skills	Avoid staff who are trained in community organizing	Provide information so consumers believe they need what you already think they need

Source: Adapted from Steckler and Herzog (1979).

proposals, planners may avoid the assault on comprehension that can paralyze citizen action. A hospital administrator's inflated claim to expertise to gain the consent of consumers in a health-planning agency may be countered by marshaling dissenting expertise or by exploring the issue to clarify just what expertise is appropriate in the case at hand. Finally, planners may counteract the management of citizens' beliefs or knowledge by promoting project-review criticism and debate and by further politicizing planning processes. "Politicizing" here means more democratically structured, publicly aired political argument, not more covert wheeling and dealing.

In land-use and health-planning processes, such corrective actions are variants of organizing strategies in communities and bureaucracies. They seek to enable informed participation that recognizes the rights of others but is skeptical of the purported benevolence of established interests that stand to reap substantial private gains from proposed projects.[29] Informing the "affected but unorganized" earlier rather than later in the planning process is one simple rule of thumb that helps to counter the varieties of misinformation: commonplace acts of checking, double-checking, testing, consulting experts, seeking third-party counsel, clarifying issues, exposing assumptions, reviewing and citing the record, appealing to precedent, invoking traditional values (democratic participation, for example), spreading questions about unexplored work of Allan Jacobs in San Francisco and of Norman Krumholz in Cleveland.)[30]

Yet what is crucial here is not any new progressive social technology or political gimmickry. Planners already have a vast repertoire of practical responses with which they can counteract misinformation: commonplace acts of checking, double-checking, testing, consulting experts, seeking third-party counsel, clarifying issues, exposing assumptions, reviewing and citing the record, appealing to precedent, invoking traditional values (democratic participation, for example), spreading questions about unexplored possibilities, spotlighting jargon and revealing meaning, negotiating for clearly specified outcomes and values, working through informal networks to get information, bargaining for information, holding others to public commitments, and so on.[31]

Progressive planners, therefore, must learn to anticipate misinformation before the fact, when something may still be done to counteract it. The more traditional perspectives treat information problems as either inevitable or ad hoc (see Table 1), and as a result, planners often respond too late. The practical problem, then, is not to invent new strategies in response to misinformation— such strategies abound. Instead, the planner must be able, as the progressive view suggests, to anticipate and counteract the practical misinformation likely to arise in various organizational and political processes (see Table 2).

With such vision, progressive planners can then draw on a repertoire of responses to counteract the disabling effects of misinformation in the planning process. Only if planners anticipate these problems can they counteract misrepresentation with checking and testing of data. Only then can they defend against false appeals to trust by checking the record of past promises. Only by anticipating misinformation can planners resist obfuscation with clear and powerful writing. Only then can they address the manipulation of consent by invoking shared tradition, precedent, or established rights. The progressive approach thus draws on the vast store of strategies that planners and citizens already possess; it also suggests that planners and citizens can anticipate misinformation in time to *use* those strategies effectively, rather than looking back regretfully and saying, "Well, what we should have done was . . ."

These responses involve risks to planners that depend both on the internal support for planners in planning departments and on the external support planners receive from other agencies, community groups, or established figures.[32] How much risk is involved should be neither minimized nor exaggerated, but further assessed in theory and in practice.[33]

Planners as Sources of Misinformation

Planners themselves can produce misinformation. They often work within pressing time constraints, with limited data. In addition, they often face organizational and political pressures to legitimate existing processes, to mitigate or avoid conflict, and to gain consensus and consent from potentially warring factions (developers, community groups, labor representatives) whenever possible. Under such conditions, planners can sometimes exacerbate the problems caused by misinformation: misrepresentation of facts, improper appeals to expertise or precedent, misleading statements of intentions, or the obfuscation of significant issues. Moreover, the production of misinformation by planners often does not occur just by happenstance; rather, it may be encouraged by the very structure of the bureaucracies in which the planners work.

There can be no guarantee that planners will not produce misinformation. Yet two questions are crucial for planning practice: First, when can misinformation be ethically justified or rejected?[34] Second, if misinformation cannot be prevented, what good comes from an analysis of these problems?

The ethics regarding misinformation from planners (and from professionals more generally) has been a neglected topic in the planning profession until recently. In the last several years, a number of studies have begun to address these issues, and they provide guidance for the isolated justification—but more frequently for the rejection—of planning actions that distort communications; for instance, withholding information, or exaggerating risks or uncertainties.[35] Acts depend on particular contexts for their sense and meaning; so must any ethical justification or rejection, seeking to protect human integrity, autonomy, and welfare, be interpreted and applied anew in particular historical contexts. If general ethical principles are not applied to specific cases, planners risk becoming dogmatists, blind to the requirements of specific cases, or sheer relativists, thinking that whatever seems right in the situation will suffice. Rigid adherence to formal principle, then, may callously substitute ready-made solutions for discriminating and sensitive ethical judgments. Situational relativism, in contrast, actually provides an ethics of convenience for the powerful. When the situation decides, then those with the power to define the situation really decide, and "right" is reduced to "might." Thus, at either extreme, questions of genuine justification in practice become meaningless.[36] How then are planners to apply general principles protecting integrity, autonomy, and welfare to concrete cases?

We might ordinarily wish to discourage lying, for example, because of the corrosive effect it has on social trust, but in some special circumstances we might justify it: such as deceiving a violent assailant about the whereabouts of his or her victim who has taken refuge in our house.[37] Similarly, misinforming actions by planners may at special times be justified, too, but only under particular and rare conditions, and hardly as often as might be supposed: when reasonable alternatives (as judged by a diverse, informed public) are not available; when the informed consent of others may be available (a client requests a rough summary of issues, not a more precise technical analysis); or when substantial and serious harm may be done otherwise. Each of these conditions is quite "soft" and open to a range of interpretations, but each may nevertheless be useful for the evaluation of planners' possible misinforming actions.

In the face of ever-changing historical circumstances that demand practical action, any general ethical analysis must be largely indeterminate. Yet the analysis of misinformation still can serve a politically critical function. Only after the types of misinformation that may be produced by planners are distinguished can concrete alternatives in specific circumstances be examined—and only then can we turn to the questions of justification or rejection. This chapter cannot offer ethical judgments independent of all practical cases, but it can and does serve, first, to identify the types of misinformation (whether produced or faced by planners, or both); second, to identify a repertoire of responses to misinformation; and third, to suggest how ethically to evaluate practical strategies for presenting, withholding, checking, or challenging information in the planning process. How, then, can planners work in the face of power?

The Structural Sources of Misinformation

In practice, how planners respond to misinformation will depend in part on their view of the sources of that misinformation. If they perceive misinformation to be accidental or unique to particular communities or types of projects, they are likely to work in a more ad hoc manner than if they view it as structural, to be routinely expected and countered. Questions about the sources of misinformation therefore become immediately practical. What types and mechanisms of power are faced by planners and by citizens affected by the planning process, and how influential are these modes of power? How does such power work, and how is it limited or vulnerable?

Extending Steven Lukes's cogent analysis, we can explore three answers to these questions.[38] Each answer will suggest different strategies for progressive planners to employ. One exercise of power can be understood by focusing—as the pluralists do— on decision making. Decision-makers can inform or misinform citizens effectively by virtue of their ability to prevail in formal decision-making situations.

A subtler exercise of power occurs in the setting of agendas— controlling which citizens find out what and when, about which projects, which options, and what they might be able to do as a result. Such power is immediately reminiscent of the information-brokering roles often attributed to planners: Shaping who finds out what and when often shapes action (and inaction).[39]

Yet another, still more insidious, exercise of power exists in the ability of major actors to shape the self-conceptions, the sense of legitimate expectations, and finally the needs of citizens: for example, the conceptions that citizens must acquiesce in the face of big government and big business; that socialism for poor and middle-income people is perverse, but appropriate for the wealthy who control investment; that individual market consumption will fulfill all needs; and that collective action is not a public responsibility but a nuisance.[40] Difficult to measure, this form of power nevertheless seems undeniable.

Each of these three modes of power can thwart the efforts of planners and informed citizens who seek to participate in a democratic planning process. Each of these modes—control of decision making, agenda setting, and needs shaping—can create misinformation that not only subverts informed and articulate citizen participation, but also weakens working relationships between planners and citizens. In health planning, for example, hospitals that propose expansion often utilize the pomp and circumstance of their medical staff to manipulate the trust and consent of consumer members of health-planning boards.[41] Consumer participation may then become characterized by passivity and deference, and progressive planning staff who question the need for expansion may come to be viewed with suspicion by the consumers. In such a case, the hospital staff members exert power not through decision making, but through their ability to shape agendas of discussion and citizens' perceived needs. But how are these agendas and self-perceptions shaped? Why do the consumer board members listen?

Power as Political Communication

Hospital staff members in the above example are able to exert power because the information they present—and the way they communicate—is highly political.[42] They very selectively inform and misinform citizens. They may call attention to particular apparent needs and obscure others, whatever the resources available to meet those needs. Appealing to the public trust in their reputation and their record of community service, hospitals may stress pressing community problems and their devotion and commitment to addressing them. They may appear to welcome legitimate, open discussion and public education while simultaneously ignoring the inability of significantly affected populations to join in those discussions. They may omit a careful analysis of public-serving alternatives to the proposed expansion and thus misrepresent the actual planning options faced by the health-planning body. In each of these cases—and they are all common enough, as any review of public participation in planning reveals—the established and often private "developer" can exert power through the control of information.

By informing or misinforming citizens, power works through the management of comprehension, or obfuscation; of trust, or false assurance; of consent, or manipulated agreement; and of knowledge, or misrepresentation.[43] Each of the three modes of power works in this way, either to thwart democratic participation and encourage passivity, or to encourage articulate political action and the realization of a democratic planning process (see Tables 2 and 3).[44]

Anticipating Misinformation: Progressive Planning Responses

The progressive planner seeks to anticipate and counteract misinformation that hampers publicly accessible, informed, and participatory planning. Each mode of power (decision making, agenda setting, and needs shaping) and each dimension of misinformation (obfuscation, false assurance, pretension to legitimacy, or misrepresentation of facts) may present distinct obstacles to progressive planning practice, and each obstacle calls for a distinct response.[45] As discussed here, planners can prepare participants in the planning process to face such misinformation—sometimes preparing them with facts, sometimes with questions and arguments, sometimes with expertise, and at other times just with an early warning.

Planners can respond to decision-making power by anticipating political pressures and mobilizing countervailing support.[46] Anticipating the agenda-setting attempts of established interests, planners can respond through a variety of informal, information-brokering roles, keenly attuned to the timing of the planning process, its stages and procedures, and the interests and perceptions of the participants all along the way. In addition, planners may work to include or seek ties to those traditionally excluded, encouraging attention to alternatives that dominant interests might otherwise suppress. As presented here, then, progressive planning practice represents a refinement of traditional advocacy planning, a refinement based on the practical recognition of systematic sources of misinformation. Finally, planners who anticipate the attempts of established interests to shape the perceived needs of citizens may not only work against such needs-shaping rhetoric, but they may also encourage, or ally themselves with, progressive, local organizing efforts. In the face of these modes of power, no single type of planning response will be sufficient. No doubt many strategies will be necessary if planning practitioners are to respond to, and indeed empower, citizens who hope to have an effective voice regarding the issues that affect their lives.

Conclusion

The power available to progressive planners encompasses the information strategies of the technician, the incrementalist, and the liberal-advocate, but it is more extensive still. Recognizing structural, routine sources of misinformation, the progressive planner seeks to anticipate and counter the efforts of interests that threaten to make a mockery of a democratic planning process by misrepresenting cases, improperly invoking authority, making false promises, or distracting attention from key issues. In environmental planning this means beginning with the demand that impact reports be intelligible to the public and not simply commented on at public hearings once they are written. It means countering corporate misrepresentations of costs, risks, and available alternatives, too. In health planning this means attending to preventive health care as well as to curative medical care, to workplace threats as well as to medical responses. In neighborhood planning it means tempering the exaggerated claims of developers and demystifying the planning process—and the rest of local government—itself. In each area, progressive planners can encourage and inform the mobilization and action of affected citizens.

Just as each form of misinformation is a barrier to informed public participation (see Table 2), so might an analysis of these barriers help citizens and planners alike to identify, anticipate, and overcome such obstacles to a democratic planning process. Planners can work to distinguish inevitable from avoidable distortions, ad hoc from structural distortions, and they may respond to these accordingly, so protecting reasonably informed planning and empowering citizen action as well.[47] Indeed, in a political world, any rationality in planning and administrative practice can be maintained only if analysts carefully assess the institutional contexts in which they work—as we will see in the next chapter. Anticipating and working to counteract distortions of communication that weaken democratic planning, then, progressive planning—structurally critical yet hardly fatalistic—is at once a democratizing and a practical organizing process.

Chapter Four

The Politics of Muddling
Through

What actions are rational for planners and administrators to attempt depends on the situations in which they work. Pressed for quick recommendations, planners cannot begin lengthy studies. Faced with organizational rivalries, they may justifiably be less than candid about their own plans. What is sensible to do depends on the context one is in, in ordinary life no less than in planning and public administration. The situation is a bit like that of the recent immigrant who kept stuffing a vending machine with quarters and getting pieces of pie from the tray below. To his friend, who found him doing this and yelled at him to stop immediately, he said, "What's it to you if I keep winning?"

In public administration, planning, and policy studies more generally, the situation is not as funny. The "vending machines" are erratic. They cost more. And the advice of friends, falling into two broad categories, has generally been unsatisfactory. One friend, taking the familiar rational-comprehensive position, promises that "you get what you pay for": To solve problems you must define the problem carefully, collect all relevant information, rank values, evaluate alternatives, and select the best strategy. Another old friend is one day an incrementalist and the next day a "satisficer," choosing not to optimize but to satisfy lowered expectations instead. This friend suggests that "you get what you can see": To cross an intersection, why look all the way across town?

Neither of these recommendations helps much in practice. The rational-comprehensive formulation can be a recipe for failure, and the incrementalist formulation could have us cross and recross intersections without knowing where we were going. This chapter presents a resolution to this quandary that lies at the very heart of administrative theory and practice. By assessing degrees of complexity in decision-making situations, planners and decision-makers may be better able to adopt a strategy to fit each situation, thus avoiding both impossible information-processing demands and unsatisfactory, "making-do," settling-for-less strategies. In particular, we will refine the practical strategies of bounded, constrained rational decision making by taking into account—and suggesting strategies to overcome—politically structured, unnecessary constraints on planning and administrative action.

This chapter has three sections. The first briefly summarizes the two major problem-solving recommendations offered by the public administration literature to date: the comprehensively and boundedly rational approaches. The second section reformulates the nature of the "boundedness" of rationality, suggesting practical strategies that are appropriate under different decision-making conditions. In Charles Lindblom's terms, then, the chapter's third section analyzes the politics of "muddling through" by assessing degrees of complexity in the decision-making situation. The conclusion summarizes the practical implications of this analysis for the work of public administrators, planners, policy analysts, and others.

The Rationality Debate: Comprehensive or Bounded?

Consider the basic positions in the debate over the comprehensiveness or boundedness of rationality. The rational-comprehensive position abstracts from actual decision situations. It asks ideally, "How should we solve problems rationally?"

The rational-comprehensive position, abstracting from the messy "real world," assumes that decision-makers have

1. a well-defined problem;
2. a full array of alternatives to consider;
3. full baseline information;
4. complete information about the consequences of each alternative;

5. full information about the values and preferences of citizens; and

6. fully adequate time, skill, and resources.

These assumptions are so strong that they make the rational-comprehensive position seem like a caricature, but this would be an unfair and misleading inference. The inclination, if not the temptation, to "get all the facts" is a strong one. The requirement to take a "systems" (or integrated, comprehensive) approach to a problem before spending money on it has been commonplace.[1] The rational-comprehensive worldview is deeply rooted in Western thought; it achieved perhaps its most classic formulation in Descartes's *Discourse on Method*. Indeed, to the extent that these assumptions might be approximately fulfilled, we might really be able to solve problems, to find best solutions, and to do so not by arbitrary guesswork. At the same time, of course, as virtually everyone agrees, this model is impossible to follow in any strict sense, because radically simplifying steps are immediately necessary in any practical application.

Herbert Simon and James March proposed another way to think about and, more important, to act on problems. They suggested not an abstract approach, but a behavioral one: Look and see, they suggested, how skillful decision-makers behave, and learn from them. What are the real conditions under which they work, and what do they actually do?[2]

Simon and March proposed that actual decision-makers face

1. ambiguous and poorly defined problems;
2. incomplete information about alternatives;
3. incomplete information about the baseline, the background of "the problem";
4. incomplete information about the consequences of supposed alternatives;
5. incomplete information about the range and content of values, preferences, and interests; and
6. limited time, limited skills, and limited resources.[3]

Under these "bounded" conditions, the world looks very different from the way it looks to the rational idealist. Charles Perrow summarizes succinctly the implications of this view of the bounded rationality of decision-makers:

Given the limits on rationality, what does the individual in fact do when confronted with a choice situation? He constructs a simplified model of the real situation. This "definition of the situation," as sociologists call it, is built out of past experience (it includes prejudices and stereotypes) and highly particularized, selective views of present stimuli. Most of his responses are "routine"; he invokes solutions he has used before. Sometimes he must engage in problem solving. When he does so, he conducts a limited search for alternatives along familiar and well-worn paths, selecting the first satisfactory one that comes along. He does not examine all possible alternatives nor does he keep searching for the optimum one. He "satisfices" instead of "optimizes." That is, he selects the first satisfactory solution rather than search for the optimum. His very standards for satisfactory solutions are a part of the definition of the situation. They go up and down with positive and negative experience. As solutions are easier to find, the standards are raised; as they are harder to find, the standards fall. The organization can control these standards and it defines the situation; only to a limited extent are they up to the individual.[4]

Under conditions of bounded rationality decision-makers "do what they can." But they might simply be "making do." The "satisficing" position is more realistic than the optimizing alternative, but it may be so narrowly realistic that it is not helpful. It provides no way, apparently, to distinguish more or less efficient solutions, more or less recognition of good alternatives, more or less insensitivity to important values lacking well-organized defenders. "Satisficing" and incrementalist strategies respond to the radically constrained situations faced by decision-makers of all sorts; yet these strategies may well, in turn, radically constrain the options available in actual decision-making situations.[5] While the rational-comprehensive formulation may reach for the sky, the boundedly rational and incremental formulations may tie our hands. Only by examining how problem resolution may actually be bounded in specific cases will it be possible to select appropriate strategies of response, action, and decision making.

Re-Bounding Rationality: The Political Boundedness of Decision Making

To make the strongest possible case for the boundedness of rationality, Simon stressed the decision-making constraints of cognitive limits—for example, brain capacities that were (a) relatively independent of specific political structures, and (b) arguably part of the human condition—hardly subject to change. Limited brain or computational capacity, he suggested, was part of the decision-making situation itself, and this alone rendered the rational-comprehensive assumptions irrelevant to actual decision making.[6] This argument is forceful, but it does not go far enough. Two practical questions arise.

First, what about those additional practical constraints that are *not* independent of specific political structures, constraints that are indeed politically structured and that press on public administrators and decision-makers? Second, what about those constraints on information that are *not* part of the human condition, constraints such as those that produce correctable communications problems? These questions suggest that the boundedness of rationality is itself quite variable. Some bounds may be politically structured, others may not. Some bounds or constraints may be necessary, unchangeable, symptoms of the human condition; others may be unnecessary and therefore avoidable (see Table 1).[7]

What difference might it make to recognize these various kinds of constraints? If we treated necessary constraints simply as if they were transient, we would be foolish. Conversely, if we treated transient bounds as if they were necessary and unchanging, we would be self-defeating. If we treated systematic constraints as if they were ad hoc, we would be dangerously misled. And if we treated ad hoc constraints as if they were systematic, we would be paranoid.

Again, what is practical—and rational—to do in a situation depends in part on the structure of that situation.[8] An analysis of the decision-making situation itself, in addition to following the very general rules suggested by March, Simon, and Lindblom, is therefore arguably essential to acting rationally and sensibly in that situation. But how can the decision-making situation be assessed?

The debates among rational-comprehensive, satisficing and incremental, and more political positions center on assumptions made about the actual decision-making setting. From the rationalist's idealized situation runs a continuum reaching to highly politically structured (and distorted) decision-making situations. It will be helpful to consider this continuum by beginning with the idealized assumptions and then slowly relaxing them. In each decision-making situation, different practical strategies will seem appropriate, depending on the level of complexity and boundedness present (see Table 4).

TABLE 4. *Rationality and Practice in Administration and Planning*

Type of Boundedness of Rationality	Conditions of Administrative/Planning Action					
	Agent	Setting	Problem	Information	Time	Practical Strategy
Comprehensive (Unbounded)	Rational actor	One room, closed system	Well-defined	Perfect	Infinite	Optimize/solve (algorithm, technique)
Cognitive limits (Bounded I)	Fallible actor	Room open to environment	Ambiguous scope, basis of evaluation	Imperfect	Limited	Satisfice/hedge, lower expectations
Socially differentiated (Bounded II)	Several actors; varying skills, insight; co-operative	Several rooms, phones, socially differentiated	Varying interpretations	Varying quality, location, accessibility	Varying with actors	Network/search and satisfice
Pluralist (Bounded III)	Actors in competing interest groups	Rooms in organizations, variable access	Multiple definitions (senses of value, right, impacts)	Contested, withheld, manipulated	Is power	Bargain/increment, adjust/check
Structurally distorted/political-economic (Bounded IV)	Actors in political-economic structures of inequality	Rooms within relations of power: differential resources, skill, status	Ideological definitions; structurally skewed	(Mis)information ideological; contingent on participation, "consciousness"	Favors "haves"	Anticipate/counteract, organize/democratize

Here is the crux of the argument. Depending on the conditions at hand, a strategy may be practical or ridiculous. With time, expertise, data, and a well-defined problem, technical calculations may be in order; without time, data, definition, and expertise, attempting such calculations could be worse than a waste of time. When information is needed in a complex organizational environment, intelligence networks will be as important as documents. In an environment of interorganizational conflict, bargaining and compromise may be required. Administrative strategies are sensible only in a political and organizational context—but what are the most important aspects of that context? (See the successive rows of Table 4.)

Comprehensive or Unbounded Rationality

Begin by considering the decision-making situation at its simplest. Assume that there is only one decision-maker to consider and that he or she is a utility-maximizing, economically rational actor. The setting is the decision-maker's office, by assumption a closed system. The problem is well defined; its scope, time horizon, value dimensions, and chains of consequences are clearly given or available in the closest file drawer. Information is perfect, complete, accessible, and comprehensible. Time is infinitely available.

Under these conditions there is a clear and distinct practical strategy to adopt: rational problem-solving or optimization through available algorithms and solution techniques. When problems are tame, information available, and time of no consequence, rational problem-solving is the order of the day. A single best answer is likely to be found, waste will be avoided, and political compromise will be irrelevant (for there is no one for our decision-maker to compromise with). (See the top row of Table 4.)

The Politics of Muddling Through

Bounded Rationality I: Cognitive Limits

Now let us relax these assumptions, and begin to constrain the decision-making situation. We retain the assumption of one agent, but now this decision-maker is fallible: Not always following the mathematical dictates of utility maximization, the agent permits hunches, intuitions, loyalties, and doubts to creep into the picture. The setting is now less isolated; it is open to the environment, allowing our decision-maker to view the behavior of others and allowing others to look, if not barge, in. The problem is now no longer so well defined; its scope is a bit ambiguous—are new funding sources in the picture or not? Next year's potential clients? Potential political supporters? Evaluating the problem—knowing what counts as success—becomes a little less clear. Is a client-certification rate of fully 60 percent good, or is only 60 percent bad? Information is now imperfect; some of the statistics are not clear, and important questions seem not to have been asked at all. It would be nice to know more, but time is now a scarce resource. A decision must be made within the month, and other pressing work needs attention, too (see Table 1, quadrant 1).

Under these conditions, the optimizing strategy is no longer likely to be practical or desirable. "Satisficing" will be necessary: Expectations of success will have to be lowered from finding the optimal decision to reaching a satisfactory one. A satisfactory, if suboptimal, decision will have to suffice. Investigations into consequences and environmental changes now become bets to be hedged. Shortcuts must be taken, estimates made, approximations settled for. With the realistic constraining of the decision-making situation from ideal conditions to organizationally situated ones, what is practical shifts from an optimizing to a satisficing strategy, as Herbert Simon has argued most compellingly (see Table 4, row two).

Bounded Rationality II:
Social Differentiation

If we relax the assumptions of the decision-making situation even further, still more constraints must be faced. Our fallible actor is no longer alone, but in a world populated by other actors, decision-makers, staff, and clients, whose skills and insights vary, even though they may still be assumed to be fully cooperative. The decision-maker's setting is no longer the single office but now includes several offices, each inhabited by a relevant person, all connected by telephone, mail, or computer services. The setting is now socially differentiated; a division of labor creeps in. Interpretations of the problem are also differentiated now: Clients are likely to perceive a problem differently than the staff does, and the decision-maker no doubt appreciates aspects of the situation that neither clients nor staff do (and vice versa). Information is now not only imperfect but is also of greatly varying quality, in equally varying locations, with less than simple accessibility. Time now becomes a socially precious resource. Not only is it limited, but different actors will also have different amounts of time to devote to the decision or problems at hand (see Table 1, quadrant 2).

In this situation, satisficing alone will no longer do. It must be supplemented by strategies of search through social intelligence networks. Simon has written about search as an information-gathering venture, for the most part, but here search is a deeply social process. Search depends on the ongoing cultivation, maintenance, and nurturance of networks: strings of good working relationships with contacts in other agencies, at various levels of government, in the nonagency community and the private sector, and so forth. Here the decision-making situation is no longer simply in a cognitively bounded or limited environment; it is now socially differentiated, and decision-making strategies must take that environment into account. So settling for less will no longer suffice. Our decision-maker must now be able to gather information by bridging organizational boundaries, by using social networks, and by tapping sources of expertise (see Table 4, row three).

Bounded Rationality III: Pluralist Conflict

In practice, of course, decision-makers face opposition and suspicion from other actors, as well as intermittent support. The real world of administration is hardly wholly cooperative. Other actors usually have allegiances and interests of their own. They may act to protect their own agencies; they may pursue profit, status, or other rewards. The public works department will not always see eye-to-eye with planning; the housing authority staff's position on a particular project may differ from that of the staff of the redevelopment agency. Private developers are at least as likely to resent the planning department's review procedures as they are to let them go unchallenged. Neighborhood residents may be expected to resist perceived threats to their local environment. Interests differ, the pluralist political theorists claim, along interest-group lines: Every organization reflects a particular mobilization of interest and bias, and planners and public administrators routinely find themselves confronted by diverse and conflicting claims of competing interests, articulated by competing actors.[9]

Thus in a pluralist world the decision-making setting becomes more complex. In addition to mere social differentiation, competing organizations further complicate the practical decision-making environment. Until fairly recently, for example, health planners worked in settings mandated by Congress. At state and regional levels, those planners and staff members of regulatory agencies worked with public and private hospitals, organized groups of physicians, a multiplicity of health-care "provider" agencies, and health-care "consumers," too. Beyond a simple differentiation of groups, then, the pluralist decision-making setting can now be characterized by differences in levels of organization, access, and interests.

Definitions of problems in a pluralist environment are multiple. Different interest groups have different senses and valuations of the problems at hand. In health planning, for example, the "problem" of whether or not to allow a local hospital to expand will be posed in significantly different ways by providers, consumers, and, perhaps, independent staff. The hospital will define the problem as one of maintaining access to high-quality care. The planning staff may define the problem as one of inflationary duplication of services sought by an oligopolistic supplier of services. Consumers may define the problem as a matter of access and control; they may feel that other services that are not yet available are even more important to obtain.

Information, similarly, now becomes a political resource. It will be contested, withheld, manipulated, and distorted. The problem of gaining access to pristine information now gives way to a set of problems about knowing what and whom to trust, what can be done in the face of misrepresentation, and so on. And time is now a coveted resource. Time allows search and research, contacts through networks, attention to cultivating support and resisting opposition, and further strategic action (see Table 1, quadrant 3).

Under these conditions, strategies of search and "networking," marshaling expertise, tips, and wise counsel, are not enough. In the face of pluralist competition and conflict, bargaining and adjustment are necessary—as Lindblom, perhaps most lucidly of all, has demonstrated.[10] It is not enough to seek guidance in order to devise solutions in a differentiated environment. That environment is composed of conflicting interests, and incremental bargaining is the order of the day, given the assumptions of pluralism (see Table 4, row four). Short-term political compromise becomes a practical incremental strategy, one that is all the more defensible if, indeed, there are "watchdogs" for all affected interests.[11]

Again, as the decision-making situation grows more complex, the appropriate practical strategies also become more complex: Practical strategies change as the practical environment changes. We must consider, now, one final layer of complexity: structural distortions of the decision-making situation, and the interventions required to counteract those distortions.

Bounded Rationality IV: Structural Distortions

In practice, pluralism may provide more consolation than guidance, for it suggests not only that conflict is ubiquitous but also that there may be little pattern to the conflicts that planners and decision-makers might expect and be prepared to handle. If every actor is simply seen to be a member of an interest group like any other actor, then there is no distinction to be made, for example, between the claims of a developer seeking speculative profits and those of a neighborhood resident seeking not to be displaced from his or her home.

"Power" seems to play a weak role in the pluralist account—which is peculiar for a political theory—because a rather strong assumption is made: the assumption that power is diffused so widely in the society that all important affected interests have an effective voice or "watchdog," as Lindblom put it in his classic essay "The Science of Muddling Through."[12] Calling this assumption into question is hardly radical. Is effective political power really so diffuse? Poverty in America abides. Unemployment early in the Reagan administration reached levels exceeded only by the Great Depression. Despite gains, women continue to earn roughly two-thirds of what men do for comparable work in similar jobs. Territorial and residential segregation remains extensive. Unemployment among nonwhites is staggeringly higher than among whites. Concentration of wealth is extensive, and the ability to invest and shape the direction of productive resource use is hardly democratically distributed. Indeed, by definition, investment in a capitalist political-economy is quite unlikely to be democratic, Swedish amalgams notwithstanding. This litany has a simple point: Power and the ability to act and invest in this society are unequally distributed, and those inequalities provide and shape the context in which planners and public administrators, and decision-makers more generally, work and act.

To say that all claims express interests does not mean that all claims are equally sincere or warranted or respectable. There is simply no reason to accept as equally deserving of public consideration a claim by the owner of a small business seeking a zoning variance and a claim by an avowed bigot seeking to send people of one race to another country, people of one gender to the kitchen, or people of one religious persuasion to the jails. Should planners, public administrators, and decision-makers who serve the public give equal attention to all of these views? Do they owe equal consideration to all views presented to them, to all claims made on them? To the hypothesis that the earth is flat? Clearly, the answer is no.

Instead, planners, public administrators, and decision-makers might well expect that the actors in their political-organizational environment are not simply randomly and diversely interested atoms, colliding and competing with one another in groups of molecules in Brownian motion. These social actors instead are often positioned with and against one another in social and political-economic structures that display significantly nonrandom continuity. The unemployed are unlikely to disappear tomorrow. The downtown business interests are unlikely to stop asking for tax abatements tomorrow. The unorganized and the poor are unlikely to suddenly appear informed on the issues that affect their communities and be ready to "participate" in the formally democratic processes of local government. Whether the actors in the decision-making environment fall neatly into two classes (as orthodox Marxian theory would have it) or not, significant, highly structured, and highly organized differences appear among vast portions of the population along lines of race, gender, ownership of productive resources, and wealth. Pluralist assumptions about the equality of effective voice, in short, seem unrealistic, and Lindblom himself admits as much.[13]

If they relax the assumption that the decision-making situation can be characterized by equality of resources or power, decision-makers might rather expect actors to occupy positions in historical, social, and political-economic structures; the decision setting then is characterized not by random plurality, but by highly structured plurality, where structure and power are rarely neatly separable (see Table 1, quadrant 4). In such settings, definitions of a problem come to reflect their social sources (see Table 4, row five). In the planning process, developers appeal to the prerogatives of private property; bureaucrats appeal to the principles of formal equality and procedural democracy; and community organizations appeal to the diffuse tradition of direct democratic participation. Information blurs into misinformation as selective attention shades into self-serving presentations and misrepresentations of the likely consequences of a program or project. The decision-makers' information is as likely to reflect the interests (balanced or not) of the participants in the decision-making process as it is to portray any independent objective "reality" surveyed from some detached Archimedean vantage point. And time, under these conditions, is power, but, again, power that is not likely to be distributed equally. The "haves" often have more time than the "have-nots," who usually have to worry about problems that are much more immediate and pressing than the varied decisions faced by planners and public administrators who work for city hall, nonprofit private agencies, consulting organizations, or regional and civic associations.

Under these conditions, incremental strategies are hardly responsive to the realities at hand. Indeed, they may avoid unpleasantries, but social justice is likely to be the price of such convenience. Many critics, of course—themselves hardly radicals—have noted that incremental, pluralist strategies are likely to be profoundly conservative.[14] Thus, the strategies that are appropriate under decision-making conditions of severe structural distortion and inequality are restructuring strategies: strategies that work toward effective equality, substantive democratic participation and voice, and strategies that work away from the perpetuation of systematic racial, sexual, and economic domination.

What are such strategies? Several alternatives can readily be considered. First, the traditional Rooseveltian liberal tack of redistribution might be adopted, wherein efforts are channeled in remedial or compensatory ways. Affirmative action, categorical antipoverty grants, and special community-development efforts are commonplace examples of such redistributive strategies. Second, the approach seeking to formulate and implement "nonreformist reforms" might be adopted, whereby effort is directed to empower populations who might then act further to alter the structures of power in the society.[15] Whereas Medicare and Medicaid were reformist or redistributive, Ronald Dellums's (D.-Calif.) proposal for a democratically controlled national health service (improving on the British system) seeks a nonreformist reform, as does "Workers' Right to Know" occupational health and safety legislation recently adopted in communities and states throughout the nation.[16] Such legislative changes act to alter the balance of power in society so that the structures of care (and risk) might be further altered.[17]

Third, more directly nonreformist efforts might be attempted: the work of planners and public administrators might be directed specifically to social and labor movements working to attain structural changes in the present political-economy. Work aimed toward immediately nonreformist ends may be as ordinary as providing information or expertise, but identifying and supporting an actual force that is able to effect major political-economic change is crucial. There is little consensus on examples of such forces in the United States today, and pointing elsewhere—for example, to the sweeping changes effected by the Sandinista forces that overthrew the Somoza regime in Nicaragua—makes things no simpler for practitioners in the United States. Some will argue that parts of the labor movement are such a force; others suggest that diverse social movements are now the bearers of significant change.[18]

In any case, if the pluralist assumption of significant, effective political equality of power is recognized as a political ideal rather than as an accurate description of contemporary U.S. society, then the incremental and bargaining strategies that seemed appropriate

under those assumptions are no longer so obviously sensible. Instead, strategies that anticipate and counteract structural inequalities of power must be devised and put into practice. Such strategies
are likely to be most familiar to us as variants and kin of political and community-organizing strategies, as suggested in the last
chapter.[19] Some strategies focus on the regulation of capital—for
example, by linking revenues from downtown urban development
projects to neighborhood housing needs. Other strategies seek to
empower the disenfranchised—for example, by developing locally
based community development initiatives. Still other strategies
seek political-economic restructuring by supporting gender-, race-,
or class-based movements. In the face of structural imbalances of
power and life-chances, active interventions seeking social justice
are required, interventions that go beyond liberal-pluralist bargaining and incrementalist strategies.[20]

Conclusion

Different contexts, then, call for correspondingly different practical strategies of action. We have reviewed a repertoire of such
strategies. As the contextual complexity of the decision-making
situation grows, an increasingly sophisticated set of decision-
making approaches is required.

We have presented a bare-bones treatment of the basic assumptions that may be used to characterize decision-making situations.
It worked from the most abstract and idealized assumptions (one
agent within a closed system, given a well-defined problem, perfect
information, and time to spare) to the most concrete and messy
assumptions: actors playing their parts within structures of power,
problems ambiguous and ideologically contested, time and information each an element of the play of power. These strategies are
not neatly exclusive. Instead they form a repertoire from which
skilled practitioners can draw. They are cumulative: At each level of
complexity, elements of the previous strategies can also be brought
to bear. Even in the face of pluralist or structurally distorted conditions, "satisficing" strategies may play a role, if no longer the
predominant one under these more complex environmental constraints. (Table 4 also illustrates the constraints schematically pre-

sented in Table 1. Each row in Table 4, from row two through row five, represents a quadrant of Table 1.)[21]

Several other implications for planning and public administration follow. First, even if one accepts that practical strategies of action must be context-sensitive, it is not a simple matter to know in practice what the actual decision-making context is.[22] Precisely because so many ambiguities can be involved in deciphering the context at hand, political ideologies often substitute for thorough analyses. Yet just as some actors may invoke explicitly political ideologies, others may be tempted to deny the political character of problems altogether and treat the environment as if political considerations, pluralist or structural, were irrelevant.[23] Others may characterize the environment as pluralistic and seek correspondingly less technical resolutions of the issues at hand. *Because the context of action is typically ambiguous, practitioners must have theories—must make bets—about the character of the situations they find themselves in:* How will the other agencies act in this situation? What should we watch out for? Who will be with or against us?

Significantly, different theories or bets about encompassing social structures will lead to different practical expectations on the job, to different predictions, and so to different practical schedules and senses of timing as well. The decision-maker who perceives a freely functioning, competitive market—say, for housing—is likely to act differently on given problems than will the decision-maker who perceives instead a struggle between three well-defined interest groups. Likewise, both of these practitioners will recommend different strategies than will the actor who views the housing situation as a conflict between owning and working classes in the broader society.

Second, if being practical depends strongly on context, then ironically the domains of "the practical" and "the technical" will not be the same. Technical solutions depend on a stable context and on a problem that can be isolated from that context. Practical solutions depend on the peculiarities of a specific context that define the given problem. Being practical means responding to the demands of a situation with all its particularities. Being technical typically means using a generalizable technique; being practical means using ordinary skills on a unique, context-dependent problem. The two strategies may well be entirely different enterprises.[24]

Third, if practical strategies are context dependent, and contexts vary widely and are always changing, then rational action and decision making will fail in a technical search for a one-best-recipe. Instead of recipes, repertoires of strategies are called for and should be investigated in diverse decision-making situations.

Fourth, if contexts can hardly be posited once and for all, clearly and distinctly, then the role of administrative theory in decision making takes on a new coloration. The role of theory is not to predict "what will happen if . . ."; instead, it is to direct the attention of the decision-maker, to suggest what important and significant actors and events and signals to be alert to, to look for, to take as tips or warnings. Thrown into situations of great complexity, decision-makers need theories to simplify their worlds, to suggest what is most important to attend to and what can safely and decently be neglected.[25]

Fifth, and finally, there is an ordered way to understand what some of the shouting is about in the political world of planning and public administration (see Tables 1 and 4). Pluralists and Marxists, for example, differ most fundamentally over the issue of structural and systematic social biases (see Table 1). Comprehensive planners and incrementalists, satisficers and the politically minded, "realists" and "idealists" all differ over the issues of constraints on action and decision making: Which have to be accepted as part of the human condition? Which are changeable? How important is social structure? How important is independent, willful action? These differences—and their practical implications—can now be ordered in a systematic way.[26]

At the beginning of this chapter our friend was putting quarters into the vending machine, making his selection, and winning pies all the time. We may often be in similar situations if we fail to understand the decision-making environments within which we act. Perhaps now, though, we will understand more clearly how the practicality of what we do, however differently constrained or bounded, depends on our reading of the contexts we work within. Perhaps, as we now spend our quarters in our vending machines, we might stop with what we can eat or share, and spend the rest of our budgets on more productive ventures, or other pleasures.

Part Three

Anticipate Organizational
Power and Conflict

Chapter Five

Three Views of Planning Organizations

Planners work in complex networks of organizations. But what should they expect from their organizational environments: rationality or arbitrariness, support or perpetual resistance, interagency coordination, or coalition and class politics? What difference do organizational settings make? Problems of acting effectively in organizations confront planners every day. Many planners are struck by the "craziness," the unpredictability and incomprehensibility of their work settings.[1] One of every two planners seems to employ both technical and organizational-political skills, while an additional one in five identifies predominantly with political and interactive roles.[2] Common sense—which is not always so common—suggests that the organizational environment of planning will substantially influence the reception, appreciation, and effectiveness of planners' work. But the planning literature provides no framework for a practical and politically critical understanding of organizational action that can inform progressive planning practice. This chapter seeks to provide that framework.[3]

When planners report that their political and organizational environments are "crazy," they lead us to ask, "Is there any method in that madness?" Popular thinking and academic organization theory provide two possible answers to this question, answers we may call the instrumental and the social views of organizational life.[4]

The Instrumental View of Organizations

Perhaps the madness is transitory, while method is the real bedrock of the organizations with which planners work. For years, the popular and academic imaginations have seen organizations as efficient mechanisms or organisms with integrally related and coordinated parts. The view of human organization as method writ large, as a regulated or self-regulating structure of means and ends, dies hard.

Even our ordinary language encourages this instrumental view. Planners describe other organizations predominantly by function: the Public Works Department monitors and constructs public works projects; the Bureau of Building Inspections inspects buildings and plans; trade associations protect the interests of their members; and so on. Staff members are described in the same way: "On our staff we have an architect, a community planner, a real estate specialist, and an environmental planner"—each role is designated here by instrumental function, not, for example, by political ideology (e.g., conservative, socialist, liberal). In the instrumental view, the real structure of an organization is an idealized flowchart of functional relations. This perspective, of course, is virtually apolitical; "politics" is likely to be a shorthand for "all those things that get in the way of problem-solving."

The instrumental view is partially true but it is also quite misleading. Task specialization does exist in almost any large organization, and it is usually expressed in terms of the functional needs of the organization. In a city planning department, architectural staff members use specialized skills to review plans. Community planners serve intelligence functions for community organizations and planning staff alike, and still other staff members produce maps, plans, layouts, and other "graphics." Elsewhere in the city, an engineering department hires engineers to design sewer projects and hires construction workers to build them. A city attorney's office will seek legal and research skills. So, indeed, organizations are partly instrumental, but they are far more than that.

How many people can these organizations hire? How are their projects and their goals selected? Do these organizations depend on good relationships with anyone else? Or with anyone who might influence their budgets? In a world where any one organization's staff must frequently work with staff from many other agencies, how cooperative or competitive are these interorganizational relations? Are there internal rivalries, cliques, friendships, or hatreds within as well as among these organizations? Is anyone concerned about his or her personal career and prospects for advancement? These are not simply instrumental questions; they are deeply social as well. These questions involve not just the organization's means and ends, but also the character of the ongoing relationships that make the performance of any task possible in the first place.

Thus when planners report that the world is not as logical as it appeared to be in school, or when they suggest that even the most technically skilled specialists are sometimes ignored because of "politics," they are telling us that organizations are not well-ordered systems of means and ends and that the instrumental view does not adequately describe practical reality.

The Social View of Organizations

The social view of organizations emphasizes not the method but the madness, the madness that always makes the efficiency and power of available methods somewhat vulnerable. All the technique in the world will come to naught in an organization if cooperation does not exist. The computer specialist depends on good relations with many people: those who maintain the equipment, those with access to data, those who support the specialist's work in a time of shrinking resources or in the face of demands for additional staff for other departments.[5] Organizational morale and staff motivation are far from trivial issues. Instrumental output and the daily working environment both depend on good internal working relations in which staff insecurities, fears, and suspicions can be eased and where cooperation, pride in one's work, and innovation can be fostered. This is true in public or private settings, in a for-profit firm or a nonprofit agency.[6]

The social view of organizations focuses on the ways organization members sustain more or less meaningful relationships every day.[7] The instrumental or functional aspect of work is only one, albeit a significant, part of healthy organizational life. With each project they undertake, planners develop and remake their working relations with supervisors, co-workers, and other agency staff, to say nothing of neighborhood residents and, at times, politicians. Some of these relationships grow stronger. If the assistant director finds a planner's last project excellent and completed promptly, she may be willing to give still more responsibility to that planner next time. Of course, some relationships weaken. A planner who sees that a consultant is misrepresenting plans for a project under review will learn to watch out in future meetings, to expect future deception, and to be more careful when they next discuss project plans.

Like the instrumental view, the social view of organizations is also apolitical. "Politics" becomes a matter of interpersonal relations. "Culture" substitutes for, rather than complements, political-economic structure. Indeed, in the social view structure can be quite ill defined, and goals can be ambiguous, multiple, and conflicting. The social view leaves us thinking not only, "Yes, all those social issues matter!" but also, "It's an amazing wonder that anything works at all!"

Although the social view contains more than a grain of truth, it also has its limits. Even though it easily accounts for the self-protective behavior prevalent in many organizations, it does not account for the influence of broader social and political interests, structures, and movements. It therefore cannot easily address the issues of organizational growth and decline; radical inequalities of power, status, and income; or the historical and systematic exclusion of women, people of color, and those of certain political beliefs from positions of influence.

Organizations as Instrumentally Productive and Sociopolitically Reproductive

Consider a third, more critical view that builds on the insights of the instrumental and social perspectives. What do organizations do? They put forward selective claims and arguments. Our insurance company tells us we are entitled to benefits or we are not. The state highway department tells us the road should go here or there. The grocery store tells us that if we want to purchase this product, we need to pay a certain sum. The planning department sends reports to the planning board, tells community associations about forthcoming projects, and recommends patterns of future development. According to this view, organizations are structures of practical communicative action, and thus they not only produce instrumental results but also reproduce social and political relations.[8]

Consider what happens when a planner works with a consultant, a community resident, or a staff member of another public agency. The planner does not just present and collect information, reach agreements, set meeting times, and call for further work to be done—all these the production of instrumental results. The planner also establishes, refines, and recreates, and thus reproduces, social relations of trust or distrust, cooperation or competition, amiability or hostility, encouragement or discouragement, and so on. Every organizational interaction or practical communication (including the nonverbal) not only produces a result, it also reproduces, strengthening or weakening, the specific social working relations of those who interact.

To acknowledge a nonverbal cue in a meeting, for example, may indicate not only agreement to help to change the course of the discussion (an instrumental goal) but also support, cooperation, and willingness to enter into a coalition with the sender of the signal and against others (the reproduction of very practical social and political relations). Planners seek goals and produce results, then, but they also "reproduce" a fabric of social and political relationships with others at the same time. In the following sections, the term "reproduction" will refer to that ongoing strengthening, altering, or weakening of those social relations, without which the production of desired results (e.g., plans, reports, recommendations) would not be possible.[9]

Even in the review of strictly technical work, the discussion, refinement, and acceptance of technical judgments are themselves structured by social rules and conventions.[10] The judgment that a particular load-carrying beam will not have sufficient strength may be a technical judgment made in the review of building plans by an engineering technician on the planning or permits department staff. The judgment that zoning in one municipality will harm another municipality's development may be technical, to be made by a planner in an intermunicipal review process. Yet the fact that these judgments can be made and have effect at all is the result of the socially established institution of the review process. Technical judgments can make a difference, not because they are technical, but because they can be *authoritative*.

Thus, technical judgments can yield instrumental results be-

cause the institutional roles of those who make them and those
who need them are socially and politically legitimated or reproduced.[11] Once reported or uttered, even the most technical judgment becomes an integral part of the political world; it becomes
inescapably political, seeking legitimacy by appealing to the consent of those concerned with the merits of the case at hand.[12]

Reproducing Knowledge, Consent, Trust, and Formulations of Problems

Planners, then, can expect the organizations with which they work
not only to seek certain ends but also to reproduce, or refashion,
social and political relations.[13] We will explore below how such
reproduction works.

By selectively restricting the information they make available,
organizations shape "who knows what when," and, in particular,
what concerned citizens know about the conditions in their communities. In response, of course, practitioners struggle to get better
information. Environmentalists, for example, may try to question
energy producers about their plans; ombudspersons may call upon
an agency to clarify eligibility criteria; and journalists may investigate the distribution of community grants. As organizations develop or restrict information, they shape others' knowledge and
beliefs; and just as significantly, they shape others' abilities to act
and organize.

A developer, politician, or planner may try to gain consent for a
favored proposal by appealing to precedent, legislative mandate,
or administrative regulations. A local merchant may fight the
threatened loss of parking spaces by saying, "But the street's always been this way; that's how the neighborhood shopping area
should be!" A public works department may claim jurisdiction over
the arterial road pattern and yet find itself ignored by the state highway department, which claims still other authority. Each party here
invokes legitimate authority and appeals to the consent of others.
By gaining and managing such consent, organizations extend their
power and seek to influence, if not co-opt, their opposition.

As they build dependable working relationships with community residents, agency staff, and others, planners establish informal
networks of trusted and cooperative contacts. Most often, the per-

son "in the know" has a full address book, not an encyclopedic mind, and the ability to get to (and then be trusted by, inform, and learn from) key people throughout government, business, and community organizations. Members of public and private organizations alike continually maintain and extend these contacts; as cooperation and trust are developed, so are practical intelligence networks and bases of future coalitions.

In addition, when they frame problems selectively and so influence what others come to regard as relevant in the case at hand, developers, business interests, agency staff, and community members not only express their interests but also attempt to marshal effective political arguments. In a community-development effort, for example, planners may wish to focus attention on the need to provide low-rent housing as one part of any larger project. Business interests and investors, though, are likely to call attention to issues of their financial risk, and to their desire to assure a healthy return on the capital they invest. This ability of planners, developers, or community organizations to pose problems in particular ways depends in part on their credibility, their political resources and constraints, and their wealth. Thus, it should surprise no one that public problems are often posed not by progressive planners in terms of the democratic control of investment to meet public needs but rather by those who control capital investments in terms of their own desires—to ensure returns on investments that are supposedly to benefit the broader public through a "trickle down" process. Too little notice is given, however, to the fact that in such development efforts the poor often receive a trickle, while those with the capital to invest seem to drink quite a bit. As organizations frame problems, then, they highlight or neglect both needs and opportunities, and they enable or discourage political participation, action, and coalition formation in turn.

Thus, as structures of communicative relations, organizations both produce instrumental results and reproduce social and political relations of knowledge (who knows what), consent (who accepts whose authority and who resists), trust (who has established networks of cooperative contacts), and the ways we formulate problems (who considers which issues and neglects which others).[14] In this way social relations of power are built up and reproduced, and these organized, contingently reproduced relations form the background against which any particular exercise of power must be understood.[15] Yet crucial questions remain: Can planners expect any systematic pattern to this reproduction of social relations? Are these reproductive processes random? What do planners need to know or learn to begin to answer these questions?

Judgments Required in Practice

When we recognize that organizations not only produce instrumental results but reproduce social and political relations as well, we can immediately draw practical inferences for planning. Consider, for example, what knowledge practicing planners need, what they must learn as they face new projects. Three kinds of knowledge and skill are essential. These are put into practice in the form of technical, practical, and critical judgments.

Technical and Practical Judgments

When recruiting staff, for example, what qualities might planners seek? Does it all depend on the project at hand? Hardly. In part, of course, each project or branch of a planning department will call for distinct skills, and new recruits must have these, be able to brush up on them, or learn them quickly. The design-review section will need people with architectural skills. The graphics section will appreciate people who have an aesthetic sensibility as well as the ability to draw a straight line. The data section will need people with computing and data-analysis skills. These specific technical skills are all necessary at times, but they are far from sufficient.

Whoever is hired will be called on not only to check designs, draw, compute, or calculate but to work with others too. They will do technical work, but they will also encourage other staff members or bore them, befriend or antagonize them, cooperate with and assist them, or keep to themselves. They will be a source of new ideas and insights, or they will be reticent, doing only what is asked of them. When working with other agencies or members of the public, they will extend the welcome of the planning department or make enemies by putting others off, making the planning department more vulnerable than ever. These are not simply issues of technical training; they are the practical matters of maintaining, improving, and reproducing the planning department's social and political relations both within the department and with others.

These issues extend far beyond personnel decisions. When a developer proposes a new project, or when a public works department receives funds to begin a massive new construction project, or when a new community group or local political organization is formed, planners similarly need both technical and practical information. They need the former in order to review complex proposals and assess possible physical, social, and economic consequences. Yet if they are to obtain any such technical information and work with it, the planners will need the practical knowledge of whom to talk to, whom they may find cooperative and whom not, whom to seek out and whom to avoid, in either the public or private sector. They will need to know—in the developer's consultant's firm, the public works department, or the local community organization—who can speak for that organization and who cannot, who can be trusted to have accurate information and who is not particularly reliable, who resents the nosiness of the planning department and who welcomes the department's involvement.

Planners need to learn the history of those involved in new projects: Did they start a similar project three years ago and then change their minds in midstream? Have they had problems with a planning department staff member who has since left, or do they perhaps hold a grudge against one who still works there? Have they gained support in the past from planning commissioners, the mayor, or city supervisors? Have they had trouble with community organizations? Are their time schedules for project development credible? When they seem less than happy about the planning department's review process or overall involvement, are they simply disgruntled, or do they threaten to bring serious political pressure to bear on the department?

These questions point to practical issues that planners must appreciate and anticipate. As new projects are proposed and developed, planners need technical knowledge and the ability to gather and assess it, and they need practical organizational knowledge and the ability to learn the various "rules of the game." Without practical knowledge and skill, planners with technical virtuosity may find their ideas ill timed, distrusted, barely heard, and little appreciated. Conversely, without technical skills and knowledge, planners may find themselves appreciated as cooperative people and good talkers, with nothing to say.

Critical Judgment

But technical and practical organizational knowledge alone will not help planners come to grips with problems of equity, the concentrated accumulation of wealth, and the perpetuation of widespread poverty and suffering. Planners who hope to serve fundamental human needs must be able to recognize both the practical forces that work to meet those needs and those forces that serve the interests of the relatively few. Planners need to know that in the instrumental production and sociopolitical reproduction of every organization lie fundamental issues of justice and domination.

Do the people affected by a particular organization have a democratic voice in determining either how that organization produces instrumental results "for" them, or, still more significant, how it reproduces the social and political relations that shape their lives?[16] Do patients in long-term care facilities and hospitals have a voice in those institutions? Do workers in industrial and chemical plants have a real voice regarding the organization of work or the toxicity of the substances to which they are exposed? Do community residents have a real voice in the locational decisions of the industries that "provide" their jobs? Do neighborhood residents have a real voice in the building decisions of local developers? These questions suggest the challenges that face planners who seek a more just and democratic society.

As various organizations and their members reproduce the social relations of knowledge, consent, trust, and the ways problems are formulated, so do they reproduce the social relations of the broader society. As medical-care organizations, for example, reproduce citizens' knowledge of their own health, so are citizens made aware or kept ignorant of the causes of illness, the available modes of prevention or redress, and the health of the health-care delivery system itself. As public agencies promote political participation and democratic control or, alternatively, discourage such political action, so do those organizations reproduce relations of power and consent, or deference, quiescence, and "apolitical" political identities.[17]

If public and private organizations alike cater to individual pref-erences and ignore issues of social responsibility, for instance, by promoting market models emphasizing fee-for-service or user-fee allocation schemes, they may weaken cooperative social and com-munity ties.[18] Compare, for example, policies of neighborhood re-habilitation that seek to keep communities intact with those of ur-ban renewal that often scattered community residents, in terms of the reproduction of social relations of trust, cooperation, and community.[19]

When public and private organizations attend to particular problems and neglect others, they reproduce the citizenry's "com-mon sense" and their sense of the more and less important issues of the day. Today it is common sense for a person of moderate means to avoid buying a gas-guzzling car. Not too long ago that was not true. It is not just the price of gas that makes the difference, but the public's expectation that today's price will not decrease substan-tially tomorrow. Such public expectations are shaped not through the instrumental production of commodities and goods but through clear and credible claims on the public's attention. To take another example, the extent to which the development of solar energy is pursued will be a matter not only of its technical feasibility (for that is in part yet to be explored) but also of the public attention that can be aroused to consider its potential.

Citizens are profoundly affected, therefore, not only by what gets *produced* by public and private organizations, but also by how these organizations *reproduce* social and political relations of knowledge and ignorance, consent and deference, trust and depen-dency, and attention and confusion. When citizens lack a demo-cratic voice in the reproduction of these relations, planners can ex-pect to find needless human suffering and political domination.[20] Instead of finding an informed citizenry knowledgeable about pol-icy options and social needs, planners will find affected citizens ignorant about alternative policies and about the planning or policy-making process itself. Instead of finding citizens organizing politically and participating actively in the planning process, plan-ners may find them depoliticized and quiescent, deferring to ap-parent status, title, or expertise. Instead of finding community members with thriving, cooperative community organizations, planners may find them isolated from and distrustful of one an-other, yet trusting in the good intentions of established powers and thus all the more dependent on them. Instead of finding citizens clearly articulating their own needs and concerns, planners may find them convinced by the formulations of others and yet hardly clear about their own needs or opportunities.[21]

Where employers, for example, deny citizens access to information about workplace exposure to toxic chemicals, workers are kept ignorant and vulnerable. Where corporations deny citizens participation in influential decisions (regarding possible plant closings, for example), those citizens will be dominated and manipulated. Where overtrained professionals lead citizens to inflated expectations of professional service delivery (e.g., highly specialized medical care) to the exclusion or weakening of personal and social networks, citizens will be rendered less able to act cooperatively for themselves. Where self-aggrandizing investors lead citizens to neglect policies that might indeed serve the public (e.g., soft energy paths), citizens may well be confused about their actual policy options and be led to waste scarce resources of time and effort.

So citizens may well suffer more than the private appropriation of the fruits of their labor, as Marx suggested. They may also, just as fundamentally, suffer the appropriation of their informed knowledge, consent, trust, and sense of their own needs. Citizens may thus be exploited not only through the lack of democratic control of what public and private organizations produce in this society but also through the lack of democratic control of the social relations those same organizations reproduce. Control and consent are appropriated from citizens, but so too are their dependency and trust, their knowledge and belief, and their attention and sensibility.[22]

Political-Economy and the Reproduction of Social Relations

Recognizing these threats to participatory planning and policy-making processes, a critical theory of power and organization asks how these threats are sustained and can be resisted. In a society whose capital accumulation and investment is privately rather than democratically controlled, it follows that the organizational form of that capital, its investment, and the state agencies protecting it will also be nondemocratically controlled. Thus, planners can expect (with a few exemplary, democratically structured exceptions) that the organizations in and with which they work will systematically reproduce sociopolitical relations that (1) ignore ways to socialize and democratize accumulation; (2) discourage widespread participation and representation that might reveal the contradictions between private accumulation and public needs; (3) deter cooperative, well-organized, community-based organizations that might press to meet social needs to the detriment of concentrations of private capital; and (4) distract public attention from social needs and instead focus on the promotion of individual consumption.[23]

Once planners can anticipate how the organizations with which they work render citizens powerless, they can begin to respond. By seeking to play an educative and organizing role, informing citizens about forthcoming projects and ensuring citizens access to relevant information, planners may resist social relations of knowledge that might otherwise leave citizens practically ignorant. By aiding citizens' political and community organizing toward democratic control of resources and investments (e.g., in cases of threatened public services, or school or plant closings), planners may work to alter political relations of consent that would otherwise allow formally democratic but substantively autocratic policies to ensue. By encouraging citizens' local autonomy and the protection of social networks as countervailing influences to professional power, planners may mitigate the dependency and helplessness that current service-delivery organizations, however unintentionally, create. By broadening the content of alternatives presented to affected citizens in community, labor, and environmental organizations, planners may work to expand citizens' vision, to clarify real policy and productive possibilities, and to focus public attention on actions that directly address the needs of the poor, the underserved, and the powerless.[24]

Contributions of a Critical View of Organizational Action

How can planners put into practice the contributions of the third—the synthetic and critical—view of organizational life? We will consider four points. First, planners can understand and be sensitive to their political and organizational environments in more sophisticated ways than those offered by the instrumental or social views of organizational behavior. Planners can expect organizations to have two related faces: one producing instrumental results, the other simultaneously, but less visibly, reproducing social and political relations involving knowledge (who knows what), consent (who exercises power and who obeys), trust (who cooperates with whom), and the formulation of problems (who focuses on or neglects which problems).

Second, planners can expect to need more than technical, instrumental knowledge in order to be effective. The planner who is good with the calculator but who cannot cooperate with anyone will not last long. As the social and reproductive views of organization both suggest, planners need organizational skills and knowledge as well as technical competence. They need to be able to work with others, to develop trust, to locate support and opposition, to be sensitive to timing, and to know the informal "ropes" as well as the formal organization chart.

Third, as social relations are maintained in nondemocratic ways, as accountability of authorities is limited and the representation of the unorganized, the poor, and the underserved is weak, so planners can expect affected citizens to be: (1) uncertain and uninformed about policy opportunities and consequences, yet believing that others "know better"; (2) cynical about the promise of their own participation and deferential to those with expert, official, or investor status, consenting through deference, not participation; (3) doubting their own social and community capacities for cooperation, and trusting instead in the good faith of professionals or the hidden hand of market advocates; and (4) confused about and distracted from planning and policy options that could address social needs in more than a "trickle down" fashion—so that neighborhood planning, rehabilitation, and public housing, for example, seem to be distant alternatives to, rather than substitutes for, urban gentrification. By anticipating these obstacles to the public's ability to organize and control democratically the productive resources of the society, planners can learn how to counteract the powerlessness of citizens in community organizations, in unions, in environmental organizations, and in the broader polity.

Finally, planners will not only need to know how citizens can be rendered ignorant, powerless, dependent, and confused by private capital-accumulating or public bureaucratic organizations; they will also need to learn how to support citizen organizations and movements that work to overcome these problems, to democratize the social relations of production. Planners can work in part to organize (or, alternatively, to disorganize) effective citizen action and mobilization. They can work, for example, with community organizations and unions to get information about possible plant closings that threaten local communities. Planners can encourage rather than preempt citizen action, politicization, and community organization to improve local planning processes. They can also work to support networks and coalitions of groups pressing for increased public access to, participation in, and democratic control over resource allocation and investment (in local housing or health-care planning, for example).[25] Planners can work through these networks and groups to call attention to policy alternatives that serve the public and that might otherwise be ignored or suppressed by the narrower initiatives of private-sector investors.

By learning how the public welfare is threatened, how the powerless are kept powerless, and how the poor are kept poor, planners can also learn how to counteract these conditions: to organize, politicize, and empower citizens to create the possibility of genuinely democratic politics. In such practical education lies the contribution of a critical account of organizations and organizational action.

Chapter Six

Planning in the Face of
Conflict: Mediated Negotiation
Strategies in Practice

In the face of local land-use conflicts, how can planners mediate between conflicting parties and at the same time negotiate as interested parties themselves? To address that question, this chapter explores planners' strategies for dealing with conflicts that arise in local processes of zoning appeals, subdivision approvals, special permit applications, and design reviews.

Local planners often have complex and contradictory duties. They may seek to serve political officials, legal mandates, professional visions, and the concrete requests of particular citizens' groups all at the same time. They typically work in situations of considerable uncertainty, great imbalances of power, and multiple, ambiguous, and conflicting political goals. Many local planners, then, may seek ways to negotiate effectively, as they try to satisfy particular interests, and to mediate practically too, as they try to resolve conflicts through a semblance of a participatory planning process. But these two tasks—negotiating and mediating—appear to conflict in two fundamental ways.

First, the interestedness of a negotiating role threatens the independence and presumed neutrality of a mediating role. Second, although a negotiating role might allow planners to protect less powerful interests, a mediating role threatens to undercut this possibility and thus to leave existing inequalities of power all too intact.[1] How can local planners deal with these problems? We discuss their strategies in detail below.

This chapter first presents local planners' own accounts of the challenges they face as they simultaneously negotiate and mediate in local conflicts over land-use permits. Planning directors and staff in New England cities and towns, urban and suburban, shared their viewpoints with the author during extensive open-ended interviews. The evidence presented here, therefore, is qualitative, and the argument that follows seeks not generalizability but strong plausibility across a range of planning settings.

Second, we will explore a repertoire of mediated negotiation strategies that planners use as they deal with local land-use conflicts. We assess the emotional complexity of mediating roles and ask: What skills are called for? Why do planners often seem reluctant to adopt face-to-face mediating roles?

Finally, we will address the implications of these discussions. How can local planning organizations encourage effective negotiation and equitable, efficient mediation? How can mediated negotiation strategies empower the relatively powerless instead of reproducing existing inequalities of power?

Local Land-Use Conflicts

Let us first consider the settings in which planners face local conflicts over land-use permits. Private developers typically propose projects. Municipal boards—typically, planning boards and boards of zoning appeals—have authority to grant variances, special permits, or design approvals. Affected residents often have a say, but sometimes little influence, in formal public hearings before these bodies. Planners report to these boards with analyses of specific proposals. When positive, the staff reports often recommend conditions to attach to a permit or suggest design changes to improve the final project. When the reports are negative, there are other arguments to be made and reasons to be given.

Some municipalities have elected permit-granting boards, and others have appointed boards. Some municipal ordinances mandate design review; others do not. Some local by-laws call for more than one planning board hearing on "substantial" projects, but others do not. Nevertheless, for several reasons, planners' roles in these different settings may be more similar than dissimilar.

Common Planning Responsibilities

First, planners must help both developers and neighborhood residents to navigate a potentially complex review process; clarity and predictability are valued goods. Second, the planners need to be concerned with timing. *When* a developer or neighborhood resident is told about an issue may be even more important than the issue itself. Third, planners need to deal with conflicts between project developers and affected neighborhood residents that usually involve several issues at once: scale, the income of tenants, new traffic, existing congestion, the character of a street, and so on. Such conflicts simultaneously involve questions of design, social policy, safety, transportation, and neighborhood character. Fourth, how much planners can do in the face of such conflicts depends not only on their formal responsibilities but also on their informal initiatives. A zoning by-law, for example, can specify a time by which a planning board is to hold a public hearing, but it will not typically tell a planner how much information to give a developer or a neighbor, when or with whom to hold informal meetings, how to hold the meetings, whom to invite, or how to negotiate with either party. So within the formal guidelines of zoning appeals, special permit applications, and site-plan and design reviews, planning staff can exercise substantial discretion and exert important influence as a result.

Planners' Influence

The complexity of permit-granting processes is a source of influence for planning staff. Complexity creates uncertainties for everyone involved. Some planners eagerly use the resulting leverage. As an associate planning director explains, beginning with a truism but then elaborating:

Time is money for developers. Once the money is in, the clock is ticking. Here we have some influence. We may not be able to stop a project that we have problems with, but we can look at things in more or less detail, and slow them down. Getting back to [the developers] can take two days, or two months, but we try to be clear: "We're people you can get along with." So many developers will say, "Let's get along with these people and listen to their concerns." . . . But we have influence in other ways, too. There are various ways to interpret the ordinance, for example. Or I can influence the building commissioner; he used to work in this office and we have a good relationship, so his staff may call us about a project they're looking over and ask, "Hey, do you want this project or not?"

Planners think strategically about timing not only to discourage certain projects but also to encourage or capture others. The associate director explains: "On another project, we waited before pushing for changes. We wanted to let the developer get fully committed to it; then we'd push. If we'd pushed earlier, he might have walked away." A director in another municipality echoes the point: "Take an initial meeting with the developer, the mayor, and me. Depending on the benefits involved—fiscal or physical—the mayor might kick me under the table: "Not now," he's telling me. He doesn't want to discourage the project . . . and so I'll be able to work on the problems later." For the astute, it seems, the complexity of the planning process produces more opportunities than headaches. For the novice, no doubt, the balance shifts the other way.

But isn't everything, in the last analysis, all written down in publicly available documents for everyone to see? Hardly. Could all the procedures ever be made entirely clear? Consider the experience of an architect-planner who grappled with these problems in several planning positions. The following conversation took place toward the end of our interview. The planner pulled a diagram from a folder and said, "Here's the new flowchart I just drew up that shows how our design-review process works. If you have any questions, let's talk. I think it's still pretty cryptic." The zoning appeals planner, who was standing nearby, interjected: "If *you* think it's cryptic, just think what developers and neighborhood people will think!"

Both planners shook their heads and laughed, since the problem was all too plain: the arrows on the design-review flowchart seemed to run everywhere. The chart was no doubt correct, but it did look complicated.

I recalled my first interview with the zoning appeals planner. I had asked a deliberately leading question: "But what influence can you have in the process if everything's written down as public information, if it's all clear there on the page?" The zoning appeals planner had grinned from ear to ear: "But that's just it! The process is not clear! And that's where I come in."

The architect-planner developed the point further: "Where I worked before, the planning director wanted to adopt a new 'policy and procedures' document that would have defined every last item. We were going to get it all clear. The whole staff spent a lot of time writing that, trying to get all the elements and subsections and so on clearly defined. . . . But it was chaos. Once we had the document, everyone fought about what each item meant." So clarity, apparently, has its limits!

Different Actors, Different Strategies

Planning staff members describe almost poignantly the different issues that arise as they work with developers and with neighborhood residents. The candor of one planning director is worth quoting at length:

It's easy to sit down with developers, or their lawyers. They're a known quantity. They want to meet. There's a common language—say, of zoning—and they know it, along with the technical issues. And they speak with one voice (although that's not to say that we don't play off the architect and the developer at times—we'll push the developer, for example, and the architect is happy because he agrees with us). . . .

But then there's the community. With the neighbors, there's no consistency. One week one group comes in, and the next week it's another. It's hard if there's no consistent view. One group's worried about traffic; the other group's not worried about traffic but about shadows. There isn't one point of view there. They also don't know the process (though there are those cases where there are *too many* experts!). So at the staff level (as opposed to planning board meetings) we usually don't deal with both developers and neighbors simultaneously.

Although these comments may distress advocates of neighborhood power, they say much about the practical situation in which the director finds himself.

All people may be created equal, but when they walk into the planning department, they are simply not all the same. This director suggests that getting all the involved parties together around the table in the planners' conference room is not an obviously good idea, for several reasons. (It is, however, an idea we will consider more closely below.)

First, the director suggests, planners generally know what to expect from developers: The developers' interests are often clearer than those of the neighbors, and project proponents may actually want to meet with the staff. Neighborhood residents may be less likely to treat planners as potential allies; after all, the planners aren't the decision-makers, and the decision-makers can often easily ignore the planners' recommendations. Because developers may cultivate good relations with planning staff (this is in part their business, of course), while neighborhood groups do not, local planning staff may find meetings with developers relatively cordial and familiar, but meetings with neighborhood activists more guarded and uncertain.

Second, the planning director quoted above suggests that planners and developers often share a common professional language. They can pinpoint technical and regulatory issues and know that the other understands what is being said. But he implies that on any given project he may need to teach the special terms of the local zoning code to affected neighbors before they can really get to the issues at hand.[2]

The planning director makes a third point. Developers speak with one voice; neighbors do not. When planners listen to developers, they know who they are listening to, and they know what they are likely to hear elaborated, defended, or qualified next week. When planners listen to neighborhood residents, though, this director suggests, they cannot be so sure how strongly to trust what they hear. "Who really speaks for the neighborhood?" the director wonders.

So planners must make practical judgments about who represents affected residents and about how to interpret their concerns. This director implies, therefore, that until a way of identifying "the neighborhood's voice" is found, the problems of conducting joint, mediated negotiations between developers and neighbors are likely to seem insurmountable. We return to this issue of representation below.

Inequalities of Information,
Expertise, and Financing

What about imbalances of power? Developers, typically, initiate site developments. Planners respond. Neighbors, if they are involved at all, then try to respond to both. Developers have financing and capital to invest; neighbors have voluntary associations and no capital, but lungs. Developers hire expertise; neighborhood groups borrow it. Developers typically have economic resources; neighbors often have time, but not always the staying power to turn that time into real negotiating power.

Where power relations are unbalanced, must mediated negotiation simply lead to the co-optation of the weaker party? No, because as we will see below, mediated negotiation is not a gimmick or a recipe; it is a practical and political strategy to be applied in ways that address the specific relations of power at hand. When either developers or neighborhood groups are so strong that they do not need to negotiate, mediated negotiation becomes irrelevant, and other political strategies will be appropriate. But in cases where both developers and neighbors want to negotiate, planners can then act both as mediators, assisting the negotiations, and as interested negotiators themselves. But how is this possible? What strategies can planners use?

Planners' Strategies: Six Ways to Mediate
Local Land-Use Conflicts

Consider the following six mediated negotiation strategies that planning staff can utilize in local land-use conflicts. These are "mediated" negotiation strategies because planners employ them to assure that the interests of the major parties legitimately come into play. These are "negotiation" strategies because (except for the first) they focus attention on the informal negotiations that may produce viable agreements even before formal decision-making boards meet.

Strategy One: The Planner as Regulator

The first strategy is a traditional response to local land-use conflicts, pristine in its simplicity, but obviously more complex in practice. A young planner who handles zoning appeals and design review says: "I often see my role as a fact-finder so that the planning board can evaluate this project and form a recommendation; whether it's design review, special permits, or variances, you still need lots of facts."

Here of course is the clearest echo of the planner as a technician and bureaucrat; the planner processes information, and someone else takes the responsibility for making decisions. But the echo quickly fades. A moment later, this planner adds: "Our role is to listen to the neighbors, to be able to say to the board, 'Okay, this project meets the technical requirements, but there will be impacts.' The relief will usually then be granted, but with conditions. . . . We'll ask for as much in the way of conditions as we think necessary for the legitimate protection of the neighborhood. The question is, is there a legitimate basis for complaint? And it's not just a matter of complaint, but of the merits."

This planner's role is much more complex than that of a fact-finder; it is virtually judicial. She implies, essentially, that she is not just a bureaucrat, she is a professional. She needs to think not only about the technical requirements but also about what is legitimate protection for the neighbors—now she has to think about the merits. Thinking about the merits, though, does not yet mean thinking about politics, the feelings of other agencies, the chaos at community meetings; it means making professional judgments and then recommending to the planning board the conditions that should be attached to the permits. But let us now consider a slightly more complex strategy.

Strategy Two: Pre-Mediate and Negotiate

When developers meet with planners to discuss project proposals, neighborhood representatives rarely join them. Yet planners might nevertheless speak for neighborhood concerns as well as speak about them. A planning director in a municipality characterized by well-organized, vocal, and influential neighborhood groups notes, "We temper our recommendations to developers. While we might accept A, the neighbors want D; and so we'll tell the developers to think about something in the middle—if they can make it work."

Here, the planner anticipates the concerns of affected residents and changes the informal staff recommendation accordingly to search for an acceptable compromise with the developers. He explains: "What we do is 'pre-mediate' rather than mediate after the fact. We project people's concerns and then raise them; so we do more before [an explicit conflict arises]. . . . The only other way we step in and mediate, later, is when we support changes to be made in a project, changes that consider the neighbors' views; but that's later, after the public hearing."

Unlike the planner-regulator quoted above, this planning director relies on far more than his professional judgment when he meets with a developer. He will negotiate for a project that satisfies local statutes, professional standards, and the interests of affected residents, too. His calculation is not only judicial, but explicitly political. He anticipates the concerns of community members and seeks to represent neighborhood interests—but without neighborhood representatives.

Such pre-mediation—articulating others' concerns well before they can erupt into overt conflict—involves a host of political, strategic, and ethical issues. What relationships does the planner have with various neighborhood groups? In what senses can the planner know what the community wants? To which key actors might the planner steer the developer? How much information and advice should the planner give, or withhold?

Such questions arise whether or not project developers ever meet with neighbors. In many cases, where "neighborhoods" are sprawling residential areas and where "the interests of the neighbors" seem difficult to represent through actual neighborhood representatives, the planners' pre-mediation may be the only mediation that takes place.

Strategy Three: The Planner as a Resource

The planner's influence might be used in still other ways. The director continues: "Regardless of how our first meeting with a developer goes, we recommend to them that they meet with neighbors and the neighbors' representatives [on the permit-granting board]. We usually can give the developer a good inkling about what to expect both professionally and politically. The same elected representative might say that a project is okay professionally, but not okay for them in their elected capacity. We try to encourage back-and-forth meetings."

The director, then, regularly takes the pulse of neighborhood groups and elected representatives. Working in city hall has its advantages, he says: "We'll discuss a project with the representatives; we see them so much here—just in the halls—and they ask us to let them know what's happening in their parts of the city." So the director listens to the developers, listens to the neighbors, and encourages "back-and-forth meetings."

A planning director who seldom met jointly with neighbors and developers had an acute sense of other strategies:

We . . . urge the applicants, the developers, to deal directly with the neighborhood for several reasons: First, if the neighbors are confronted at a hearing with glossy plans, they'll think it's all a *fait accompli*. So they'll just adopt the "guns blazing, full charge ahead" strategy, since they think it'll just be a "yea" or "nay" decision. Second, we tell them to talk to the neighbors, since if they can come up with something that the neighbors will okay, it'll be easier at the Board of Appeals. Third, we try to get them to meet one on one, or maybe as a group, but in as deinstitutionalized a way as possible, informally. We try to get the developers to sell their case that way; it'll get a much better hearing than at the big formal hearings.

But why should planners be reluctant to convene negotiating sessions between developers and neighbors, yet still be willing to encourage both parties to meet on their own? Why don't these planners embrace opportunities to mediate local land-use conflicts face-to-face? One planner could hardly imagine such a mediating role: "Work as a neutral between developers and neighbors? I don't know how I'd approach it. I'd just answer questions, suggest what could be done, and so on. That's what our role should be— although we should reach compromises between developers and neighbors. But we have to work within the rules. That's my reference point: to say what the rules of the game are. That's the job."

This planner's image as a "neutral" between disputing parties is less that of a mediator who facilitates agreement than it is of a referee in a boxing match. The referee assures that the rules are followed, but the antagonists might still kill each other. No wonder planners find the prospect of such mediation unattractive. A senior planner envisions further complications:

If I could be assured I could be wholly independent, then I could mediate—but I still have to pay my bills. . . . The planning department always has some vested interests, as much as we try to stay objective, independent. . . . I work for a mayor, for the elected representatives, for fourteen committees. . . . So there's always the question of compromise on my part: if the mayor says, "Tell me how to make this project work," for example. It took me a long time before I was able to say, "I'm going to have to say no." We have a very strong mayor.

Strategy Four: Shuttle Diplomacy

A planning director proposes yet another way to facilitate developer-neighbor negotiations: "I feel more comfortable in shuttle diplomacy, if you will: trying to get the neighbors' concerns on the table [and then] to get the developers to deal with them. . . . I'd rather bounce ideas off each side individually than be caught in the middle if they're both there. If both sides are there, I'm less likely to give my own ideas than if I'm alone with each of them."

Shuttle diplomacy, this director suggests, allows planners to address the concerns of each party in a professionally effective way. He explains:

If I'm with the developer, I feel I can make a much more extreme proposal—"knock off three stories"—but I wouldn't dare say that if neighbors were there. The neighbors would be likely to pick up and run with it, and it could damage the negotiations rather than help them. . . .

I'm a little reluctant to propose an idea to a developer with a neighborhood representative there. I'm willing to back off on an issue if the developer has a good argument, but the neighborhood might not, and then they might use my point as a club to hit the developer with: "Well, the planning director suggested that; it must be a good idea," and then I can't un-say it.

This planning director is as concerned about how his suggestions, queries, and arguments will be used as he is about what should be altered in the project. The director recognizes clearly that when he talks, he acts politically and inevitably fuels one argument or another. He not only conveys information in talking, but in talking he acts practically, influentially. He focuses attention on specific problems, shapes future agendas, legitimates a point of view, and suggests further arguments. The director continues:

I might not want to concede to a developer that there won't be a traffic problem, because I want to push him to relieve a problem or a perceived problem. . . . But I could say to the neighbors aside, "Look, this will be no big deal; it'll be five trips, not fifty." I can say that in a private meeting, but in a public meeting if I say it to a neighborhood representative I'm insulting him, even if the developer snickers silently. . . . So I lose my ability to be frank with both sides if we're all together. Not that this should be completely shuttle diplomacy, but it has its place.

These comments suggest that planning staff can certainly mediate conflicts in local permit processes, if not in ways that mediators are typically thought to act. The planners may not be independent third parties who assist developers and neighbors in face-to-face meetings to reach development agreements, but they may still mediate such conflicts as "shuttle diplomats."[3]

Consider now the work of a planner who works as an officially interested mediator.

Strategy Five: Active and Interested Mediation

We can consider a case that involves not a zoning appeal but a rezoning proposal. One planner, who had earlier worked as a community organizer, convened a working group of five community representatives and five local business representatives to draft a rezoning proposal for a long stretch of the major arterial street in their municipality. She reflects about how she acts as a mediator, dealing with substantive and affective issues alike:

Am I in a position of having to think about everyone's interest and yet being trusted by no one? Sure, all the time. But I've been in this job for seven years, and I have a reputation that's good, fortunately. . . . Trust is an issue of your integrity in the planning process. I talk to people a lot; communication is a big part of it. . . . My approach is to let people let off steam—let them say negative things about other people to me, and then in a different conversation at another time, I'd be sure to say something positive about that person—to try to let them feel that they can say whatever they want to me and to try to confront them with the fact that the other person isn't just out to ruin the process. But I'd do that in another conversation; I let them let off steam if they're angry.

This planner is well aware that distrust on all sides is an abiding issue, so she tries to build trust as she works. She tries to assure others that she will listen to them, and more—that she will acknowledge and respect their thoughts and feelings, whatever they have to say. She pays attention first to the person, then to the words. Then, as she establishes trust with her committee members and with others, she can also make sure, carefully, that real evidence is not ignored.

Realizing that anger makes its own demands, she responds with an interested patience. She seeks throughout to mediate the conflicting interests of the groups with which she is working:

I also make a point to tell each side the other's concerns, categorically, not with names, but all the other side's concerns. . . . Why's that important? I like to let people anticipate the arguments and prepare a defense [that will] either stand or fall on its own merits. For people to be surprised is unfortunate. It's better to let people know what's coming so they can build a case. They can hear an objection (if you can retain credibility) and absorb it; but in another setting they might not be able to hear it. . . . If they hear an objection first as a surprise, you're likely to get blamed for it.

If concerns are raised in an emotional setting, people concentrate more on the emotion than on the substance—this is a concern of mine. In emotional settings, lots gets thrown out, and lots is peripheral, but possibly also central later.

This planner is keenly aware that emotion and substance are interwoven and that planners who focus only on substance and try to ignore or wish away emotion do so at their own practical peril. Yet she is saying even more.

She knows that in some settings disputing groups can hear objections, understand the points at stake, and address them, whereas in other settings those same points may be lost. She tries to present each side's concerns to the other so they can be understood and addressed. Anticipating issues is central; learning of important objections late in the process will be costly, emotionally and financially, and planners are likely to share the blame.[4] "Why didn't you tell us sooner?" the refrain is likely to sound.[5]

Consider next, then, this planner-mediator's thoughts about the sort of mediation role she is performing:

But what I do is different from the independent mediator model. In a job like mine, you have an ongoing relationship with parties in the city. You have more information than a mediator does—about the history of various individuals, about participating organizations, about the political history of city agencies, and so on. You also have a vested interest in what happens. You want the process to be credible. You want the product to be successful—in my case I want the city council to adopt the committee's proposal. And you're invested . . . both professionally and emotionally. And then you have an opinion about particular proposals; you're a professional, you should have one, you should be able to look at a proposal and have an opinion.

Thus, she suggests, mediation has its place in local land-use conflicts, but the rules of the game will not be those that labor mediators follow. Indeed, planners who now mediate local land-use conflicts are not waiting for someone else to write the rules of the game; they are writing them themselves.

Strategy Six: Split the Job—You Mediate, I'll Negotiate

Consider finally a planning strategy that promotes face-to-face mediation with planners at the table, but as negotiators or advisors, not as mediators. A planning director explains: "There's another way we deal with these conflicts; we might involve a local planning board member. For example, if there's a sophisticated neighborhood group that's well organized, we've brought in an architect from the board who's as good with words as he is with his pencil. . . . The chair of the board might ask the board member to be a liaison to the neighborhood, say, and sometimes he'll talk just to the neighbors, sometimes with both."

Here a facilitator comes from the planning board with highly developed "communications skills." How does the planner feel in these situations?

It's more comfortable from my point of view—and the citizens'—to have a board member in the convening role. I'm still a hired hand. It seems more appropriate in a negotiating situation to have a citizen in that role and not an employee. . . . Since they've come from the neighborhoods, a board member is in a better position to bring neighbors and developers together, if they behave properly. Some board members are good communicators; some are more dynamic than others in pressing for specific solutions.

This planner identifies so strongly with the professional and political mandate of his position that a role as neutral convenor or
mediator of neighborhood-developer negotiations is not really
imaginable. But that does not prevent mediation; it means rather
that the planner retains a substantively interested posture while
another party, here a planning board member, convenes informal,
but organized, project negotiations between developers and neighbors. He illustrates the point:

Take the example of the Mayfair Hospital site. The hospital was going to
close, and the neighbors and the planning board were concerned about
what might happen with the site. So Jan, from the planning board, got
involved with the hospital and the neighborhood to look at the possibilities. Both the neighbors and the hospital set up reuse committees, and
Jan and I went to the meetings. There was widespread agreement that the
best use of the site would be residential—the neighbors definitely pre-
ferred that to an institutional use—but then there was a lot of haggling
over scale, density, and so on. Ultimately, a special zoning district was
proposed that included the site. The neighbors supported it, and it went
to [the elected representatives] where they voted to rezone the several
acres involved.

When local planners feel they cannot mediate disputes themselves, then, one strategy may be to search for informal, most likely
volunteer, mediators. These ad hoc mediators may be borrowed
from respected local institutions, and their facilitation of meetings
between disputing parties can allow planning staff to participate as
parties professionally interested in the site in question.[6]
Together, these six approaches form a repertoire of strategies
that land-use planners can use to encourage mediated negotiations
in the face of conflicts in local zoning, special permit, and design-
review processes. To refine these strategies, local planning staff can
build on several basic theories, techniques, and criticisms of conflict resolution (Fisher and Ury 1983; Raiffa 1982; Bacow and
Wheeler 1984; Susskind and Cruikshank 1987; Amy 1987). In the
next section we will consider the distinctive competences and sen-
sitivities required by these strategies.

Diplomatic Skills

More than the lack of independence keeps planners from easily
adopting roles as mediators. The emotional complexity of the me-

diating role makes demands that are quite different from those that planners have traditionally been prepared to meet. The community organizer turned planner quoted above makes the point brilliantly: "In the middle, you get all the flak. You're the release valve. You're seen as having some power—and you do have some. . . . Look, if you have a financial interest in a project, or an emotional one, you want the person in the middle to care about your point of view— and if you don't think they do, you'll be angry!" When asked, "So when planners try to be 'professional' by appearing detached and objective, does it get people angry at them?" she responded, "Sure!" This comment cuts to the heart of planners' professional identities. Must "professional," "objective," and "detached" be synonymous? If so, this planner suggests, then planners' own striving for an independent professionalism will fuel the anger and resentment of the same people those planners presume to serve.

Thus we can understand the caution with which a planner speaks of his way of handling emotional participants in public hearings: "How do I deal with people's anger? I try to keep cool, but occasionally I get irritated. But that's how we're expected to behave, to be rational. It's all right for citizens to be irrational, but not the staff!" How does one keep cool, be rational, and still respond to the claims of an emotional public at formal hearings? This planner elaborates: "It's one thing to begin the discussion of a project [to present our analysis] and anticipate problems. But it's another thing to *rebut* a neighborhood resident in public in a gentle way. . . . Part of the problem is that if you antagonize people it'll haunt you in the future. . . . We're here for the long haul, and we have to try to maintain our credibility."

The planner's problem here is precisely not the facts of the case; the facts may be clear enough. But how should the planner present the analysis that he feels must be made? Judging *when* to say what matters: "The biggest problem I have in the board meetings is when to respond and when to keep quiet. In a hearing, for example, I can't possibly respond to all the accusations and issues that come up. So I have to pick a direction, to deal with a generally felt concern. It's just not effective to enter into a debate on each point in turn; it's better to clarify things, to explain what's misunderstood."

This planner does much more than recapitulate facts. He tries to avoid an adversarial posture, even when he feels the situation to be conflictual. He listens as much to each person as he listens to each point. He knows that points and demands and positions may change as issues are clarified, but that if he cannot respond to people's underlying concerns, he is in trouble. Because he and his staff are there "for the long haul," he wants to be able to work with neighbors, community leaders, and elected representatives alike not just now but in the future too. So this planner knows that on any one project he must pay as much attention to the relationships involved in the review process as he pays to the project itself. How he relates to the parties involved in any local dispute, therefore, is as important as what he has to say.

Another planner points to the skills involved here:

Who would I try to hire to deal with such conflicts? I'd look for someone who's a careful listener, someone who's good at explaining a position coherently, succinctly, quietly, in a calm tone . . . someone who could hear a point, understand it whether he or she agreed with it or not, and who could then verbalize a clear, concise response. Most people, though—myself included—try to jump the gun and answer before it's appropriate. So I want someone who's able to stay cool and stay on the issues.

A community development director first mentions "a good listener" and then elaborates that in conflictual situations, he would want to hire

someone who won't say, "I know best," who won't get people's backs up just by their style. I'd want someone with some openness, with a sense of how things work, who won't accept everything, but who won't offend people.

They have to have critical judgment—to leave doors open, to give people a sense of involvement, and a sense of the feasible—they can't be convinced of something that's not likely to work, just for the sake of getting agreement.

This planning director also points to the balance necessary between what planners say and how they say it. He looks for substantive judgment and the skills to manage a process, too. Referring to the demands of working with developers as they navigate the approval process, the director stresses the role of diplomacy: "We [planners] have access to information, to resources, to skills . . . so developers usually want to work with us. They have certain problems getting through the process . . . so we'll go to them and ask, 'What do you want?' and we'll start a process of meetings. . . . It's diplomacy; that's the real work. You have to have the technical skill—that has to be there—but that's [only] the first 25 percent. The next 75 percent is diplomacy, working through the process."

Percentages aside, the point remains. To the extent that planning practitioners and educators focus predominantly on facts, rules, likely consequences, and mitigation measures, they may fail to attend to the pressing emotional and communicative dimensions of local land-use conflicts. Because the planning profession has not traditionally embraced the diplomat's skills, it should surprise no one that planners envision mediating roles with more reticence than relish.

In the following section, we will turn to administrative and political questions. What, initially, can be done in planning organizations to improve planners' abilities to mediate local land-use negotiations successfully? What about imbalances of power?

Administrative Implications for Planning Organizations

What does the analysis above imply for policy-makers and planners who wish to build options for mediation into local review processes? Mediation offers several opportunities under conditions of interdependent power: a shift from adversarial to collaborative problem-solving; voluntary development controls and agreements; improved city-developer-neighborhood relationships that enable early and effective reviews of projects; more effective neighborhood voice; and joint gains ("both-gain" outcomes) for the municipality, neighbors, and developers alike. Such opportunities present themselves *only* when no single party is so dominant that it does not need to negotiate at all.

The strategies reviewed above are already used in diverse settings. Which strategy a planner uses, and when, depends in large part on practical judgment: What skills does the planner have? Are developers or neighbors or other agency staff willing to meet jointly? Is there enough time for early, joint meetings? Are the practical and political alternatives for any one party so attractive that they see no point in mediated negotiations?

No single strategy is likely to be desirable in all circumstances.

So no one approach is likely to provide the model to formalize into new zoning or permit-granting procedures. But to say that these strategies should not be formalized does not mean that they cannot be regularly employed. How then can planners refine these mediated negotiation strategies in local zoning, permit, and design-review processes? Five points should be considered.

First, planning staff must distinguish clearly two complementary but distinct mandates they typically serve: (a) to press professionally, and thus to negotiate, for particular substantive goals (design quality, or affordable housing, for example); and (b) to bring about a participatory process that gives voice to affected parties (thus, like mediators, facilitating negotiations between disputants).

Second, planners need to adopt, administratively if not formally, a goal of supplementing formal permit-granting processes with mediated negotiations. Such negotiations cannot and should not substitute for existing political processes, but they should provide all parties with opportunities to craft workable and voluntary tentative agreements before formal hearing dates.[7]

Third, planning staff should examine each of the six strategies reviewed above. What skills do the planners need to develop to employ each of these strategies appropriately? The size of the agency, local zoning and related by-laws, the political histories of elected officials and neighborhood groups all have to be considered in adopting one or more of these strategies.

Fourth, planning staff must be able to show others—from developers to neighborhood groups to public works department staff to elected and appointed officials—how and when mediated negotiations can lead to "both-gain" (if not "win-win") outcomes and so improve local land-use planning and development processes. Planners also have to be clear about what mediated negotiation will *not* do: It will not solve problems of radically unbalanced power, for example. It can, however, refine an adversarial participatory process into one that is partially collaborative. It will not solve problems of basic rights, but it can often expand the range of affected parties' interests to be taken into account. Mediated negotiations will neither necessarily co-opt project opponents (as skeptical neighborhood residents might suspect) nor stall proposals and projects (as skeptical developers and builders might suspect). Yet when each side can effectively threaten the other, when each side's interests depend on the other's actions, then mediated negotiations may allow voluntary agreements, incorporate measures of control on both sides, allow "both-gain" trades to be achieved, and do so more efficiently for all sides than pursuing alternative strategies (e.g., going to court or, sometimes, community organizing).

Fifth, planners need to create an administrative process to match incoming projects with one or more of the mediated negotiation strategies discussed above and to review their progress as they go along.[8] With staff training in negotiation and mediation principles and techniques, planning departments would be better able to carry out these strategies effectively once they have organized administratively to promote them.[9]

Dealing with Power Imbalances

The six mediated negotiation strategies we have considered are hardly neutral. Inevitably, planners who adopt them must decide either to perpetuate or to challenge inequalities of information, expertise, political access, and opportunity. We will briefly consider how each approach, in turn, might address power imbalances.

Planners who provide just the facts, or information about procedures, to anyone who asks for them seem to treat everyone equally. Yet where severe inequalities exist, treating the strong and the weak alike ensures only that the strong remain strong and the weak remain weak. The planner who pretends to act as a neutral regulator may sound egalitarian but is nevertheless acting, ironically, to perpetuate and ignore existing inequalities.

The pre-mediation strategy involves substantial discretion on the part of the planning staff. If staff members fail to put the interests of weaker parties "on the negotiating table," then here, too, inequalities will be perpetuated, not mitigated. If the staff defends neighborhood interests in the development negotiations, they may indeed challenge existing inequalities. But which "neighborhood interests" should the planning staff identify? How should neighborhoods—especially weakly organized ones—be represented? These questions are practical and theoretical at once, and they have no purely technical answers.

At first glance, the strategy of letting developers and neighbors meet without an active staff presence seems only to reproduce the initial strengths of the parties. Yet depending on how the planners intervene, one party or another might be strengthened or weakened. At times, planners have helped developers anticipate and ultimately evade the concerns of oppositional neighbors. Yet planners might also provide expertise, access, information, and so on to strengthen a weaker neighborhood's position.[10]

The same discretion exists for planning staff who engage in shuttle diplomacy. Here a planner might counsel weaker parties to help them both before and during actual negotiations by identifying concerns that might effectively be raised, experts or other influentials who might be called on, and pre-negotiation strategies and tactics to be employed. The practitioner of shuttle diplomacy need not appear neutral to all parties; he or she needs instead to appear useful to those parties.

Planners who act as interested mediators face many of the same problems and opportunities that shuttle diplomats confront. In addition, though, the activist mediator may risk being perceived by planning board members, officials, or elected representatives as making deals that preempt their own formal authority. Thus, the invisibility of the shuttle diplomat has its advantages; the planners can give counsel discreetly, suggesting opportunities and packages but avoiding the glare—and the heat—of the limelight.[11]

Finally, the strategy of separating mediation and negotiation functions also involves substantial staff discretion. Here, too, the ways that mediators and negotiators consider the interests and enable the participation of weaker parties will affect existing power imbalances. Because negotiations always involve questions of relative power, they depend heavily on the parties' pre-negotiation work of marshaling resources, developing options, and organizing support.[12] Thus, progressive planners will need both organizing and mediated negotiation skills if conflicts are to be addressed without pretending that structural power imbalances do not exist.

Note that power structures involve collective relationships and require collective strategies (e.g., social movements) if they are to be challenged. The question to be asked here is not, "Can mediated negotiation strategies change power structures?" (they cannot) but rather, "Can mediated negotiation strategies support wider, collective efforts to change such structures?" (they can).

To focus on power structures while neglecting planners' strategies will produce paralysis, not empowerment. The planner who explicitly calls attention to class-based power imbalances, for example, may achieve no obviously better results in any practical sense than an activist mediator who acts on such knowledge without explicitly framing the planning negotiations in class-based terms. Yet to focus on strategies alone while neglecting power relations will produce not efficacy, but naïveté. For planners who seek to defend and empower the relatively powerless, then, mediated negotiation strategies must complement pre-negotiation organizing strategies. Both organizing and mediated negotiation work require planners to exercise political judgment and skill—to be able to listen sensitively and critically, to speak cogently and persuasively, and to encourage and mobilize action.[13]

Conclusion

The repertoire of mediated negotiation strategies discussed above inevitably requires that planners exercise practical judgments, both politically and ethically. These judgments involve who is and is not invited to meetings; where, when, and what kind of meetings are held; what issues should and should not appear on agendas; whose concerns are and are not acknowledged; how interventionist the planner's role is; and so on, as we have seen.

In local planning processes, then, planners often have the administrative discretion not only to mediate between conflicting parties but also to negotiate as interested parties themselves. Planning staff can routinely engage in the complementary tasks of supporting organizing efforts, negotiating, and mediating. In these ways, local planners can use a range of mediated negotiation strategies practically to address power imbalances of access, information, class, and expertise which perpetually threaten the quality of local planning outcomes.

Mediated negotiations in local land-use processes are no panacea for the structural problems of our society. But when local conflicts involve many issues, when differences in interests can be exploited by trading to achieve joint gains, and when diverse interests rather than fundamental rights are at stake, then mediated negotiation strategies for planners make good sense, politically and practically.

Part Four

Focus on What Counts: Planning and Design as Practical Communicative Action

Chapter Seven

Listening: The Social Policy of Everyday Life

In planning practice, fact and feeling, reason and emotion are often tightly intertwined. Whether a long-time neighborhood resident faces unwelcome change or a developer faces financial risk, anger and fear are always close at hand. In such situations, planners must deal as much with people's passions as with their earnestly certain predictions. But how is this possible? Planners not only must be able to hear words; they also must be able to listen to others carefully and critically. Such careful listening requires sensitivity, self-possession, and judgment. This is a critical part of paying attention—to other people and to substantive issues. This chapter focuses on the work of listening not only in planning and administrative practice but in everyday life as well.

We weave the texture of social policy in our everyday lives, as planners or as ordinary citizens, in our work or family settings, and in our personal affairs with friends or neighbors. By ignoring or paying attention to the issues of the day, we either neglect or nurture engaged and caring lives with one another. A friend or coworker may be in trouble, or a colleague may sit through a meeting in stony silence. They may be distressed over personal troubles, societal issues, or both, inseparably.[1] How we respond, or fail to do so, makes up the politics of our everyday lives. We may simply hear chatter, or ignore silence, and go about our business, or we may listen and respond.

To examine such politics, this social policy-making of our everyday or professional lives, this chapter contrasts the "hearing" we commonly do with the "listening" we can often do so much more powerfully. This contrast will show us the fabric of social policy we can create, add to, or tear apart in our daily lives. We can then uncover real opportunities that we so often fail to see and act on. If we simply hear words but do not listen to one another, our actions are likely to be irrelevant, if not reactionary. Yet if we listen so that we respond with sensitivity and care, our actions may be freeing, empowering others rather than mechanically generating feedback.[2]

Webster's New World Dictionary defines the verb "to listen" as "to make a conscious effort to hear; attend closely, so as to hear." It defines the verb "to hear" as "to become aware of (sounds) especially through the stimulation of auditory nerves in the ear by sound waves; to listen to and consider: i) take notice of; pay attention to; ii) to listen to officially; give a formal hearing of (a law case, etc.); iii) to consent to, grant; iv) to be a member of the audience; v) to permit to speak; to be informed of, be told, learn; vi) to have a normally functioning ear or ears; be able to hear sounds; to listen; to get news, learn, be told (of or about)." The meanings overlap, but two differences stand out: Listening is clearly active, while hearing is often more passive; and hearing is often formal, institutionally defined, as in "to grant a hearing," while listening seems more ordinary, if not more intimate. These differences are political and practical, too, as we will see.

Hearing is easy. Listening seems, mistakenly, not to be. We can hear words, but miss what is meant. We can hear what is intended, but miss what is important. We can hear what is important, but neglect the person speaking. As we listen, though, we can learn and nurture relationships as well. Listening is an action of being attentive, a way of being in a moral world. We can make a difference by listening or failing to do so, and we can be held responsible as a result. Many people know this, of course, especially those who have ever been told pointedly, "You're not listening!"

Listening involves subjects—speakers and listeners together—rather than objects. In contrast, hearing has an object, a message sent to be received. Only hearing, we subordinate the uniqueness of the speaker to the literal meaning of his or her words. Listening, we understand the meaning of what is said in the context of the speaker's life. When we only hear, we later find ourselves needing to say, "Well, that may be what they meant, but what they *said* was . . ." And we know this is usually a feeble excuse, hardly justifying our failure to understand. In hearing, we have only information flow; in listening, we have a world of relationships, a moral world of actors.[3] In listening, we pay attention not to the sound of the person, but to the person of the sound; we pay attention to practical meaning and possible implications, not to "dictionary meaning." Yet we often seem to understand listening far less than we understand hearing—or, perhaps worse still, we reduce it to hearing. But not listening is dangerous.

Failing to listen, we fail to learn, and we also damage our working relationships with others. If they do not listen carefully to members of the public, planners will lose any reputation for responsiveness or fairness, any public trust they might have had. Such planners may appear faithful to their bureaucratic obligations, but they will seem blind to their public duties.

Our failure to listen neglects far more than information; it denies a common membership in a common world of action—the city, the organization, or more private relationships. We can quickly cut ourselves off from others, weaken our ties, undercut mutual trust, and undermine our abilities to act together in the future. In the endless meetings of organizational life, listening is crucial if we are to learn what others care about or fear, what common interests we might share, what arguments or strategies or offers we might try tomorrow.

In the face of an uncertain future and the interplay of ambiguous and conflicting interests, a planner's ability to listen is tied to his or her ability to hope. Listening to the passionate voices of project proponents and opponents alike, planners must explore possibilities that no party may yet have considered. Posing questions to project developers, staff members of other agencies, and city residents, planners must probe for deeper interests, for still undisclosed but relevant information, for new ideas about possible strategies, agreements, or project outcomes. Listening to neighbors in discussions of local development proposals, a planner might transform expressions of futility into careful, strategic thinking about political interventions. Listening to developers' fears about the financial hazards of dealing with unexpected delays, planners might suggest yet unexplored project designs.

To listen well inevitably means to ask questions about deeper interests, future possibilities, and reformulations of the problems we seem to face. To ask such questions is at once to educate and to organize, to probe for new possibilities of action, to call into question conventional assumptions and expectations, and to assess new strategies and relationships.[4]

But why do we so often fail to listen critically? Listening can make us vulnerable, while simply hearing provides distance. Listening is work, and other work may call. Hearing is less demanding, if also less rewarding. To listen requires care, while hearing requires the more passive receipt of literal information—and sometimes we just do not care. In listening we create a relationship, a sense of mutuality, a "we," but in hearing, the flow of information is the only connection between sender and receiver. When planners face heated arguments, for example, but hear only words, they may easily dismiss the ambiguities of interests as expressions of anger, muddleheadedness, or inner confusion. The impulse to avoid ambiguity can have substantial psychological costs (Baum 1987). Yet when planners *listen* in such situations, they will be far more likely to expect and respect ambiguities of meaning, probe and explore them, and actually build on them to reach practical agreements.[5] Hearing passively records; listening helps us to learn: "Sure, they were talking about housing units, but another real concern they have is about their power in this process!"

The Practice of Critical Listening

We hear with our ears, but we listen with our eyes as well as our ears: We see gestures, expressions, and postures. "There's more to seeing than meets the eyeball," a philosopher of science once remarked. Seeing that reddish-pink color in the sky as a sunset depends on our prior understanding no less than on the direct evidence of color. Similarly, there is more to listening than meets the eardrum, far more than the hearing of words. How a planner listens will depend as much on his or her knowing the speaker as on hearing the speaker's words.

The differences between hearing and listening are differences between two ways of being-in-the-world, just as Martin Buber's I–It relations constitute a posture and a mode of being-in-the-world that differ from I–Thou relations. Hearing is an I–It orientation;

listening is an I–Thou relationship. But what can we do and bring into being when we listen? Five points deserve our attention.

First, in many interactions, by being attentive—demonstrating an attitude of caring involvement, inquiry, and wonder—our listening can foster mutuality and dialogue. John Friedmann quotes Karl Barth in this regard: "You and I must speak with one another, must listen attentively to one another. . . . That is the human meaning of dialogue."[6] To paraphrase the insight of the planner-mediator quoted in the last chapter: If planners do not acknowledge others' passionate concerns, the planners will add fuel to the fires, and they will risk being burned as a result.

As an expression of concern for serious conversation and dialogue, the listening that planners do may make trusting relationships possible. By offering reciprocity, their listening can work to create a sense of mutuality in place of the suspicions of a vociferous collection of individuals. As they search for possible meanings, for underlying interests, and for key experiences, planners can encourage others' voice, action, and self-understanding.[7]

Second, questioning is essential to listening well. Asking good questions can be an archaeological and interpretive digging into what matters, and, in this way, listening can reveal and clarify unspoken significances, values, and concerns.[8] Listening can thus both express care and reveal it in the life of others; as a result, a planner who probes more and presumes less can learn a good deal about the interests and fears of neighborhood residents and developers alike. Mary Belenky and her colleagues put it well: "Just as it takes a long while to develop the capacity to pose questions for yourself, it takes a good deal of time before you can imagine and appreciate the questions that others pose for you; and it takes even longer to understand the importance of posing questions to others" (1986, 188).

Third, by exploring meaning and implications, attentive listening can assess fundamental ambiguities of intentions and obligations.[9] When a city council member asks a planner in a public meeting for "proof," the planner must listen carefully: Is the council member grandstanding, concerned about data, or simply hoping to delay the proceedings? Sorting out the ambiguities here is a supremely practical challenge facing planners every day. By attending to the person and the situation of the speaker as well as to the words heard, when we listen we explore intended and contextual meaning as well as literal meaning.

Fourth, by creating a sense of publicity, our manifest listening works to prevent illusion, self-deception, and, at the extreme, solipsism (Barber 1984). When we act within a shared language—whether of zoning, environmental quality, or rates of return—rather than treating language as a tool, our listening can act as a corrective to others' self-deception, not necessarily with explicit criticism, but perhaps by bringing speakers back to our shared language and the rules of its ordinary use. We see this most clearly, no doubt, in personal relationships. Pictures can hold us captive, as Wittgenstein put it, and so a friend's listening can sometimes set us free.[10]

Fifth, listening can be an act of respect, showing that we "take the other seriously," rather than treating him or her as a tool or an object or a numbered client. The experience of a former welfare department caseworker, now a planner, illustrates the point beautifully:

First I thought I could at least be polite, that I'd be dealing with the poorest and the most downtrodden of society, that even if I didn't have the power to do much, I could be polite. But then I saw that some people were just so personally obnoxious that it was the most I could do to be business-like. Being polite to them was more than I could do. Then, some people just expected the agency to give them hell, and they acted like it.

There was one woman—she was just impossible to deal with. She just yelled and screamed and pounded her fists on my desk—and nothing I could say did anything. There wasn't anything I could do; I'd try to talk to her, but she'd yell and demand this and that—she was just irate. Then once I couldn't take it anymore. I threw my casebook down on the floor, slammed my fist, and yelled right back at her. What happened? She had a big smile on her face, and in the first calm and steady voice I'd ever heard out of her, she said, "Well, there! You'll be all right yet!" I was astonished. It seemed I hadn't really been paying attention to her, taking her seriously, really listening to her, until then.

In listening critically, then, we can express concern and build relationships. We can pose problems to uncover interests, fears, and new possibilities. We can explore ambiguity rather than shun it. We can respect difference, and look for ways to go on together.

Confronting Systematically
Distorted Communications

Our work of listening also has an inherently critical and judgmental character that brings several philosophical traditions into focus. In both the American pragmatist and the European neo-Marxist traditions, "praxis" refers to that type of social action in which theory does not direct but rather frames and is refined in turn through practice (Bernstein 1971). The activity of listening, as we have discussed it here, is an everyday and deeply political form of praxis. Furthermore, in the European tradition of the "human sciences" and more recently in its American variation of interpretive social science, "hermeneutics" refers to the interpretation of meaning beneath surface or literal meaning (as in the origin of hermeneutics, biblical exegesis). Thus listening is also a deeply hermeneutic activity. When we recognize that listening is truly a hermeneutic praxis, we discover a powerful integration of pragmatist and neo-Marxist concepts of action with phenomenological notions of interpretation. When we listen well, we integrate hermeneutics and critical theory, phenomenology and the critique of ideology, and put them into practice together.

But is such listening simply utopian? Hardly. For were we not able to listen critically, we would never be able to identify, assess, and counteract manipulative strategies, ideological claims, racial and sexual biases, or even plain misunderstandings. We may suspect, for example, that a project advocate is not telling the whole story, that neighbors are missing vital information, that a public official is deliberately exaggerating a position, that committee members are confusing discrete issues, or that project opponents are grasping at straws. In such cases, simply hearing what is said will not get us very far; we need to listen critically to interpret just what is happening and to gauge then how to go on. To listen in this way, we need a working theory of the context we are in: Is the community member yelling because he has lived in his now-threatened house for ten years, or because he feels the planning department has betrayed the neighborhood, or because that's just his way of making an emphatic point?[11]

Hearing virtually ignores context, but listening is immediately practical.[12] We hear words, but we listen to people in situations of stress, anger, inequality, fear, suspicion, potential profit or loss. Sensitive to exaggeration, grandstanding, or false promises of co-operation, our listening is a critical response in everyday life and in our professional and political practice as well.[13] Faced with the arguments of a project developer or opponent, planners must not expect complete candor but must listen for proponents' and opponents' real concerns and interests, for their strategies, for what is negotiable and what is not. Is this developer simply out to make a quick profit and leave town? Do the neighbors want to stop the project for racist reasons?

Listening, then, is our mode of practical interpretation in the face of power. But how do we bring theory to bear as we listen? How do we identify systematically distorted or ideological claims and respond to them? How do we already at times recognize and respond to systematically distorted communications—or carry out the classical critique of ideology—as we listen critically? Careful empirical research here could uncover and elaborate a fascinating repertoire of political skills and strategies.[14]

Notice that to listen critically we must be able both to *understand* meanings and to *explain* social and political influences on them. Too often in discussions of social science and interpretation the tasks of understanding and explaining have been posed as exclusive choices.[15] Planners cannot afford to choose only one or the other of these tasks. When a developer or a citizens' group makes a threat, planners need simultaneously to understand what's been said and to explain the pressures that led to it. If past threats have not been carried out, the planners might explain this one as "just bluffing." Alternatively, a recent change in local economic conditions or in a political campaign may lead the planners to explain the same threat as quite real.

Ethnic identity and cultural style can matter enormously, too. What one party may take as an emotional loss of control, another party may recognize as an expression of seriousness. A member of one ethnic group may interpret words uttered in a cool, detached way as a signal of disrespect, a lack of compassion and concern. A member of another ethnic group may interpret those same words as a signal of self-controlled and even-handed consideration (Kochman 1981).

If planners attempt only to explain behavior—"He's just out to make a big profit" or "He's just playing to an audience"—without trying to understand what this developer, this neighborhood leader, or this politician means, they will quickly undercut the working relationships they need to get their work done. Yet if planners focus too closely on the meaning of what is said without being able to explain the influence of outside, possibly systemic, pressures on what they hear, they are likely to be short-sighted, if not perpetually misled.[16]

Failures of Listening Can Reveal Ideological Influences

If our listening serves as a corrective to the distorted, ideological claims we face in daily political and professional life, then when we fail to listen well we allow such claims to have influence, to go unchallenged. To understand how this can happen, we should recapitulate the subtle ways in which we can fail to listen.

We may focus on the utterance and not the person. When planners make this mistake, they may find themselves saying after a meeting, "I don't know where she's coming from, but what she said was . . ." Here they attend to messages rather than to actors, to signals sent rather than to lives lived—as the detachment of "what she said" rather than "where she's coming from" suggests.

We may not be familiar, or competent, with the language, dialect, style, or jargon with which we are faced.[17] We may say we are "talking past one another," or, since we both seem to be making sense, but not to each other, we may say, "We're just in different worlds!" We can both be speaking English, agreeing that the sun rises in the east, and so on, but we can be in very different (meaningful) worlds nonetheless. To listen we need to share a way of speaking together in which communication, and not just word recognition, is possible. If we are captive to different language styles, we will be prisoners within radically different practical worlds.[18]

At times, we may demand excessive clarity, precision, or definition from others and avoid our own responsibility to draw out implications and think, pay attention to meaning. Just as facts do not speak for themselves, neither do spoken words automatically express their implications to us. We must be prepared to draw and interpret the implications of what a supporter, an opponent, a friend, a foe, a lover, or a co-worker has said. To neglect this responsibility can easily lead us not to expect it of others. Then we would be in danger of realizing another self-fulfilling prophecy: expecting and thus fostering passive and dumb audiences, ourselves included.

We may not recognize the context of what we hear, and so we may misinterpret and misunderstand. To understand what we hear, we have to know some history—what the speaker has done, what important events make up the backdrop of the speaker's words. We will understand the same words quite differently if they are spoken in a speech, in intimate conversation, on a theater stage, or as an example of what someone else has said. In conversations with lawyers or physicians, their professional role and our client relationship may define the context in which we listen.[19] For the psychoanalyst, clarifying the client's context of early childhood experience is central to the practice of listening, understanding what words really mean, as analysis proceeds. For community organizers, program administrators, managers, and planners, the same argument holds: If we misjudge the context, we are likely to go wrong.

But contexts can change. "I love you" or even "I understand" can mean extraordinarily different things as time passes, as a relationship changes, progresses, or falters. The same political promise will have different meanings and take on different significance and implications as political-economic conditions change. When a promise has been broken twice before, the context of the third promise is no longer what it once was; although we may hear the same words, "I promise that . . . ," we will be likely to listen and act differently than we did at first. Thus to listen well, we must pay attention to changes not only in what we hear but in the contexts in which we hear as well. Hearing the same words and presuming the same context when the world has in fact changed can lead to disaster—and it is not listening.

In addition, our concern with "good reasons" can preoccupy us with the abstractions of arguments and lead us to neglect the people in front of us. In our everyday lives, we make this mistake when we say: "That's just (Marx/your mother/your father/your latest cult-hero) talking." Our distrust of political rhetoric can lead us to dismiss a speaker when we feel we're hearing a "political line." When planners attend only to reason or evidence, they can easily appear disrespectful of others' experience and insensitive to their feelings when they say: "Yes, I heard what she said, but she didn't have any reason to feel that way, or say that." Listening means paying attention to people—and not subordinating empathy to an interest in the abstract qualities of argument.[20]

We may also be predisposed not to listen. As speaking is a mode of action, so is listening, and for any individual, both are particular ways of using language. But some things are harder to talk about than others, and some kinds of participation are easier to engage in than others. Religious, family, and political backgrounds all shape the conversation we find difficult, riddled with self-deception, or heretical. Some people cannot talk about socialism; others cannot talk about psychoanalysis. Some people cannot talk about God; some cannot talk about gender equality. Here listening fails, and relationships fail.

Furthermore, if we do not respect other people's fallibility, our listening can only fail. If we expect others to speak as perfectly programmed machines, we will hear sounds, and be disappointed no doubt, but we will not listen. If we expect to hear only arbitrary babble from people we hardly consider to be politically autonomous human beings, we will be unable to listen, too. We cannot listen either to machines or to a chaos of noise, though we can hear both all too well. To be able to listen, we must respect the life of the person speaking; without that, we have only prejudice, stereotype, the racism and sexism that deny the lives of others—and we have no possibility of building a common world.

Finally, we may forget the relation between part and whole, between this person and the broader social structure, between what C. Wright Mills called "personal troubles" and "public issues."[21] We may attend only to the speaker or only to the setting. We fall too easily into the attitude that people's beliefs come from "within their heads," or perhaps not from them at all but from "the economic system" or their parents. To take an example from social work: "The client's tendency was to locate the problem and the blame outside himself, while the worker tended to see the client himself as contributing significantly to his own problem."[22] To focus only on social structure neglects the person; to attend only to the individual may be to blame the victim and neglect fundamental needs to restructure our social and political institutions.[23]

Conclusion

In planning or everyday life, then, listening necessarily addresses questions of possible actions, the pervasive questions of "what can be done." Whether we hear the frustration of a developer, the fear of a neighborhood resident, or the puzzlement of a colleague, in listening we share the perpetual questions of others: "What can I do? What should I do? Why?" The listener recognizes these questions whether they are heard explicitly or not; in ignoring or responding to these, the listener is a political actor, organizing or disorganizing hope, neglecting or addressing the art of the possible. In so doing, planners must continually face the claims of power and ideology and address opportunities to counteract them.

Finally, as it is an act of participation, listening is inescapably political.[24] When planners speak the language of a particular group, they do so not just to be clear, but to shape a course of action. They act as they speak. Because we learn language and the world together, we cannot have much of a world together if we do not listen.[25] Only through our shared work, language, and interaction do we have a meaningful world of which we are intelligible, moral members.[26] In a world where people do not listen to one another, there may be decision, force, and violence, but there can be no collective mobilization or organizing, no collective social or political life.

So too in our efforts to work and organize with one another: Developing the ability to listen critically is a political necessity. Listening well is a skilled performance. It is political action, not simply a matter of a friendly smile and good intentions. Without real listening, not simply hearing, we cannot have a shared, critical, and evolving political life together. In listening we may still better understand, explain, and cut through the pervasive "can't," the subtle ideological distortions we so often face, including of course our own misunderstandings of who we are and may yet be. Listening well, we can act to nurture dialogue and criticism, to make genuine presence possible, to question and explore all that we may yet do and yet become.[27]

Chapter Eight

Designing as Making
Sense Together

Architecture, as practiced by design professionals, is a kind of ne-
gotiation process.

—Dana Cuff

If the work of listening is so poorly understood and yet so politically vital, how inadequately appreciated and understood is the
work of *designing*! How can we understand the incredible richness
of what designers and design professionals actually do when they
craft, review, and reformulate project designs?[1] This chapter proposes a deceptively simple answer to this question: Using practical
conversation as its medium, designing is a deeply social process of
making sense together.

Let me begin with a story. As I left a metropolitan planning
office recently, I stood in an elevator with two architects. One held
project drawings; the other held a model of an office complex.
They had just finished another meeting with the planning staff.
The younger of the two men asked his colleague, "Well, scream
now, or scream later?" I braced myself. The older man answered,
"It was actually a pretty good design review." As we parted company on the street below, I asked if the staff had wanted lots of
changes. They both nodded, one perplexed, the other knowing.
One pointed to the model and gestured: "They want this [section]
rotated something like this. We'll see." The process obviously
would continue.

This vignette raises several questions. First, whether design originates in intuition or inspiration, the unconscious or acculturation, it materializes through the social processes of review and evaluation, criticism and modification, partial rejection, partial adoption. When designers sketch, look again, and modify, they have internal conversations with themselves, just as later they will have more social conversations with others—sketching, presenting, modifying, and refining designs with other architects, planners, clients, and politicians. We need to explore how these conversations work.

Second, the story suggests that if designers focus too narrowly on the design problem or individual design "methods," they risk being victims of design processes in which they are only participants, not all-powerful masters. So we must ask how designers can design effectively if they cannot be assured of influence and power.

Third, the contrast between the young architect's perplexity and the older architect's appreciation of the review suggests the importance of understanding design activities as socially structured practices. Practical expectations and daily experience can then be adjusted accordingly; less confusion and disruption may result; and review processes could come to be viewed as constructive rather than inquisitorial. But what notion of design practice can help designers anticipate these interactions?

In this chapter, we will explore designing not only as a form-giving practice but also as a practice of "making sense together" in practical conversations. By drawing, sketching, revising, or offering plans together, designers make and challenge their common sense in various cultural and ideological contexts.[2] Their conversations take place in specific institutional settings: in the school studio, in the firm's work spaces, in the planning department's conference room, in the client's offices. These settings influence designers and their designs just as those settings are influenced by them. In such settings, design conversations may be replete with contradictions, informed by traditions and ideologies, subject to and contingent upon political and economic pressures. Yet discussions of design practice have focused more on the products of individual designers than on the interactions that influence the realized designs.[3]

When form-giving is understood more as an activity of making sense together, it can then be situated in a world where social meaning is a perpetual practical accomplishment. Designing takes place in institutional settings where rationality is precarious at best, conflict abounds, and relations of power shape what is feasible, desirable, and at times even imaginable. By recognizing design practices as conversational processes of making sense together, designers can become alert to the social dimensions of design processes, including organizational, institutional, and political-economic influences that they will face—necessarily, if also unhappily at times—in everyday practice.[4]

To develop my argument, I will first consider the conventional view that design is a search through a solution space of alternatives.[5] This powerful yet problematic understanding of design activity is explored by considering a concrete example drawn from a neighborhood planning process concerned with the design of a small urban park. Second, I will present a detailed discussion of form-giving as the practical work of making sense together.[6]

Urban Design and Community Planning

The following exchange took place at a community planning meeting in a small northeastern city. The meeting was organized by the Neighborhood Housing Services Office to discuss proposed improvements for a one-square-block neighborhood park. Residents near the park were skeptical of so-called improvements, fearing that changes in the park would attract loud and disruptive late-night visitors and that any new benches would simply be vandalized.

At one point, following a good deal of discussion, the city planner asked the crowd of thirty local residents, "What about benches—putting in some benches along with better lighting?"

"No benches," one resident retorted. Another said, "Fine—if they stay and aren't torn up."

So the planner asked the architect, "Russ, would you talk about the vandal-proof benches?"

"Well, some are cast iron; others are wood on a concrete pad."

The discussion shifted as the planner tried to elicit other responses. She asked, "What about a drinking fountain?" Protests of "No!" erupted. A resident explained: "These people who come late at night don't drink water! They bring pop cans and drop them."

The planner then asked, "Where should the refuse cans go?" and a couple of residents suggested, "At the entrances."

"At the entrances?" the planner probed.

"Yes," came the residents' reply.

Another resident spoke up: "I don't think you need a gazebo in the middle of the park at all; but I'd like a bench under a tree—I'd use it." Another responded, "There's already one there—but it's usually well occupied. There's usually a wino sleeping on it."

Here the architect, who had been silent for some time, attempted a noncommital statement ("Well, why don't I take a look at it?"), but implied that the final details might be left to his judgment. The response was telling: "Well, I wouldn't leave it up to *your* judgment," said one resident. "No offense—nothing personal, I mean." And then she exclaimed, "Oh my, I just heard what I said!"

Notice that the object of this part of the meeting was in a very real sense urban design. Planners, an architect, community organizers, and community residents assembled to discuss plans for the local park. The meeting was itself one part of the larger design process. The participants considered various design elements: ordinary or "vandal-proof" benches, better lighting, a gazebo structure, a drinking fountain. And not only did the planner and the architect collect comments from the community, but they also worked to shape a design consensus.

In addition, the ambiguities in the meeting are instructive. Just what *are* the roles of the architect, the planner, and the resident? Who had the power to formulate a final design, much less to implement it? This was hardly clear. Moreover, the very parameters in which the final design was to be realized were not well specified; how well specified can vandalism be?[7] Were the planner and the architect just going through the motions of soliciting comments, or not? Will the neighborhood association take this meeting as a closing or an escalating step in the process of park design?

Notice that these problems of roles, power, parameters, cooptation, and community activism and resistance create practical ambiguities for observers and participants alike. The planner cannot easily predict neighborhood sentiment and political pressures on the planning department. As an outside consultant, the architect can predict even less, possessing a still fainter sense of the connections between his early sketches and what will eventually be built. Staff members from the local housing service may not be insiders with either the planners or the community, and what they know and whom they trust vary as a result. Finally, local residents are often unsure about their ability to influence city hall, with which they associate the planners, and they often feel more vulnerable than efficacious as a result.

In interactive settings such as the one described above, how does a design emerge? We may begin to answer this question by asking how the "search" and "sense-making" metaphors of designing capture the interactive dynamics involved.

Design as a Search Process

The notion of designing as a search process might be used to understand this brief case example, though it seems to lead to immediate difficulties. The meeting could be considered a place where the planner, the architect, and the community residents were searching for at least a satisfactory solution. But just who is conducting the search? By answering "the designer," we only replace a problem with a label.[8] Any theory of design must address this problem: the relation between the design professional and the people affected by the designer's work.

Further, the parameters of the "solution space," the conceptual space in which possible solutions might be found, in even this simple case are not clear. Community sentiment in particular seems difficult to specify in advance. Some people were worried about a lot of kids making noise in the park at night; others were worried about "winos." Still others were concerned about transients. Some worried about safety, while others called attention to aesthetics. Everyone, though, seemed to agree that "improving the park" could cause as much disruption as pleasure for local residents.

For several people, the solution space was their present way of life, the status quo. Even though the planner spoke in terms of "improving" the site, they responded, in essence, "If isn't broken, don't fix it. We want the park just as it is." For others at the meeting, the various ways of controlling noise, enhancing aesthetics, controlling low-status users, and so on may have abstractly defined the possible solution space. But does this help us to understand what happened at the meeting? Surely different participants there interpreted the basic parameters of noise, aesthetics, and visitors (intruders?) differently.

Issues of interpretation emerge once the planner, architect, or community resident asks how specific criteria should be used to evaluate a given proposal. Because the criteria are often ambiguous, the question of meeting criteria calls for judgment and interpretation—an application of a general norm (maintaining simplicity of form, for example) to a particular case. What is required here is not simply a comparison of well-defined combinations of design elements with well-defined, unambiguous criteria, but skilled interpretation as well. Such interpretation involves the (form-giving) application of a general norm (for instance, maintain a clean line) to a particular case. But this is no longer just a process of "search"; it is the creation of new meaning or sense.[9]

Furthermore, the very instability of the setting (a community meeting) belies a description of the park design discussion as a rational search process. Although solutions certainly were sought, the sentiments of all present were clearly in flux, in part because of the meeting itself. Thus, the meeting was as much a search for a definition of the problem as it was a search for the problem's solution. The participants seemed to pay more attention to defining "the problem of the park" than they did to searching within any fixed parameters for a satisfactory final design.[10] Here the metaphor of a search process evaporates, for if search includes creating the values, variables, and parameters within which the search behavior is to operate, the notion loses whatever formal power it originally had. Those who advocate that we understand designing as a search process presume just what is most problematic, the work of defining the problem, as our example suggests.

Given limited elements to combine and definite parameters within which a design can be unambiguously evaluated, "search" has a powerful logic to recommend it; but stripped of its problem-defining parameters, search becomes directionless meandering.[11]

The power of the "search" metaphor may be precisely its weakness: Its technical meaning presumes a specification of a "solution space," while substantive questions of who is searching, with what interests, values, preferences, and styles, and in what organizational or procedural setting are only weakly intimated. Yet the notion of a search process has a lasting appeal, not only for its technical merits but also for its colloquial implications. Designers have the experience of searching, playing, wondering, and then at times having a solution emerge. The irony here is that designers might embrace Herbert Simon's metaphor for reasons very different from those Simon had in mind. If that is so, it is instructive, for it points to the need to develop an understanding of design practices that is experientially compelling and articulated politically and culturally as well.

Designing as Making Sense Together

Now consider the community meeting as part of a design process understood alternatively as one of making sense together in practical conversation. Does this metaphor fare any better than that of a search? Is this even a fair question, for isn't the community meeting itself a conversation? It is a fair question, for the community meeting is not a conversation in any ordinary sense of the word; the conventional bounds of ordinary conversation are far more circumscribed than the conventions of large, public, formal, and institutionally defined community meetings. Nevertheless, the notion of designing as an interpretive, sense-making process may account far more adequately for the behavior in the community meeting than does the notion of "search," for several reasons.

Facing Ambiguity:
Reading Context and Desire

First, whereas the notion of design as a search cannot account for action in the face of ambiguity, the sense-making metaphor embraces such action. A search permits the discovery of a satisfactory solution once values and evaluative positions are known. In contrast, sense-making leads us to examine the very genesis of those evaluative positions.

The meaning of a sentence, or the physical form of a park, emerges only in a context. Likewise, a native skill of speakers, and a learned skill of designers, is to fit an offered phrase, or a suggested sketch, into the context at hand. "The context," however, is never a clear given, as the search model presumes. Reading the context is a practical skill that is called into action when anyone attempts to communicate with someone else. At the stage of programming, conceptual development, or design development, an architect's attempts to "make sense" are inextricably linked to his or her active reading and anticipation of context—both social and physical.[12]

Notice what happened in the meeting when the planner asked about a drinking fountain. Her question about a functional design element was answered with a reformulation of the entire context: "No! These people who come late at night don't drink water! They bring pop cans and drop them." Functional amenities will be wasted here, the resident suggests, if a deeper problem—late-night users—is not addressed. Design proposals must make sense in context, but in which context?

Sir Geoffrey Vickers referred to this determination of context as the exercise of appreciative skills; Donald Schön and others speak of balancing or fitting the "whole and its parts"; and phenomenologists refer to the parallel interpretive work that grows out of the "hermeneutic circle."[13] In every case, gauging the context at hand is essential to making sense and, thus, to designing.

In addition to setting out and reading context, design as a sensemaking activity faces other ambiguities (elaborated in Chapter Nine).[14] How do the planner and the architect gauge the residents' intensity of feeling, or each other's? Planner, architect, and residents make sense together not only in a context but also in relation to one another, with fears and desires that are often ambiguous. Nevertheless, such emotions influence the meaning and character of design solutions. In everyday life, we draw on a repertoire of subtle strategies with which we create as well as interpret ambiguities of context and desire. So too in the work of designing. How much can we learn, practically and theoretically, about that repertoire of strategies?[15]

World-Shaping

Second, once we see designing as a collaborative effort to make sense, we can easily recognize the world-making (or worldthreatening) nature of design. One resident refers to the prospect of new benches being torn up by vandals. Another resident refers to the litter that might despoil the neighborhood park. Yet another points facetiously to the benches already in use—not by local residents, but by winos. Perhaps most significant, the architect suggests that the design decisions be left to him. Here one woman challenges his presumption of power even before she could think to do so more politely: "Well, I wouldn't leave it up to *your* judgment. . . . Nothing personal." These comments are not just about functional issues. Indeed, they speak to the relation between proposed designs and the very character and integrity of the neighborhood park. As the woman suggested to the architect, the stakes are quite a bit more than "personal."

Not only the function but the actual lived meaning of the park is at issue here. What sense does it make to have a park in which benches are torn up or used for beds, where litter mars the grounds, or decisions seem to be made without regard for the concerns of local residents? The designer's work is not just a matter of technical problem-solving. It is a matter of altering, respecting, acknowledging, and shaping people's lived worlds as well. Significantly, designers cannot freely alter such worlds because they are, in part, products of their own culture, training, and institutional settings, as we will see below.[16]

Practical Conversation and Communicative Action

Third, the sense-making account suggests that design evolves through the communicative performances of many participants in practical conversations. In the meeting above we clearly have both elementary and more complex communicative actions: questioning, stating, answering, reporting, challenging, apologizing, suggesting, qualifying, and so on. Notice how much more than information-processing, seen as the transmission of facts, goes on.[17] Factual reports about the park do not dominate the evening but are complemented by expressions of feeling, by questions that open up issues, by challenges to the appropriateness of certain moves, and so on. As the participants speak, and so act, together, they take and defend and modify positions; they create precedents, impressions, and expectations. The planner and architect, for example, may come to be seen as more or less open, more or less responsive, or more or less competent on the basis of what they say, what they claim, and how they do it.

Furthermore, the community meeting approximates a broader

conversation between professionals and affected persons. As the practical talk proceeds, proposals surface, meeting differing support and resistance. New ideas may be generated, too—ideas whose future depends as much on the forces constituting the design conversation as on their technical or aesthetic merits (Schön 1983).

The design conversation above is political and also quite practical. Neither the professionals nor the community residents came to the meeting to discuss trivia. Residents came to express concerns or to protect their park. The professionals may have come to solicit ideas, to test community sentiment, or even to co-opt residents by giving them "a chance to be heard." In both cases, the notion of design as a process of sense-making via conversation accounts for such political phenomena more adequately than the notion of "search" does. Whereas the formal process of searching in a "solution space" calls for the logical pre-definition of all alternatives, the conversational model allows for the native, historically rooted abilities of participants to create new meanings together, regarding both means and ends. The communicative and interpretive account of making sense together allows for an openness of meaning precluded by the alternative notion of "search."

Conversation and Learning

Fourth, the analysis of potentially conflict-ridden design conversations (e.g., criticism in design reviews) illuminates processes of learning. In a search process, learning seems restricted to the adoption or rejection of more or less promising paths to a solution. In the sense-making model, however, learning involves not only changes in strategies but also changes in the very parameters of the definition of the problem. In architectural practice, there are many occasions, both formal and informal, of design criticism: design presentation, evaluation, review, checking, and inspection.

At the community meeting, not only were technologies discussed (vandal-proof benches), but planner, architect, and community residents alike had the opportunity to listen to one another and evolve a sense of what was important and what was to be done. In addition, the sense-making process allows for contradiction, for we might wonder whether anyone speaks for the late-night park users or the winos driven to use park benches for their beds.

Political-economic contradictions between public and private purposes may well show up conversationally as "contra-dictions":
structural problems of the national economy will be expressed
locally as conflicting and contradictory claims about social needs
and opportunities, and designers can expect to face these conflicting claims in their practice.[18]

Practically Situated Action

Fifth, design does not happen in a vacuum. Speech or gesture, line
or sketch wholly in the abstract would be meaningless. The sense-
making account situates the designer's work in a historical, practical context. The institutional and organizational settings count:
design proposals must be formulated within the bounds of resources such as time, information, historical legacy, political ideologies, and cultural styles, as well as capital.[19]

In the community meeting cited above, the work of park design
takes place in part in the very neighborhood where several of the
participants live. These citizens explain how they have used the
park and present relevant histories of the site. They also report
their experiences of planners, for as one resident said earlier, "You
know, we had the most beautiful city in the U.S. until the planners
came in!" The significance of this comment may lie more in its current implications than in its reporting of any historical fact: It
clearly indicates to the professionals the historical and politically
charged context in which their very conversation takes place. Design conversations are bounded by contextual constraints, to be
sure. Thus, as we saw in Chapter Four, an analysis of the social
and political character of these constraints is crucially important
to the defense, negotiation, and realization of specific design
proposals.[20]

Reproducing Identity and Social Relations

Sixth, the study of ordinary language use gives us a striking insight
into the richness of design processes. In ordinary speech, speakers
reproduce their contextual relationships with one another while
they simultaneously communicate messages with certain contents.
Thus, the previous sentence implicitly invokes this chapter and

your reading of it as its context just as it makes an explicit claim about ordinary language use (Watzlawick, Beavin, and Jackson 1967). Much of the care that architects take with clients, for example, reflects an intuitive sensitivity to the simultaneous recreation of social roles that occurs along with discussions about form and function.

In the community meeting, the architect, the planner, and the community residents speak about design issues, and as they do so they also play particular, if ambiguous, social roles: They create and recreate their social identities ("planner," "architect," "local homeowner") and their relationships.[21] Depending on what is said, and how it is said, as suggested above, the architect or planner may come to adopt a new role, may come to be regarded as "thoughtful" or "pushy," "aggressive" or "astute," "muddleheaded" or "professional," and so on.

What is fascinating here in the language of design is this: The work of the designer creates not only an object but also the designer's own evolving self. When Moshe Safdie, for instance, designed Habitat or the Jerusalem windows, he not only created those built forms; he also "created" (and became) a highly esteemed personage, a Moshe Safdie different from Mrs. Safdie's son Moshe. Design activity, then, reproduces designers just as it produces designed objects.

As Chapter Five argued, such refashioning of identity and reputation happens in all interaction. Selves are produced and presented just as objects are—as all talk of professional credibility and trust suggests as well. Thus, if designing is understood as a process of sense-making, we can recognize immediately not only that it is productive and instrumental, but that it is reproductive and social identity–shaping as well.

Political Rationality

Seventh, the sense-making, conversational model raises an obvious and important question: Who participates in the conversation, and who makes sense on whose terms for whom? Here the historically situated nature of designing (what Herbert Simon might describe as its necessarily "bounded rationality") assumes a political and ethical character. One can reject authoritarian design strategies without taking the posture that design should proceed by popular vote. Legitimate design authority and its constitution are at stake.

If we are not to hold that whatever is designed is designed well, we must invoke some standards of criticism and judgment. How such standards develop is of enormous importance to the history of all the design professions. If certain designs have rarely been explored because of hegemonic ideologies of gender and housework, for example, we might expect new opportunities to be revealed as designers seek to free themselves from unnecessarily restrictive conventions. To recognize such conventions as ideological may seem to help little, yet it points to the possible systematic, rather than ad hoc, stifling of historical design practices, as Delores Hayden has brilliantly shown.[22] Such problems recall the possibilities discussed in earlier chapters: Might the design conversations that now take place *at times* be systematically but unnecessarily restricted, biased, or distorted? To resist such impoverishment, designers must explore how power and ideology influence the most elemental communicative moves in the design process: sketching, showing, proposing, checking, reviewing, presenting, and so on.

Again, of course, in the case of the community meeting one might ask how the meeting was called; just who attended; whether or not anyone was intentionally or unintentionally excluded; whether past meetings had created precedents that hindered the design discussion; and whether the professionals present were open to new design ideas, or whether they were co-opting the residents who attended, letting them blow off steam while the design work had already been completed. Even if the community setting were altered and just one designer worked with a client's program, the same questions would arise with respect to both the structure and ambiguities of the program and the discretion to be exercised by the designer. The notion of design as a "search" might lead us to ask if any possible combinations or design options were suppressed, but it would give us little way of pursuing the question.

The idea of design as making sense together in conversation takes us further because it requires us to place the participants in the conversation in their institutional and historical settings. As a result, we see the issues of systematic exclusion and bias writ large. Rationality in design, therefore, depends on both an analysis of functional performance and an account of aesthetic and historical legitimacy. In the community meeting, the rationality of putting a gazebo in the center of the park is assured neither by the architect's judgment nor by the residents' vote.[23] Designers who are blind to such issues of bias, institutional distortion, and ideology risk being unhappily surprised in design processes by others who recognize the costs involved.

Conclusion

I have tried to show in this chapter that designers design with others as much as they do with their heads or hands and that, furthermore, wherever the creative impulse originates, the development, refinement, and realization of design is a deeply social process. In order to capture the practical, interpretive, and institutional dimensions of that process, this chapter has proposed an alternative conception of designing as the interactive work of making sense together in practical conversation.

Toward that end, we first explored a fragment from an actual community planning meeting to illuminate a variety of organizational, cultural, political, and rhetorical dimensions of even the most simple urban design problems. We also observed that the notion of design as a formal search process leaves much to be desired. Indeed, the notion of search seems ill suited to account for the generation of the solution space, the resolution of ambiguity (in design criteria, for example), and the fluidity of the preferences of clients, beneficiaries, and others.

Second, we considered seven aspects of design practices seen as the work of making sense together. This formulation allows us to understand design practice as action in the face of ambiguity, action that recreates the lived worlds of inhabitants, action that is fundamentally *communicative* in character. Potentially integrating "contra-dictions" with learning processes, designing is always acting in a practical context.

Furthermore, because it is a form of communicative action, designing is both instrumentally productive and socially reproductive—accomplishing ends and reproducing social and political relations of status, power, and culture at the same time. Finally, such a situated, conversational account of design practices raises historical and normative questions about the possible biases (ad hoc and systematic, necessary and unnecessary) that design processes and practices might manifest—biases that sensitive and critical designers can work to counteract.

These aspects of the sense-making conception of design practice need further elaboration and criticism. With such elaboration, design practice will be recognizable as more than a cognitive search process and rather as a fully embodied, institutionally located, practically constrained, politically contingent, ambiguity-resolving process—as a social process of making sense together, in which giving form and making sense are profoundly coterminous.

Part Five

Use Planning Theory
to Anticipate and Respond
to Problems of Practice

Chapter Nine

Understanding
Planning Practice

The ultimate objective of repoliticization . . . should be to resur-
rect the notion of democracy, which is far too important an ideal
to be sacrificed to capitalism. . . . The problem is not that capi-
talist societies accumulate, but the way in which they do it. In
order for the beneficiaries of accumulation to remain a narrow
group, a boundary is established beyond which democracy is not
allowed to intrude. . . . The time has come to think, not about
demolishing accumulation, but about democratizing it. The way
to eliminate the contradictions between accumulation and le-
gitimation is to apply the principles of democracy to both—to
give people the same voice in making investment and allocation
decisions as they theoretically have in more directly political
decisions.

—Alan Wolfe

Planning theory is what planners need when they get stuck: another way to formulate a problem, a way to anticipate outcomes, a
source of reminders about what is important, a way of paying attention that provides direction, strategy, and coherence. In this
chapter we will argue that the talk and listening of planners is at
once practical, interpretive, and deeply political. To be rational,
effective, and ethical, too, planners must anticipate and counteract
pressures that stifle public voice, that manipulate democratic processes of consensus-building, and that ignore the many in need so
that a few may prosper. In this chapter we will also formulate

a broader research agenda: What questions must we explore to understand still more insightfully the pitfalls and possibilities of planning in the face of power?[1]

Practical Planning Theory

This chapter draws in part from the author's field research in an environmental review office of a metropolitan city planning department.[2] The planning staff assessed development proposals for the city, reviewed them for "significant adverse environmental impact," and then issued either a "negative declaration" or a requirement for an environmental impact report. Some of the proposals obviously did not involve significant impacts, but a few others were so large that full-blown environmental impact reports were clearly required. Most proposals, however, fell between these two groups. In such cases, the planners had to check likely impacts quite carefully, often having to negotiate with the project sponsor or developer for design changes that would minimize potentially adverse environmental impacts. In such cases, the review planner was reviewing, to be sure, but he or she was also actively participating in project planning and redesign. Using simple examples of such project-review activity, this chapter presents a more ambitious general argument: that a critical theory of planning practice can be empirically based, practically fitting, and ethically instructive, too.

In a nutshell, the argument is as follows: A critical theory of planning helps us to understand what planners do as attention-shaping, communicative action rather than as instrumental action, as means to particular ends.[3] Planning is deeply argumentative by its very nature: Planners must routinely argue, practically and politically, about desirable and possible futures. If they fail to recognize how their ordinary actions have subtle communicative effects, they will be counterproductive, even though they may mean well. They may be sincere but mistrusted, rigorous but unappreciated, reassuring yet resented. Where they intend to help, planners may instead create dependency; and where they intend to express good faith, they may raise expectations unrealistically, with disastrous consequences.

But these problems are hardly inevitable. When planners recognize the practical and communicative nature of their actions, they can devise strategies to avoid these problems and to improve their practice as well. In addition, they can recognize the organizational and political contexts of their practice as structures of selective attention, of systematically distorted communications. Both developers and neighborhood residents are likely to withhold information; access to information and the ability to act on it (i.e., expertise) are unequally distributed; the agendas of decision making are politically and selectively structured; and citizens cannot participate equally in decisions affecting them.[4]

We need to know more than whose ends or interests planners may serve. How do planners politically shape attention and communicate? How do they provide or withhold information about project alternatives to affected people? Do planners speak in a way that people can understand, or do they mystify citizens? How do planners encourage people to act, or rather discourage them with a (possibly implicit) "Leave it to us"? What can planners do (working with others, no doubt) to counteract unnecessary, deeply ideological formulations of community problems? How can they work or organize to enable citizens' learning, participation, and self-determination?

A Critical Theory of Planning Practice

Critical theory, as we draw on it here, assesses social and political-economic structures as systematic patterns of practical communicative interaction.[5] These relations of power and production do not merely transmit information; they also communicate and reproduce political and moral meaning, organizing support, consent, trust, and political belief.[6] The critical, ethical content of the theory focuses attention on the systematic and unnecessarily distorted nature of communicative interactions, on the promises, appeals, reports, and justifications that so shape the lives of citizens of our societies. In the United States, for example, citizens are faced with such influences when politicians or administrators pretend a political problem is simply a technical one; when private, profit-seeking interests (such as the nuclear construction industry or the pharmaceuticals industry) misrepresent benefits and dangers to the public; when professionals (such as physicians, planners, or social workers) create unnecessary dependency and unrealistic expectations in their clients; or when the established interests in a society avoid humanitarian social and economic policies (such as comprehensive health services) with misleading rhetoric and falsehoods, claiming, for example, that "the public sector is always, inevitably, less efficient than the private sector." Such distortions are profoundly practical communicative influences—instances of hegemonic power—with immobilizing, depoliticizing, and subtle but effective disabling consequences. To isolate and reveal the power of such systematically distorted communications, critical theorists contrast them with the ordinary communication of mutual understanding and consensus that makes any shared social knowledge possible in the first place.

The central theme of critical theory involves the precariousness of social action in general and democratic action in particular. Bureaucratic and market pressures alike threaten participatory political processes and communities of trust and solidarity. Social interaction too depends in part on the possibility of mutual understanding. Were such understanding not possible, neither political criticism nor the most elemental technical analysis would make much sense. Thus the prerequisites of mutual understanding suggest a critical but abstract reference point, the possibility of democratic argumentation "free from domination," which can help us to assess the distorting influences of concrete productive relations and the structure and policies of the state. Recall that some communicative distortions (e.g., imperfect information) are unavoidably present in the structure of any political-economy as well as in face-to-face communication. Nevertheless, as Chapters Three, Four, and Five argued, many distortions are avoidable, politically contingent, and thus alterable. These distortions are artificial, and the illusions and misinformed consent they promote may therefore be overcome.[7] Such distortions include, for example, the self-serving legitimation of great inequalities of income and wealth; the consumer ideologies inherited from and generated by the way capitalist productive relations are organized; the manipulation of public ignorance in defense of professional power; and the stultifying racial, ethnic, and sexual type-casting to which we are all subjected daily. Such politically debilitating influences are political artifacts and not natural necessities; they can be overcome. These sources of needless suffering are thus the targets of critical social and political theory and, as we have argued, of a progressive planning practice.[8]

Critical theory thus sets the stage for an empirical political analysis that exposes the subtle ways in which a given structure of state and productive relations functions: (1) to legitimate and perpetuate itself while it seeks to extend its power; (2) to exclude particular groups systematically from decision-making processes that affect their lives; (3) to promote the political and moral illusion that science and technology, through professionals and experts, can solve political problems; and so (4) to restrict public political argument, participation, and mobilization regarding a broad range of public welfare—oriented policy alternatives that are incompatible with existing patterns of ownership, wealth, and power. Because of the hegemonic power of such distorted communications, citizens of advanced capitalistic societies may remain ignorant of their own democratic political traditions and oblivious to their ability to take corrective action. Inequality, poverty, and ill-health come to be seen as problems for which the victim is responsible or as problems so "political" and "complex" that citizens can have nothing to say about them. Yet democratic politics or planning requires true consent, and such consent grows out of uncoerced collective criticism, political argument, and dialogue, not from silence or a party line.

A critical theory of planning must therefore suggest how existing social and political-economic relations actually operate to distort communications, to obscure issues, to manipulate trust and consent, to twist fact and possibility. In this chapter we will identify how basic types of distorted communication in the planning process subvert understanding and knowledge at face-to-face, organizational, and political-economic or structural levels of analysis.[9]

Attention-Shaping Through Communicative Action

Any action works not only as a means to an end but also as a promise, shaping expectations. Planners can be effective not because they put words on paper, but because they can alter others' expectations by doing so. A planner's formality may tell city residents more than the actual information he or she provides. The quality of the communication counts; without it, technical information would never be trusted, and cooperation would be impossible. With no one listening, effective work in the planning office would grind to a halt.

Consider a local planner's description of a proposed shopping center project to a neighborhood group. If the project is described in primarily economic terms, the audience will see something different from what they would see if it were described in mostly political terms. The audience would see something different still if the planner described the project in the most simple, ordinary language. But each of these descriptions would be about the same project. Which account should the planner give? Which account should be believed?[10] Planners and residents alike must make choices: what to say and what not to say, how and when to say it, and so on.

The problem is this: The planner's ordinary description of a project, for instance, is a communicative action in itself. Like all action, its success depends on intentions, interests, and an audience. Without an audience, the project description would be like a play on opening night when no one came, and it would be absolutely uninteresting and worthless, almost by definition, without intentions and interests setting it up. But with interests that make something worth describing, intentions that make the describing worth doing, and an audience to listen, the planner's description of a project can actually help get ordinary work done.

Planners do much more than describe, of course. They *warn* others of problems, *present* information, *suggest* new ideas, *agree* to perform certain tasks or to meet at certain times, *argue for or against* particular efforts, *report* relevant events, *offer* opinions and advice, and *comment* on ideas and proposals for action. These are only a few of the minute, essentially pragmatic, communicative actions that planners perform all the time, the "atoms" out of which any bureaucratic, social, or political action is constructed. We can call these acts "speech acts."[11] Without them, we could not even ask one another, "What did the project sponsor say?" Precisely because such communicative acts are effective, the phrase "Watch out—he doesn't like planners" has meaning. The pragmatic meaning to planners is: You watch out.[12] Without these elementary communicative actions, the intelligibility of our ordinary social world could not exist. Planning problems would be inexpressible, and practical action would be impossible.[13]

Such elementary communicative actions are at the heart of the possibility of any ordinary, cooperative working relationships—in everyday life, in planning, in political movements, and in society generally. Communicative action is fundamental to practical life; without it there is no understanding, no common sense, no shared basis even for disagreement or conflict.[14] Without shared, commonly structured communicative abilities, we would not be able to say "hello" and be understood, nor could planners say, "The meeting's Wednesday at seven-thirty. Come prepared." These communicative actions are ordinary and often taken for granted, but they are politically potent nevertheless.[15] Because the planners' communicative acts perform both technical and political work, we need now to understand how this work gets done.

The Structure of Practical Communicative Action: From "Enabling Rules" to Organizing Practices

These elemental communicative actions of ordinary planning practice do not just happen. They are social actions, performed in languages we can speak together. Words and noises do not just come from our mouths; we speak. We tell, or ask, or promise, or greet, or argue. And by doing these things, we act. When we speak, we participate in a structured form of social action—ordinary communicative action, which is, like all social action, already normative and rule-structured.[16] It is not up to us to decide whether or not we want to follow the rules of ordinary language use—not if we want someone else to understand what we say, promise, warn of, or call attention to. If we want to tell someone that a project-review meeting is likely to be especially important, we cannot just make up a special word to get the point across; rather, we must try hard to say what we mean, using the language and whatever frame of reference we share. If we want to be understood when we speak practically, we must follow (or put into use, or work through) the enabling rules that structure our ordinary language—or what we really mean to say will not be what anyone listening thinks we mean. The rules here are not restrictions; they enable us to act together.[17] They help us know that "Please check out the proposal" is not likely to mean "We're all done with it."[18] We can communicate pragmatically—though there are important exceptions—because when we speak or listen, we test a common set of presuppositions with one another.[19] Listening critically, we try to gauge the extent to which another speaks[20]

1. comprehensibly, for we can presume neither clear statements nor obfuscation;
2. sincerely, for we need to assess the speaker's trustworthiness;[21]
3. legitimately in the context at hand, so we can assess the propriety of the speaker's claims; and
4. accurately, so we can assess the truth of what we hear.

Mutual understanding depends on the satisfaction of these four criteria: comprehensibility, sincerity, legitimacy, and accuracy or truth. Without comprehensibility in interaction, we have not meaning but confusion. Without a measure of sincerity, we have manipulation or deceit rather than trust. When a speaker's claims are illegitimately made, we have the abuse rather than the exercise of authority. And when we cannot gauge the truth of what is claimed, we will be unable to tell the difference between reality and propaganda, fact and fantasy.

These criteria of pragmatic communication are often taken for granted. They are part of the subtle foundations of common sense. If we do not meet them, or if others do not, we face puzzlement, mistrust, anger, and disbelief; mutual understanding, trust, and cooperation are all likely to suffer.[22] Moreover, if these pragmatic criteria are not met, our shared experience and our common social and political worlds disintegrate.[23]

In planning, these criteria are particularly important for two reasons. First, planners often have little formal power or authority, so the effectiveness of their communicative actions and practical arguments becomes all the more important. Second, planners who seek to serve the public confront particular private or class interests (e.g., in corporate development) that are likely to violate these criteria systematically. Planners then have to face the results: a community group snowed by a developer's consultant, an inquisitive citizen confused by apparently "necessary" public works cutbacks, or a working-class community organization led to accept delays while wealthier neighborhoods receive prompt attention from city government. The lesson: Planning staff must learn to anticipate the practical effects both of the class-based communicative actions and practical arguments of others, and of their own argumentative practices as well.

Two Dimensions of Action: Content and Context

How does such practical communicative action work? Theorists seem to agree on one simple but fundamental point: that all practical communication requires skillful attention to both content and context. *What* a planner talks about is the content of what is said; when and in what situation and with whom the planner talks begins to define the context.

To communicate *content,* planners and their audience need to share a language—of word or gesture—first, to be able to call attention to particular things in the world, and second, to be able to say something coherent about them. A building site presents an infinity of detail, and in speaking about it, a planner not only must selectively refer to soil conditions, economic values, and so on in a particular terminology, but also must say *something* about each of these factors: for example, the soil is not stable; the cost figures are inflated; no low-income housing units are to be provided. So the content of practical communicative action involves two components:

(a) *a factual claim:* A planner may report at a staff meeting, for example, that the neighbors are worried about congestion, traffic, and noise at the site; and

(b) *a rhetorical (or comprehensibility) claim:* At a council or staff meeting the planner calls attention to something by framing it in a particular way. For example, a planner refers to "neighbors" rather than "several disgruntled families," or says they are "worried" rather than "scared to death" about a proposed project. The "same" facts can be expressed in significantly different ways.

The *context* of what a planner says is defined by the historical, political, and social relations that provide the planner with a stage from which to speak in the first place. When planners speak, they speak as actors on an organizational-political stage rather than on a Broadway theater stage—practitioners' allusions to the "theater of the absurd" notwithstanding. When planners present a report at a planning commission meeting, or a meeting of a neighborhood association, they talk "in context." If planners presented the same report in the same way in the middle of the intersection outside, however, they would get taken away to a local hospital for observation. Context counts; content alone is practically meaningless.

The context of what is said depends on more than the structural, legal-political relations that constitute the institutional and historical settings in which planners and others talk. In ordinary speech we understand joking, exaggeration, whining, parody, satire, anger, or hopelessness in another's words. Understanding here depends on our reading of the other's intentions, their expressions of self, their personal stance.[24] When we listen to others, for example, we may think, "They're angry," or "They're kidding," or "They've got an axe to grind"; our evaluations of their *intentions* help us place their words in context. At a planning commission meeting, the professional intentions of the staff members who present a report may be taken for granted by the commissioners, yet be distrusted by building developers and neighborhood residents alike. Institutional rules and roles may be clear, providing one aspect of the context, but developers may nevertheless wonder if staff members really sympathize with the neighborhood. Neighborhood residents, in turn, may wonder if the staff members are acting in collusion with the developers.

What is said and done, then, is evaluated and understood in the context at hand. But that is just the problem; the context is never simply given. The contextual or relational side of practical communicative action involves two additional components:

(c) *a claim to legitimacy:* To be understood *and* persuasive, a planner must speak differently in different institutional settings; what is appropriate at a formal Chamber of Commerce luncheon may well be inappropriate in a neighborhood church basement; and

(d) *an expressive claim:* When planners speak, they inevitably color what they say with their own intentions and emotions, however suppressed. In addition to whatever they claim factually, they may show sympathy, impatience, arrogance, worry, or concern.

The practical importance of these four claims becomes clear when any of them fail. When a planner's factual claim fails, the result is the listener's disbelief. When his or her rhetorical claim fails, the result is confusion. When the planner's claim to legitimacy fails, the result is a lack of consent. When a planner's expressive claim fails, the result is distrust.

These pragmatic claims are structural elements of the anatomy of action, but none takes place in a vacuum, separated from social actors supporting, challenging, fighting, agreeing with, or caring for one another. This analysis of action can be quite useful, not only in assessing planning and policy talk still further (ordinary language philosophers might do that), but also in investigating the character, vulnerability, and contingencies of actual planning practice. When planners listen, no less than when they write or speak, they must attend to the ways that these four communicative claims are raised; otherwise they may fail to accomplish even their simplest objectives, as we will see.[25]

Dimensions of Social Reproduction

When planners tell a neighborhood group about a proposed project, they can easily communicate more than they intend.[26] They may lapse into bureaucratic language, confusing and mystifying people.[27] They may present information but have no way of knowing what it will really mean to the audience. They may try to be even-handed, but their detached or formal manner may instead create distrust and resentment. Trying to produce results, they may instead reproduce yet other problems.[28]

Because satisfying the four criteria of mutual understanding (comprehensibility, sincerity, legitimacy, and truth) is so problematic, it reveals the ways in which everyday interaction is contingent, precarious, and subject to distortion or failure. We can use the four criteria, therefore, not to suggest imperatives for all situations (Be sincere! Tell the truth!) but to help formulate questions about the possible influence of planning practice.[29]

1. How comprehensible or obscure are the ideas and information the planner presents? Can others understand what the city, a developer, or a neighborhood group has in fact proposed, challenged, threatened, or agreed to do? What framing of problems does the planner reproduce?

2. How forthright is the planner, and with what consequences for the reproduction of others' trust? How does the planner suppress or express feelings or intentions, which others may suspect or resent, trust or distrust?

3. How does the planner legitimate his or her actions in the context at hand? Is he or she improperly taking advantage of professional status? For example, if a planner advises a developer or community organization member, "You'll have to live with this design; there's nothing you can do to change it," this may be a purely personal judgment that wrongly invokes and seeks to reproduce the legitimacy of professional authority.

4. How factually accurate is the planner? Is there evidence supporting the planner's claims? What do other accounts say? Are listeners being offered information on which they can safely act, or are they being misinformed, however unintentionally? What beliefs are being reproduced?

Asking these diagnostic questions helps us to explore how planners' talk can have practical productive and reproductive effects in the different dimensions of citizens' beliefs, consent, trust, and senses of problems.[30]

Communicative Distortions by Planners

At times, planners will not only face but also produce communicative distortions. In bargaining and many adversarial situations, planners may not tell "the whole truth, and nothing but the truth." But even when others might expect planners to distort the practical claims discussed above (to exaggerate, for example, early in a bargaining process), they will most likely also expect, in order to compensate, to be able to *check* what the planners say with third parties—for instance, to check with trusted friends or contacts in other agencies, who can be expected *not* to distort those basic claims.[31] This expectation—that the conditions of mutual understanding can indeed be satisfied—makes any checking possible.[32]

Thus, when bargaining or adversarial behavior typically results in exaggeration or misrepresentation, the requirements of ordinary understanding suggest compensatory checking strategies that help to protect us from being misled. In these situations, the four diagnostic questions (regarding comprehensibility, sincerity, legitimacy, and truth) become *more,* rather than less, important because they help us to check claims we face. To understand the duties of planners as responsible public servants, we must understand not only how at special times their misrepresentations might be justified, but also what results such actions can produce and reproduce.[33] These questions are particularly important also because of the bureaucratic and political pressures that operate on planners. Planners may often feel compelled to be less open than they might wish, but they should not be surprised, then, when they find members of the public at times suspicious, resentful, or angry.[34]

Distorted Communications and Planners' Responses

The foregoing analysis is only a slight beginning. Planners' distortions are important, but hardly more important or influential than the systematic, political-economic distortions of argument and voice that both planners and the largely unorganized public face together. How do planners face the structural management of public attention? Consider the legacies of racism and sexism that subvert the voices of women and people of color; the concentration of capital that enables a few to attend to their own needs while the needs of many go unmet; the institutional complexity that can be navigated only by those with the most organizational resources or high-priced legal representation; and the politically selective control of information. When ordinary communication is structurally and unnecessarily or deliberately distorted, democratic political action will be crippled.[35]

The socially and politically distorted claims that citizens and planners face every day can be assessed schematically (see Table 5). For each entry in Table 5, a practical question arises about how planners can work with others to prevent such distortions. Table 6 suggests strategies of response that expose or counteract the distortions in Table 5.[36] These strategies of response are varied, but

TABLE 5. *How We Experience Communicative Distortions*

	Type of Distortion (Criterion for Mutual Understanding Not Met)			
Practical Level	Comprehensibility	Sincerity	Legitimacy	Truth
Face-to-face	Ambiguity, confusion, lack of sense "What?"	Deceit, insincerity "Can I trust him?"	Meaning taken out of context "Is this right?"	Misrepresentation "Is this true?"
Organization (e.g., hospital proposing expansion)	Use of jargon to exclude public "What does this mean?"	Rhetorical reassurances; false expression of concern; hiding motives "Can we trust them?"	Unresponsiveness; assertion of rationalizations; dominance by professionals "Is this justified?"	Information withheld; responsibility obscured; need misrepresented "Is this true?"
Political-economic structure	Mystification, complexity "Do you think *they* understand what that means?"	Manipulation of the public good "That's their line"	Lack of accountability; legitimation through empty rhetoric rather than by active participation "Who are they to say?"	Policy possibilities obscured, withheld, or misrepresented; ideological claims such as "public ownership is always inefficient" "What they never tell us about is . . ."

TABLE 6. *Correcting Communicative Distortions: Organizing Practices of Planners*

Practical Level	Type of Distortion (Criterion for Mutual Understanding Not Met)			
	Comprehensibility	Sincerity	Legitimacy	Truth
Face-to-face	Revealing meaning "What does that mean?"	Checking intentions "Does she mean that?"	Determining roles and contexts "I don't need to accept that"	Checking evidence "I'll check to see if this is really true"
Organization	Minimizing jargon; creating public review committees "Clean up the language so people can understand it"	Organizing counter-advocates; checking with contacts, networks "Check with Stu to see if we can trust them on this"	Making decisions in a participatory manner; checking with affected persons "What has the neighborhood association had to say about this?"	Using independent/critical third-party expertise "Check the data and calculations to see if these figures are really correct"
Political-economic structure	Demystification; counter-skills "All this really means is . . ."	Exposing unexpressed interests "Of course they say that! They're the big winners if no one speaks up"	Democratizing the state; politicizing planning "Without political pressure, the bureaucracy will continue to serve itself"	Institutionalizing debate, political criticism; democratizing inquiry; politicizing planning "We have to show what can be done here"

they can be summarized in one word—"organizing." This can be a planner's response to disabling distortions of practical communications: the careful, political organization of attention that can counteract these influences.[37] Not only do these strategies address a wide range of obstacles to democratic political processes, but they are pragmatic as well. They seek to marshal information, to cultivate support, to work through informal channels, to counteract monopolies of expertise, and to use many of the organizing tactics discussed in previous chapters.[38]

Enabling and Disabling Practices in Planning

Now what of local planning practice? Where is the practical benefit for planners? Once we recognize planning practice as communicative and argumentative, we can reassess several organizational problems that planners face. It becomes clear now that problems will be solved not solely by technical experts, but also by pooling expertise and nonprofessional contributions too; not just by formal procedure, but also by informal consultation and involvement; not predominantly by strict reliance on data bases, but also by careful use of trusted resources, contacts, and friends; not mainly through formally rational management procedures, but through internal and external politics and the development of a working consensus; not by solving an engineering equation, but by complementing technical performance with political sophistication, support-building, liaison work—all this, organizing—and, finally, intuition and luck. Only in the most isolated or most routine cases will future-oriented planning problems be resolved by a technical planner acting alone.[39]

As we have argued throughout this book, a planner can be technically skillful but politically inept. A planner might make a formal economic calculation impeccably, but the mayor may not really "trust the numbers." Even the most technical actions (calculating a solution, making a demographic projection, reviewing architectural plans for flaws) communicate to those they serve that "this solution serves your needs" or "with this much done, you may still wish to change this parameter (devise another scenario, look and see for yourself)." In planning contexts, unfortunately, this communicative character of technical action has often been overlooked.[40] Its practical implications, particularly its costs, have often been neglected. The most well-meaning technical planning activities have at times communicated, if unintentionally, that planning is the exclusive domain of the planner, implicitly saying, "You can trust me. Leave the analysis to me." In some cases, this implied message reflected an agreed-upon division of labor, but often, it seems, it has led to trouble. It has worked to separate planners and plannedfor; it has made information less accessible to those affected by plans; it has minimized planners' abilities to learn from projectreview criticism; and it has generated public mistrust of planning staff and reinforced planners' apprehensions that public participation will inevitably be disruptive. As long as this communicative dimension of (even the most technical) planning practice is ignored, planners and citizens alike will suffer the consequences.[41]

The communicative character of planning practice involves much more than how clearly planners write or speak.[42] What planners choose to say—and choose not to say—is politically crucial. If planners take the role of "informed technocrats," for example, they can focus attention on technical issues but obscure important political relationships. Or if planners present themselves as neutral mediators, they can encourage premature consensus-building when empowerment and organizing strategies, pre-negotiation strategies, are more appropriate. If planners adopt roles that ignore the political world, they will seriously misrepresent public problems and opportunities. They will distract attention both from relations of power and, more important, from the ways that affected citizens can act to change those relations of power. Ideologies are systematic distortions of communication in precisely this sense of obscuring political possibilities. Ideologies are powerful distortions not because they are unclear. Rather, they are so clear, so transparent, that they effectively misrepresent social and political reality just as they obscure alternatives, cover up responsibility, encourage passivity and fatalism, and justify the perpetuation of needless suffering.[43]

Planners will face these problems increasingly if they do not regularly encourage political organizing and debate, the assessment of alternative definitions of problems, and the collective construction of new design and policy proposals.[44] As planners recognize these problems, they can begin to attend to the inevitably political roles they play: Should they foster or thwart informed public participation; should they preempt or enable public debate and argument; should they encourage or discourage design, project, or policy review and criticism?

Planning organizations routinely face the same problems faced by individual staff members. Those organizations may—perhaps against their best intentions—discourage public participation. If they ignore the effects of bureaucratic language, planning organizations will perpetuate the exclusion of all but the initiated. If they are perceived by the public as less than straightforward or as untruthful, planning organizations will continue to breed suspicion and hostility to professional public servants, and this will poison the possibility of future cooperation. More subtly, if planning organizations preempt community involvement by defining problems as overly technical or as too complex for nonprofessionals to understand, they may engender political passivity, dependency, and ignorance.[45] They must systematically search for project alternatives and possible political solutions and do so through community consultation, expertise pooling, and project reviews ranging from brainstorming to mediated negotiations. Otherwise, planning organizations are likely to reach agreements too quickly or inefficiently and thus miss real program or design opportunities.

Ironically, then, the overly narrow focus of technically oriented planning will, in effect, simplify practice in the short run, but will lead to inefficiency and waste. It can separate planners from the political constituencies they serve, weakening them both as they face the designs and agendas of powerful economic forces in their neighborhoods and cities. Such planning can also undercut the public accountability of planners, neglect political friends, and keep affected citizens uninformed rather than politically educated about events and local decisions. When action is at stake—not to mention planners' jobs—this can be costly. Thus planners must assess encompassing power structures and recognize how their own actions can work either to discourage or to encourage citizen organizing.[46] Planners can recognize more clearly the "leave it to us" messages that technical work may communicate. Planners can then integrate their technical work into larger organizing strategies in a variety of ways, as the following list of options suggests. To complement their technical work, planners can

1. Cultivate community networks of liaisons and contacts, rather than depending on the power of documents, both to procure and to disseminate information;
2. Listen carefully to gauge the concerns and interests of all participants in the planning process to anticipate likely political obstacles, struggles, and opportunities;
3. Notify less-organized interests early in any planning process affecting them (the more organized groups whose business it is to have such information will hardly need the same attention);
4. Educate citizens and community organizations about the planning process and both formal and informal "rules of the game";
5. Supply technical and political information to citizens to enable informed, effective political participation and negotiation;
6. Work to see that community and neighborhood nonprofessional organizations have ready access to public planning information, local codes, plans, notices of relevant meetings, and consultations with agency contacts, "specialists" supplementing their own "in-house" expertise;
7. Encourage community-based groups to press for open, full information about proposed projects and design possibilities;
8. Develop skills to work with groups and conflict situations, rather than expecting progress to stem mainly from isolated technical work or from elected officials;
9. Emphasize to community interests both the importance of building their own power even before negotiations begin and the importance of effective participation and negotiation in informal processes of project review; take steps to make expertise available to professionally unsophisticated groups in such project-review meetings;
10. Encourage independent, community-based project reviews and investigations; and
11. Anticipate political-economic pressures shaping design and project decisions and compensate for them, anticipating and counteracting private raids on the public purse by, for example, encouraging coalitions of affected citizens' groups and

soliciting political pressure from them to counter other interests that might threaten the public (Needleman and Needleman 1974; Hartman 1984).

These actions are all elements of "organizing" practices, actively mobilizing concerned and affected persons, that planners can incorporate into their practice in addition to technically calculating solutions to problems. As they work in these ways or fail to do so, planners will call attention to public possibilities or obscure them from public view.

To say that planning is political should begin discussion, not end it. If they anticipate the interests and commitments of affected groups, planners can build political support in addition to producing technically sound documents. Technical analysis cannot stand alone. Vivid studies show that the "technician" role of planning analysis is often frustrating and ineffectual if divorced from the pragmatic considerations of political communication: maintaining trust and "an ear," lobbying, addressing the specific concerns of decision-making audiences as well as the intrinsic merits of the projects themselves, and so on.[47]

The strategies indicated above raise their own problems, however. How much information should be given to which groups, and when? What can planners do to prevent such information from being ignored, misinterpreted, or manipulated? Are there forms of community planning, widespread participation, mediated negotiation, and design review that are both democratic and efficient? These are not new questions for planners, but a critical theory of planning allows us to ask and answer them in new ways: (1) by clarifying the elemental structure of practical communicative action; (2) by distinguishing pragmatic criteria with which we can assess public communications and arguments; (3) by identifying the essential types of disabling distortions to be corrected; (4) by clarifying the planner's role in perpetuating or counteracting such distortions; and (5) by locating a pragmatic and argumentative planning practice within a political-economic structure of power and ideology—treated here as a hegemonic structure of systematically distorted communication of assurance, threat, promise, and legitimation. If the elements of organizing strategies listed above are considered as isolated ideas, they are nothing new. Only if they are understood and carried out in the context of the structural analysis of systematically distorted communication illustrated in Tables 5 and 6 can they be seen in a new light, focused on new goals and objectives and put into practice in increasingly sensitive and effective ways.

Consider finally, now, the broader theoretical significance of these arguments and their implications for research and practice.

Implications for Theory, Research, and Practice

By treating planning practice as communicative action, we are given a conceptual (and researchable) bridge from analysis to implementation (via the shaping of attention), from information to organization (via the shaping and reproduction of political identity), from cognition to action (via the claims-making structure of communicative action), and thus from the analysis of abstract meaning to a pragmatic assessment of practical professional activity. Research can thus shift from the assessment of more narrow processes of experimentation and testing (social engineering from social science) to the study of processes of argumentation and dialogue, political discourse and design criticism, mediated negotiation, and democratization and organizing.[48]

Furthermore, the analysis of planning practice as communicative action has deep roots in the "ethics of ordinary discourse" we generally presuppose in daily life. We ordinarily appeal to the possibility of communication free from domination when we make claims about facts or rightness—that is, we assume we should not in principle need to coerce others to accept our claims. Similarly, planners are called on to clarify, reveal, and communicate actual possibilities of life-enhancing, emancipatory actions to citizens.[49]

Structural, Organizational, and Interactive Implications

At the *structural* level, the organization or disorganization of attention takes the form of the ability to invest or control various forms of capital. Just as capital is accumulated, controlled, and invested, so is society's attention concentrated, allocated, and organized. Such attention may be directed in two ways: first, productively, attending to some goals and not others, to the articulated needs of some and not others; and, second, reproductively, by refashioning existing social relations and conventional commitments, preferences, roles, and responsibilities.

Planners must be able to anticipate both productive and reproductive forms of attention-directing. When planners work on occupational health and safety issues, for example, the goal of minimizing risks to workers' health can be expected to conflict with the productive and accumulative goals of those who control workplaces. Furthermore, planners can expect existing class relations in the workplace to have two effects. First, they will structure such conflicts between the attention paid to safety and health versus the attention paid to profit rates. Second, the relatively powerful will also work to encourage employee attitudes of trust or resignation, of acceptance of health risks as "necessary evils" and "all part of the job," thus often discouraging employees from actively participating in decisions about the labor process.[50]

These two structural processes of attention-directing provide the context in which any planning takes place. One is accumulative; the other socializing (legitimating, politically integrating or disintegrating).[51] An important political implication follows. To the extent that these processes are contingent and contestable, planners and policy researchers must learn to anticipate this management of citizens' attention. Because these processes are indeed structural, fundamental to the organization of the political-economy, they will be regularly expectable: Planners and researchers can therefore anticipate and respond to their influences on actual planning and policy development.[52] This practical anticipation requires planners to have working theories of the institutional world in which they function.[53] Here, of course, the research questions only begin.

How do these structural attention-directing processes work in different planning domains—local, national, or international? How do they actually shape the contexts in which planners act? How well do planners now anticipate and take these influences into account in their practice? How could they do this better? What are the requirements, the obstacles? How might planners' organizing practices strengthen, or subvert, various forms of the structural processes of attention investment? Such questions must be addressed through careful case studies and comparative institutional analyses.[54]

In *organizations,* formal mandates, informal routines, and various precedents frame participants' attention in complex ways, as suggested in Chapter Five. Planners can expect organizations to achieve particular objectives instrumentally and to shape citizens' expectations communicatively as well. But what kinds of expectations will be created? Echoing Chapter Five, we have argued in this chapter that communicative action works in four dimensions: to shape listeners' senses of truth or beliefs, rightness or consent, sincerity or trust, and understanding or comprehension. Research that explores the management of attention in these dimensions can tell us much about concrete relations of power and possibility in the planning process. An organizational analysis that builds on the study of practical communicative action can also lead to further insights. In each dimension of the always contingent management of citizens' beliefs, consent, trust, and understanding, important questions arise for both research and practice.[55] How do organizations actually structure and change the beliefs of their members and those of the citizens they affect? How are factual claims substantiated? How is credibility maintained? And similarly, what processes are employed to manage consent? By what organizational processes can trust be strengthened or weakened? How do planners play a part in these processes?

In preparing for a presentation to a planning commission, a neighborhood group, or a union meeting, for example, a planner will want to know what preconceptions or beliefs he or she will have to address. What positions will the audience support or oppose? Will the planner be perceived as a trusted ally, a suspicious professional, an untrustworthy delegate from city hall, or someone with a hidden agenda?

Let us now address these same issues as research questions. To assess the organizational management of *belief* requires an exploration of organizational "intelligence," reporting and information systems, research units, the use of studies and scientific analyses, relations with the press, and so on. To analyze the management of *consent* requires assessments of formal and informal precedents, mandates, threats, and bargains; the use of symbolism and political rhetoric; and the political, legal, and ideological culture of planning organizations and of the organizations with which planners work. To study processes of gaining *trust* would lead to assessments of myriad mundane social rituals that provide planners, and those with whom they work, with the means of "checking each other out." To study the organizational management of *understanding* leads not only to questions about the use of clear and obscure language but also to far more subtle questions about the abilities of affected citizens to raise and articulate issues and concerns in the first place.[56]

These research questions all have potentially practical payoffs, and planners ignore them at their own risk. Although an analysis of communicative action can help planners and researchers to *ask* these questions, finding answers remains to be done, across various planning arenas, and more specifically in concrete planning situations. In each case, too, as we have observed throughout this volume, planners should ask how these processes that reproduce citizens' beliefs, consent, trust, and understanding are systematically skewed or unnecessarily distorted. How can these distorting influences be counteracted?

Finally, the critical planning theory presented in this chapter provides a research framework for the empirical, interpretive, and critical study of daily planning *interactions*. In the ongoing stream of their contacts with others, planners make practical claims about facts, legitimacy, intentions, and the formulation of problems. How do they do this? In what other ways, through speech, writing, argument, and silence, can they direct their own and others' attention in their everyday work?

If their statements and reports are not *believed*, planners will feel that they are wasting their time, and they would probably be right. If they cannot establish their judgments and evaluations as *legitimate*, planners will feel powerless, recognizing that they are not being taken seriously. If their expressions of intent, their desires and hopes cannot gain the *trust* of others, supreme frustration, not cooperation, is likely to result. And if planners cannot *frame* issues clearly and understandably, they are unlikely to be working as planners for long. Yet how these four dimensions of communicative action work in practice has hardly been addressed in any systematic, politically critical way in the planning literature.[57]

What, though, is normative or critical about this account of planning practice? We have seen that the analysis of communicative action leads immediately to questions of practical distortions—those that are necessary or unnecessary (unavoidable and avoidable), and ad hoc or systematic.[58] Practical questions therefore call for research on structural, organizational, and interactive levels of analysis. Planners and students alike must explore the management of citizens' attention: how authorities make decisions, how economic and bureaucratic power sets agendas, and how subtle political and cultural forces shape citizens' conceptions of their own needs. The analysis of communicative action allows these questions about power and hegemony to be asked concretely and systematically: How can affected citizens check and challenge claims that planners, developers, and other citizens make on them? What are the capacities, resources, and requirements citizens need to challenge others' claims about the facts of cases? What are the capacities and requirements needed to challenge claims of legitimacy? How might issues of trust, of false promises, be explored? What enables or punishes the abilities of citizens to articulate their own senses of need, to pose or frame problems in their own ways?

These questions take on a different form at different levels of analysis. At the political-economic level, these issues concern political legitimacy. At the organizational level, they become questions of procedural fairness and accountability. At the level of ordinary interaction they arise as questions of interpersonal ethics. Thus, a critical communicative account of planning practice seeks not only to integrate analyses of action and structure but also to combine empirical and interpretive research with normative and ethical arguments that help us counteract the obstacles to democratic and legitimate planning processes.[59]

Conclusion

By recognizing how planning practice, now understood as deeply communicative and argumentative, may distort or clarify, obscure or reveal to affected publics the prospects they face, a critical theory of planning can be practical and ethical as well. This is the contribution of a critical planning theory: pragmatics with vision—to reveal true alternatives, to correct false expectations, to counter cynicism, to foster inquiry, to spread political responsibility, engagement, and action. Critical planning practice, technically skilled and politically sensitive, is simultaneously an organizing and a democratizing practice.

A critical, argumentative account of planning practice integrates structural, organizational, and interactive levels of analysis. Planners can expect at every level to find a politics and an economics of citizens' attention: a political-economy of attention and argumentation, whose foundation is not only traditionally productive labor but social interaction more generally. At every level, planners will find dynamics of power and needless distortion that jeopardize democratic participation and autonomy, and they can recognize, anticipate, and work to counteract these influences.

Recall, finally, that this book presents an account of planning practice—an account of just one, but nevertheless essential, piece of the puzzle of creating a more just, decent, and healthy society. Inevitably, the book omits attention to closely related and crucial concerns: Political-economic dynamics, historical roots, professional variations, and psychodynamics are among the most obviously absent analyses here. But local practice counts. In their daily work, the communicative actions of planners can shape political arguments, and those arguments in turn can help to shape larger political strategies. We can hardly blame planners for the failures of social movements or credit planners for their successes, but we should recognize the part that planners, policy analysts, public administrators, and other planning analysts can play in assisting (or obstructing) larger, encompassing political forces that seek social betterment.

This book, then, is intended not as a definitive "last word," but as a step toward the renewal of structurally sensitive, practically engaged, ethically and politically critical planning theory and practice. In the face of power, justice and equality are hopes, solidarity is a source of strength, and, however daunting the odds, there is freedom in the struggle.

Chapter Ten

Supplement on Planning Education: Teaching Planning Practice

This supplement assesses an innovative experiment in the teaching and study of planning practice. At the Department of Urban Studies and Planning of the Massachusetts Institute of Technology (M.I.T.), Professors Donald Schön and Phillip Clay reorganized the graduate core course, entitled "Planning and Institutional Processes," to achieve several ambitious goals. First, they wished to show students distinctly different styles of planning practice by examining the professional work of the department's own faculty. Second, they wished to engage students in classroom exercises that illustrated these diverse forms of practice. Third, they sought to prompt students and faculty to reflect both on the many possibilities of planning practice and on their own practice as well. And finally, they brought in a visiting faculty member to assess their experiment and to work with them to formulate an agenda for further research and teaching. This supplement presents the essentials of the report of that visiting faculty member, this author.

Accordingly, this analysis of the "Planning and Institutional Processes" course seeks to inform the future teaching of practice cases, to advance faculty members' and practitioners' reflections on their own practice, and to propose elements of a research agenda for future study. To keep the personal and interactive flavor of the course, the text refers to faculty and guests—after their initial introductions—on a first-name basis, as all participants did.

The course centered on four case studies. Professors Phil Herr and Gary Hack first presented a growth-management case involving the proposed expansion of a major regional shopping center. In the second case, Professor Frank Jones discussed Ed Logue's work on community development in the South Bronx. In the third case, Don Schön presented his work of organizational diagnosis and intervention at the World Bank. Environmental planning and regulation became central in the fourth case, as Professor Lawrence Susskind assessed the role that planners may play as mediators of public disputes. The course met as a whole in ninety-minute sessions twice a week; in addition, students attended a one-hour recitation section in smaller groups.

This supplement is divided into three parts. The first part reviews the cases, if in a necessarily impressionistic way. Names of nonfaculty practitioners have been changed to protect their identities. Quotes attributed to faculty seek primarily to convey meaning; where they are not verbatim, they are close paraphrases, and they have, like the report as a whole, been reviewed for accuracy by all course participants. This report is based on the author's observation of each case and the teaching of the course as a whole.

The second part discusses significant issues (from argumentation to racism) that were problematic in the class and that call now for further attention. The final section then proposes a way of understanding planning practice that suggests how several of the major unresolved issues in the course might be reformulated. It argues that the practice of planning can be understood as the *practical anticipation* of problem situations, an anticipation thus requiring planners to be able to: (1) *envision* problematic situations; (2) *prepare and manage good arguments;* and (3) *negotiate strategically to intervene.* The final section also explores initial questions suggested by this model: How did the case presentations enable students to envision the practice situations they were asked to step into? Why is the ability to make arguments so important? What do the cases teach us about the possibilities of learning through anticipation rather than experimentation, direct experience? What sort of learning do problems of racism demand from planners? The conclusion suggests how much work remains to be done on issues of practice.

The Cases

Shoppers' Heaven:
A Growth-Management Case

"The developer of Shoppers' Heaven wants to put in a four-hundred-room hotel," Phil Herr began, "with office buildings, a fully enclosed mall, a large movie theater, walking trails, and a system of stormwater, recreational, and reflecting ponds, . . . expanding from 710,000 square feet to 1,325,000 square feet—virtually doubling the existing mall to become the largest in the state." Calling this "growth" seemed to understate the case.

For the first session, Phil displayed a series of visual images: maps of the greater Boston metropolitan area and the neighboring region, the site plan for the shopping center, and an aerial photograph of the site and its surroundings. He read from several recent *Boston Globe* clippings; coping with growth was a timely issue. Describing the history of the mall (Shoppers' Heaven had been one of the first regional shopping malls in the country when it was built in 1951), Phil continued to present the purpose of the case: These sessions should "expose you to the questions involved in such a case, the conceptual approaches that can be taken, the roles of different actors, and the political realities involved. . . . This is about comprehensive planning—how to do it and how not to do it."

After showing slides of the existing mall, a neighboring mall, and similar projects, Phil took questions. Asked "Why is there going to be so much expansion if there's no regional growth?", Phil replied with no lack of skepticism, "All over the country there are monuments to the imperfection of market studies!" Phil then showed two zoning maps: "Zoning is probably the most powerful instrument that will guide what happens in this case. But where do these maps come from?" he asked, only to answer: "From a picture of the community as a whole and a sense of the long run. . . . But we couldn't find a comprehensive plan for Farmingdale. They're not required in Massachusetts."

Phil continued by contrasting "comprehensive planning" and "disjointed incrementalism," saying of the latter, "This is what I do." Planners need to involve the public for two reasons, he argued: to learn *and* to build consensus, "but I could fill the room with planners interested only in the second."

Here Gary Hack argued that disjointed incrementalism alone would not suffice as a planning strategy; it has to be linked to comprehensive planning. Acknowledging the point, Phil discussed the difficulties of doing that and referred students to the work of Chris Alexander and (later) John Friedmann. When Don Schön asked if disjointed incrementalism inhibited the generation of creative alternatives, Gary replied that it did.

Building on the first session, Gary asked the class to consider the role of the planner as a "designer," in the "design" tradition: "One of the things designers do is make myths," Gary explained. "In this case, for example, myths about what the good suburb should look like—its scale, its structure, its relation to nature." Viewing slides of Frederick L. Olmsted's 1860s' design for Riverside, outside of Chicago, as well as slides of Forest Hills (New York), Radburn (New Jersey), Columbia (Maryland), and Britain's Milton Keynes, the students could compare differing designs along the criteria of structure, scale, mix of uses, integration with the natural environment, and others as Gary pointed them out. "You don't get a good city simply by preventing bad things from happening," he argued. "Regulation is antithetical to most designers. Designers think we can provide something to aspire to, that we can show what is possible with a wetlands, for example, that we can do more than just stop it from being destroyed."

Are such designs, or the myths that designers hope to make, only physical? Olmsted wrote about the centrality of the family to his design ideas. Today Delores Hayden explores the centrality of gender to architecture and urban design, questioning, for example, our conceptions of what is possible even in a suburban block (Hayden 1984). Don brought the session to a close by noting that for each planning strategy, comprehensive or incremental, several issues arose. How do planners taking either strategy conceive of the "public interest"? What strategic knowledge do they require? What sort of institutional role would make them effective? The traditions of design and comprehensive planning are not the same, the closing discussion concluded; members of both seek an image of the good society, but each would likely go about getting there in different ways.

In the recitation sections, Phil asked each group of students to evaluate the proposed expansion by taking on a different role; one group would assume the role of Farmingdale residents, another group would take on the role of shopping center users, and yet another would take the part of residents of the region. Each group brainstormed "goods" and "bads." From the residents' viewpoint, for example, "goods" included reuse of the land, taxes, jobs, being put back "on the map," and so on; "bads" included traffic congestion, sewage demand, lack of housing for employees, noise, and unbalanced growth, among others. Phil recorded each item on newsprint taped to the blackboard; these sheets became a public record of the students' work and centerpieces of discussion in the following sessions. Phil then asked what should be done, given those "goods" and "bads." More lists went up: build in turnpike access, job quotas, trip-management schemes, bike paths, linkage demands for housing and day-care provisions, and so on.

The following session pooled the results of the three brainstorming sessions. After reviewing the similarities and differences among the three groups' lists, Phil asked, "Well, what shall we tell the local planner and the regional planner when they come [for the next session]? What should they do? The horse is out of the barn, but there's another one there. What now? Even if we're too late to make a difference on this project, we can be helpful for the next one." The ensuing discussion identified six priorities: (1) improved planning (e.g., with mixed use and pedestrian integration) for the site; (2) increased public voice; (3) more attention to the natural environment; (4) qualitative guidelines for site planning and review; (5) state infrastructure provision; and (6) recognition of historical qualities of the site. What would the planners say?

Phil introduced the planners (Jeanne and Robert) at the next session and summarized the process the class had gone through. Turning to the students for their comments about the most important points covered, Phil found them reticent and less animated than in earlier sessions. Reviewing the lists of items on the sheets posted on the walls, Phil then asked the planners for their comments. Robert began by putting the Shoppers' Heaven proposal in context: "An even bigger project is going in down the road. . . . This came in before we had any leverage on growth control. . . . Southdale requires 65 percent open space while our ordinance requires only 10 percent." He concluded: "We're dealing with a level of power and expertise here which is beyond us!" A bit later, after a discussion of commercial "tenant selection," Robert replied, "I'd like to know how to do this—if not now, then for the next one."

Phil pressed both planners: "Why are the town and the region letting this happen?" "[Many people think] what's good for the tax base is what's good for the town," Jeanne replied. "We're trying to say that empty buildings asking for abatements aren't necessarily a good idea. There's a lot of public education to do, and on housing, too—there's a need for ordinary housing. So what if lots for $250,000 are available?"

A student asked Robert, "Would you explain your role in the process?"

"The planning board that recommends approval of projects is pro-growth," Robert answered. "I work for the Board of Selectmen. Our new site plan review process mentions the planning director (me) for the first time as part of the development process; the zoning ordinance didn't do that before."

Toward the end of the session, Phil asked, "Is there any future vision of what the town will be? Is anyone minding the store?"

"It's nobody's job to do that," Robert replied. "It is my role to raise that kind of issue, but without any authority. Our problem is not growth; it's government."

Here the students also asked—and the planners responded—about questions of taxes, political support, public sentiment, a recent proposal for a moratorium on growth, tensions between planning board and town meeting members, state legislation and jurisdictions of state agencies, planning precedents, and so on. In this discussion, institutional context and political attitudes were central, but the students were less able to take part than they had been in other sessions. The students knew about the site and could imagine impacts, but they knew little about the political and institutional world in which that site existed. They had learned about geographic rather than legal, political, and organizational space.

In the wrap-up session, Gary began the discussion by asking what the class thought the case was really about: The influence of politics? The lack of an image of the future? The need for better decisions affecting project impacts and repercussions? One summary came: "There's no planning here at all, or it's the wrong kind; planning in the public interest doesn't occur." But didn't the pro-growth planning board have a very definite idea of the public interest—the idea that the public interest is multiple, served by the hidden hand of the market, so that growth (and presumably market response) is to be celebrated?

"Even if they want growth," another student added, "the planners can still shape it."

"What has happened in this case," Phil Clay then summarized, "has been a process like planning. Let's think about what happened, and about the assumptions we made. We considered a problem, looked at different points of view, and came up with recommendations to do something. That's a planning process—one type of planning—and you played the various roles. So what assumptions were there?"

One student replied, "Well, we generated lots of options, and then could compare them across the different groups."

A second followed, with some frustration, "But one of the hundred and fifty items we talked about outweighed them all, though!"

"I felt that we got zapped," a third agreed. "We'd been thinking about pie in the sky, but then we found out that taxes were really what was important. Phil had told us, 'You can do anything here,' but the reality was so far from that."

Phil Herr responded, "We all have the ability to turn ideas off, but it's important to open them up. You people put all kinds of ideas into the planners' heads about what future project reviews could be about!"

"This last dialogue says a lot about Phil's theory of action," Don observed. "For Phil and Gary, there's a lot of power in an image—it can pull people out of the muck they're mired in; so being zapped might be a necessary part of the process—but if you thought of it that way, you might not *feel* zapped."

Phil continued, "We try hard to get people out of the position of saying 'no' to things: we want them to select positively from ideas about what's workable."

"So that's the problem Phil has as a planner—to encourage you to think, to try ideas and not be vulnerable," Don suggested.

"The brainstorming process was the first creative thing we'd done together; we don't do it much, but we should," another student said.

"If you felt that way," Don pointed out, "so might Phil's people, too, when they're participating in a local planning process; they'd feel excited, creative, like you did—and Phil doesn't put all the reality in early, so he doesn't constrain the discussion."

"Right!" acknowledged Phil. "You can ask people to generate ideas and they don't need lots of technology."

"So the problem is to involve people along the way so they don't say they know nothing," a student said.

Then another student asked, "But whose images of the community are these?"

"In my practice we deliberately accept responsibility for designing the participation; it's the lesser of several evils—preventing the 'old boys' from dominating the process. If you want," Phil said, "it's 'manipulated recruitment.'" And then with obvious satire and a laugh, he added, "But I have a pure heart, so it's okay with me." With this, time ran out, and the first case was finished.

Community Development
in the South Bronx

New York City's South Bronx gained notoriety in 1977 when President Jimmy Carter stood amid the rubble of razed and abandoned buildings to call attention to the plight of the urban poor. Carter left the South Bronx, and the Oval Office, but the problems of the neighborhood remained. How could the massive problems of such a once-thriving community be addressed? This question was the central focus of the second case study.

Frank Jones began this case with a discussion of political history. Why was the ambitious plan of the South Bronx Development Office (SBDO), headed by Ed Logue, written when it was? Why was the problem of the South Bronx brought to national attention? Indeed, what was the "problem" of the South Bronx? Was it defined by any particular criteria that helped to compare the community to other areas of the country? Or was it, as Frank suggested, a political decision that thrust the South Bronx into the political spotlight of the late 1970s? Probing for the central themes revealed in the SBDO's 1980 plan, Frank suggested two closely related ones: urban poverty, understood in the context of racism.

The South Bronx case, Frank continued, was "a story of how

you get an issue on the political front burner." As the next sessions evolved, the case put questions of race and racism on the academic front burner.

The first session continued to discuss four possible responses to the "problems" of the South Bronx—prototypical responses of a conservative, a liberal, a socialist, and a black radical. The conservative, liberal, and socialist responses can all be compared along political-economic criteria; the black radical position posits the fundamental centrality of race. Here Frank observed, "We find it difficult to talk about black radicalism in the department, and in the United States, but we have to come to grips with it; how else in situations like this could you become a good planner?" The discussion proceeded to survey a variety of institutions: the market, the state, community associations. What then of "race"? Frank offered, "I don't know any institution in America that isn't tinged with racism."

What did this imply for planning practice? Frank turned to Logue's report and asked the class for a list of its goals. What was the report really trying to do? Six goals were listed; they concerned jobs, education, housing, private investment, human services, and one less explicitly addressed in the report itself: the restoration of faith. In the discussion that followed, Frank remarked, "Restoring faith is one of the most important goals. This concerns the spirit of the people. We have to affect that, to motivate people. M.I.T. teaches you how to measure, but not how to restore the spirit of the people." This theme ran throughout the case: pervasive racism and popular spirit were counterpoints. Later, the broader problem of public perception was discussed as well.

The second session had the students take the roles of members of South Bronx District I, of consultants to members of District III, and of Ed Logue. (Logue himself would visit the class several sessions later.) Following the model of the first case, the groups discussed "goods" and "bads" from these perspectives and reported to the entire class at its next meeting. The third session had an ambitious agenda: to gather the reports from the previous group discussions; to compare the South Bronx plan to the Columbia, Maryland, experience; and to discuss the issues of "spirit" and "venom" (racism) broached at the end of the first session. After student presentations of the small-group results, Frank turned to an assessment of the Columbia experience. Here was an effort, beginning with enormous financial backing, that soon faced a host of difficulties threatening the whole enterprise, and it was a private-sector case at that. "What were the lessons?" Don asked midway through. Several were discussed: (1) the necessity of matching the scale of solutions to the scale of the problems at hand; (2) the likelihood that neither private nor public ventures were likely to meet such massive problems of community development in a profitable manner; and (3) that only "an enormously skilled development czar" (like Logue) might be able to meet the challenges of such cases. What of community participation, the students asked. And how could such a comprehensive approach ever work, if "realistically, nothing is ever comprehensive—how could you do everything at once?" the students pressed.

Phil Clay answered by suggesting a different image: "In surgery, all the organs are interconnected and adjust to one another. So in such a planning case, an intervention might have a comprehensive impact even though you do surgery only on eleven parcels."

In the last few minutes of class, Frank turned to a discussion of racism—and the tensions between blacks and Jews in particular. How might we understand the relations between the black poor and local white shopkeepers? Was the problem economic, racial, or both, hopelessly intertwined historically?

Two issues began to emerge as central to this case. Given the scale of the problems of urban poverty, and black urban poverty in particular, could anything short of a comprehensive approach ever work? But was a comprehensive approach even possible? And given the facts of black urban poverty, could any approach be sensibly discussed that did not centrally confront questions of race and racism?

The fourth session began—with some difficulty—to address issues of racism head-on. The discussion was slow, tense, awkward, and at times almost confessional. Faculty and students analyzed less, bore witness more. Don asked why the question of racism was so central. Under some conditions, Phil argued, the ways that actors perceived problems, the ways they framed practical solutions and approaches might be just as related to the issues of race as to the ways they framed their roles as participants. Others argued that race was an inescapable issue in a pluralistic, multiracial society. Still others noted the experience of being marginalized, being made to feel they were outsiders in an ostensibly democratic society. Then one student echoed a faculty member's caution about the dangers of sentimentality in discussions of racism. He said, with much frustration, "We keep presenting problems, but never concrete ways of solving them. It tickles the mind, but at this rate, I'll leave this school without learning that *this* is the way to think logically and solve these problems."

This comment sparked a discussion about just what was to be learned in a course devoted to the study of planning practice. Another student suggested that the course should focus on examples of successful planners rather than on apparently intractable problems. Don and Frank argued that in practice planners were continually being confronted with problems for which there would not be one "right answer." How, given these arguments, Frank asked, would the students judge Ed Logue's work? They would have their chance to confront that question when they met with Logue two sessions later.

In the fifth session, Frank continued to ask how Logue's performance might be judged. Logue's work had to be seen in light of the situation he inherited when he became director of the SBDO. Logue faced overwhelming complexity, poverty, and enormous physical scale. Shifting from a discussion of the South Bronx itself, Frank asked the students to consider what it must have been like for Logue himself. "Here was a man who'd received national attention for his work in New Haven, Boston, and New York State. Now he was in the South Bronx, but with little financial backing and power. I have the feeling that Logue said, 'I'll be damned if I'm getting out of here without making a statement.' I have to say, he got something done here. Somehow you've got to create a 'can-do' spirit."

"What would it take to call Logue's work in the South Bronx a success?" Frank asked. Students answered: stability in the neighborhoods, increased investment, improved services, shifts in power so the community could initiate and reject development plans, and so on. Speaking then of the plan itself, Frank confessed, "Some of you may be right to focus on the bits and pieces; no, you can't control the context, but to my mind [the plan] is wonderful—I'll say it. It's a big problem and it needs a big solution; there are always contexts you can't control."

"But you have to work without doing it all at once!" a student responded.

"Does that mean making no big plans?" asked Frank.

"No," the student replied. "Make big plans, but have small components!"

Phil brought the discussion to a close by noting that three central (and contradictory) ideas were usually debated in discussions of planning for community economic development: (a) collective ownership; (b) job development through outside firms; and (c) entrepreneurial development within the community itself. The South Bronx was no exception.

The next class session brought Ed Logue himself.

Logue's discussion with the students took the form of questions and answers following a brief (half-hour) autobiographical introduction. "See the blackboard behind you? There's absolutely nothing on it. That's what I had when I started." Beginning with the Carter years and looking ahead to the time beyond the Reagan era when "there'll be another round" for the cities, Logue provided the insider's perspective of having "been there." With stories about key actors and political details that only he could know, Logue gave the students a palpable, compelling sense of what being a planner might involve in its complexities, limits, and psychological requirements (including abiding optimism).

Asked what planning schools might better teach students in the future, Logue replied that along with analytical skills a planner had to know "how to put your arm around someone, to be able to work with different people, not to be seen as arrogant." What experience might be essential? "Two years working for a district board; that would be like a residency for a doctor; that would be enormously helpful."

Yet the ability of planners to work with others is not only an interpersonal issue; it is one of image, too. Relating an anecdote about a news reporter who had interviewed him, Logue said, "He wanted to take a picture of me next to an abandoned building. I said, 'No way.' Instead, I took him to Mr. Serra's house, where there's an outboard motorboat parked in the driveway. Do we want to change the image or not?"

Logue also asked Frank's question of how to gauge success. Anticipating the students' questions about this, he suggested, "The basic law of life in my experience is, 'compared to what?'"

The seventh session did not attempt to synthesize the previous six class meetings. Instead, Phil presented an introduction to the "political economy of community development." Reviewing conservative, liberal, and socialist perspectives of development, Phil used this concluding session to illustrate how these views might regard the South Bronx in terms of problem origin, problem diagnosis, centrality of the market, primacy of human services, ownership, locus of decision making, and policy recommendations.

In the first case study, the presentation of student ideas to the local and regional planners provided a conclusion to the planning experience; the following session evaluated its success and the process of the exercise itself. In the second case, role-playing was less central. When Logue came, the students asked and listened. When Phil presented the concluding lecture, the students asked about the implications of various positions—doing so more as observers and potential analysts, and less as analysts and planners "on the spot" themselves.

The World Bank and
Organizational Intervention

The World Bank is a peculiar institution. Lending more than 10 billion dollars each year, it is a bank, but it also houses the largest collection of planners in the world. This "bank" plans for international development, and the phrase *"lending* for *development"* captures the two, and at times conflicting, missions of this massive organization.

Don Schön introduced students to the practice of organizational intervention, first, by posing it as a problem: What was involved? Second, he described the Bank and its urban staff, with whom an M.I.T. consulting team had worked. Third, he drew on the Bank's experience with the Calcutta project to illustrate his own practice of "organizational diagnosis." The next class sessions included presentations of Don's diagnoses and practice efforts by the students to make such diagnoses. The sessions were designed to encourage the students not only to listen but also to "practice"—in both senses of that term: *trying* to diagnose a situation themselves, and *producing* an actual diagnosis.

In the first session, Don posed several questions to set the context for the case as a whole. If organizational settings shape our practice, what do we need to know in order to change those settings? What do we need to know just to cope decently in complex organizational environments? Referring to Howell Baum's essay entitled "Sensitizing Planners to Organizations" (1980b), Don explained, "I like this piece because it captures something I feel very strongly—and other practitioners do, too—that the organizational and institutional setting is fundamental, not incidental, regardless of your ideology. These organizational, interpersonal, and political issues are going to be key, and you'll have to face them. I might as well state the argument now: The radical perspective does not exempt you from the problem—nor does the liberal perspective."

Don continued by asking students to recall organizational problems they had experienced directly. "Size and impersonality," one student responded. "Staff turnover," another offered. "Personality conflicts." "Let me put my cards on the table," Don said. "I don't have to teach you organizational theory because you already have one—none of you is at a loss here—you have lots of it. The most important thing for you to do would be to examine your own theory and test it—it's important, because that theory dictates what you think and do. I don't want to give you another theory, but I do want to get you to examine your own theories. That's what we'll do over these weeks; first diagnosis, then intervention."

Don then introduced the ideas at the heart of "organizational diagnosis": being puzzled; model-building; and testing. He went on to introduce several other concepts: "espoused theory" and "theory in use," mission, task system, measures, incentives, politics, theory/ideology, development (consequences), who's who in the organization, and bureaucracy—all potentially useful to understanding an organization. With the discussion a bit overloaded here, Don continued: "These are some preliminary ideas, but I'm not sure how to get to the case. Let's start this way: What do you want to know about the Bank?" With this question, the transition to the following day's recitation was made, for in these meetings the problem would be to explore the "puzzles" the students found as they began to learn about the World Bank, puzzles such as how field staff might handle information-filtering by central Bank staff.

The recitation groups experimented with the work of organizational diagnosis. The first group did not progress beyond listing their puzzles and briefly discussing each of them. The second group began to discuss a model that made sense of several of their puzzles, but time prevented them from following through. The third group, though, discussed puzzles, proposed an explanation, considered a fact inconsistent with that explanation, and pushed on to devise a new explanation reconciling the inconsistency. Not simply listening quietly to a presentation about organizational learning, this group learned by working through a puzzle, a tentative explanation, a fact providing a possible refutation, and then finally a more powerful, richer explanation "solving" both the original question and the additional consideration rejecting the first, tentative explanation.

"We all contributed to this!" a student exclaimed. "We could never have done this individually."

"So think if we could all share our experiences—saying, 'Maybe it's like this,' rather than 'It *is* like this'—we'd get lots of possibilities, and then we'd need to *test* them," Don summarized.

Doing the work of probing puzzles, model-building, and testing as a whole, the organization referred to as this "group" had learned together. Don remarked afterward, "I didn't have to do anything; they did it themselves." What *had* Don done? He had not presented, but questioned; not told, but elicited; not analyzed, but rather managed the group's analytical performance.

Beginning with a review of the recitations, the third session was devoted to the diagnosis of the Bank that the M.I.T. consulting group had produced. "We started with individuals at the Bank," Don explained, "but then it seemed that the issue was less the individuals and more the organization and how it influenced their work." Don recalled the early meetings with Bank staff, telling the students, "I'll say to you what I said to them." Here he listed the conditions that had to be met to "learn by doing" (one of the urban staff's self-proclaimed goals), and then he claimed that these conditions could not be met at the Bank: The Bank could not detect failure, and thus it could not learn.

To explain why this was so, Don presented his diagnosis of "the learning system of the Bank." The Bank staff straddles two worlds—that of "the field" and that of headquarters, the Bank itself in Washington, D.C. At the Bank, staff faced incentives to lend, to fit projects to a macroeconomic "theology," to make a "money machine" work. In the field, life was more profane: Real problems were messy and unstable; although development seemed more important than lending, the field staff knew how officials at the Bank would read their project reports. So reports were packaged, sanitized, "smoothed." As one urban staff member said, "They [in headquarters] don't really want to know what's going on in the field. If we told them, they wouldn't fund us; so we don't want to tell them, because we do want the funding." Thus, Don argued that relations between the Bank and the field were characterized by a "systematic culture of dishonesty" that prevented the urban staff from learning by doing.

"How did the staff respond to you?" the students wanted to know. Don role-played the responses of several staff members: "He's right, you know, but it doesn't matter," one had said dismissively. Another had said, toughly, "Cost recovery is really it; I know several countries that would be bankrupt now without it. They need to understand the economic realities. Who's going to tell them? It's a tough business, this one. It's not for everybody." Still another had said, with resignation, "Well, what he says is true. I have a wife, kids in college. I play it conservative, by the book; I back up cost recovery. I do it; no one gets fired that way." And the point: No one learns when what is heard is only what is wanted, when what is reported is only what is clean.

In the fourth session, Don turned to the problem of intervention, explored possible strategies that intervenors might have taken with the Bank, and told the story of his own intervention. He began by distinguishing several concepts: the *strategy* of the urban staff (e.g., to operate on the incentive system), operative *theories of action* (espoused and in use), appeals to *public interest,* and the *planning knowledge* required to act.

Don then asked the students, "At the Bank, how would you think about going forward? What would you have done?"

The students suggested: Change the incentive structure, open communications, foster team spirit, get the overall goals straight, and more. Then Don asked, "What assumptions must be made for each of these strategies to make them reasonable?"

After a discussion of the assumptions underlying the interventions the students had proposed, Don summarized conventional intervention strategies discussed in the literature on organizational change. The central targets are typically structure, information, personality, politics, and behavior. But what strategy had Don used at the Bank? What was Don's intervention after testing his own model of field-headquarters relations with the urban staff?

This session ended with the students generally sitting on the edges of their seats as Don recounted his meetings with one initially skeptical, then supportive vice-president ("the staff may not be wholly competent, but they don't lie"), and with another top official, whom we shall call Bailey, the real power at the Bank. Deciding to meet with Bailey was not simple: "I had a problem," Don explained. "If I went to Bailey and it didn't go well, he could kill the project. If I didn't go, I risked making an enemy of him. So I decided I had to see him."

Bailey had a reputation: "extremely smart, confident, and feared within the Bank." What happened? "I went alone," Don said.

"What have you got to tell me?" Bailey began.

"For each argument of mine," Don recounted, "Bailey had one of his own: The staff are 'incorrigible optimists'; the field staff won't write accurate reports; they resist control; some like to be sloppy; we have committees dealing with accountability all the time."

"I asked," Don continued, "'When these committees talk about accountability, do you get good information?'"

Bailey replied, "No—but it's hard to get an honest reporting system anywhere."

"Bailey was 180 degrees opposite many of the staff," said Don. "I felt I'd completely failed. I thought I should not have gone alone, that by meeting alone I had allowed the staff to get off the hook, and I fell into a hole. The effect was that the project basically died."

Phil then asked, "But is there any reason to believe that it would've been any different if others had gone with you?"

"No," Don replied, "they might not have stood up and been counted."

But the urban staff's research director did follow up. Some training seminars for staff members were held. "At the moment I hear rumblings," Don concluded, "so perhaps I will return. That's the story of the Bank."

The class discussion then shifted to an assessment of the previous day's role-playing exercise that had simulated roles of World Bank officials, Health Ministry officials in a developing country, and government staff. In the simulation, the Bank officials wished to lend, the government wanted funds but without the Bank's strings, and the health officials wanted a more sensibly designed project than the one being negotiated by the other parties. The students found themselves quickly taking positions similar to those discussed in the diagnosis of the Bank. Why? Don suggested, "I think we're all programmed with theories of action that lead us to behave in ways we've seen at the Bank. If that's right, we have to change ourselves and not just the projects. I think the important question here is how to get people to face failure, to learn; this requires looking at our theories of action, at 'how do I behave?' We have to discover the answers to that question—which we don't already know—we have to look at what *we do*." In the discussion of the exercise, one student had felt narrowly committed to his role: "That's what the role said!" he explained, obviously feeling constrained. Don responded, "But your theory of action told you how to read it. Whether it was changeable or not, cast in concrete or not, that the role *didn't* say!"

This simple exchange seemed to capture a central point about the effectiveness of practitioners' theories of action. *How* roles are played, in the classroom or the agency, depends on the interpretations that we call practical theorizing, having a "theory in use." Examining those practical theories (testing them *or* changing our "programming"?) may then enable us to learn in practice.

Environmental Planning and Regulation

Lawrence Susskind began the fourth case by broadening its announced title from "Environmental Mediation" to "Environmental Planning and Regulation." The point, he argued, was to learn not only about what to do in the face of a given dispute, but also about how to rethink the structure of planning and regulatory processes.

"I teach not with cases, but with games," Larry explained. "I use scoreable games, a constrained form of simulation, to allow us to draw lessons, so we know what's worked, because now we know what '*worked*' means. Tomorrow we'll use a game designed to help states figure out how to think about the problem of siting low-level radioactive wastes. The issue will be not just power, but the wisdom of the decisions. So when I get put in the 'power tradition,' I worry, because I'm worried about the quality of what happens."

Describing the sessions to come, he summarized: "This will be not a case in the sense of Shoppers' Heaven or the South Bronx, but a look at what to do when people disagree about what to do, about what a regulation or rule should be."

Larry then recounted two instances of his own practice. In New York City, the Board of Estimate faced a decision about how to plan for the future disposal of the twenty thousand tons of garbage generated daily by city residents. When the Department of Sanitation submitted an Environmental Impact Statement (EIS) assessing resource-recovery strategies, the conflict began. Larry dramatized the situation by pointing to the conflicting claims of experts who reviewed the EIS: The Brooklyn neighbors of one proposed site engaged Barry Commoner, whose assessment in effect concluded, "Yes, the strategy's dangerous; people will die." The Department of Sanitation hired another esteemed consultant who reported, in effect, "Nope, no problem; the risk is negligible."

"Now here," Larry argued, "were all these legitimate scientists contradicting one another, and the City Council asking what should be done." The stage was thus set, for the class, and for Larry's entrance as a mediator. Each side had claimed to speak in the public interest, so the dispute provided a case not just of mediation, Larry suggested, but of environmental planning more generally. Having structured the testimony of experts in front of the City Council and the public, Larry had come to the turning point in the case: "I was stunned once I saw what the dispute was really about!" In fact, the crucial issue was the *likelihood* that the incineration strategy would meet the state standard that both sides respected as legitimate. So, without an agreement about whether the plant would meet the standard, a settlement was nevertheless reached in which a private party would be given the chance to meet the standard and to take the risks of not doing so.

"My job," Larry said as he summarized his first case, "was to facilitate a wise decision—I don't think the planners should decide the issue. The planner's job is to structure the inquiry so that elected people have a better chance of choosing well."

In the second instance, thirty-seven municipalities in New Jersey had struggled without success to devise a plan to achieve a level of regional water quality that would meet federal standards that had been violated for years. Appointed as a special master to the New Jersey Superior Court, Larry was instructed by the judge to try to produce an agreement that met a range of criteria—least cost, best engineering, and so on.

"I didn't decide the outcome, but we got an agreement," Larry explained. He indicated four central points illustrated by this situation: (1) the place of joint fact-finding; (2) the generation of options and the packaging of options into alternatives; (3) the evolution of single-text written agreements that can facilitate negotiations; and (4) the interplay of formal and informal processes.

Larry summarized, "You can't preempt the formal decision-making mechanisms of government, but you can supplement them. And with environmental planning and regulatory decisions made at local, state, and national levels through legislative, executive, and judicial mechanisms, I am suggesting that planning ought to be viewed as a supplement to these resource-allocating, policy-making activities. It can do so by structuring informal, face-to-face assisted negotiations among those affected by these decisions, along with those who have technical expertise to try to produce the wisest possible suggestions. That's an image of planning as a negotiation process, and the role of the planner in that process is as a mediator."

In the following session, six groups of students played the Rad-waste game simultaneously (a game produced by the Harvard Program on Negotiation). Each group consisted of seven parties (a state management authority, municipal governments, environmentalists, Native Americans, an antinuclear coalition, a waste-generators' association, and a governor's advisory committee) who

sought to agree on a package of ten out of twenty possible siting criteria. These groups produced three five-way agreements
by the end of the session, one six-way agreement, and one "no-
agreement." But each group had started with precisely the same
information. How could such a variation in outcomes be explained?

In the debriefing, Larry proposed the "mediator" role for the
planner as one alternative to that of the "technician" or the "advocate." Then he presented criteria by which good outcomes of a
planning process might be judged: elegance (did parties maximize
joint gains?), commitment to the agreement, legitimacy, efficiency,
and wisdom.

"These are the things a mediator asks about when looking at a
conflict situation," Larry explained. "I'd suggest this is at least as
good as what the technician's or advocate's point of view says."

Distinguishing mediated outcomes from simple compromises,
and mediation from direct negotiation, Larry argued that the public interest, "to the extent that it means anything, is not a technical
solution, and not an advocate's position. And while the pluralistic
view of the public interest is that compromise emerges from the
head-on clash of different interests, adequately represented in a
formal democratic process, I'd rather have that process be supplemented by this kind of helper in the hope of doing better in getting
a public interest that meets more of these criteria."

Turning to the Radwaste results, Larry began with a party
who'd done very well. "I took a hard line, stuck with it, and got
it," the student said.

"What will you do next time, when you have to deal with these
people again?" Larry asked. "In my experience," he continued,
"most public-sector organizations will deal with each other in the
future. They won't forget."

This was not an argument for complete candor, though. Larry
went on: "The notion of not revealing everything, but being truth-
ful about what you do reveal, is perfectly consistent with the problem of meeting again in the future."

Moving through the players' scores and probing for strategies or
the lack of them, Larry pointed to a central principle of all public-
sector negotiation: "The real issue here is how to *exploit the differences in how people value things.* That's how you get consensus
in a multiparty, multi-issue negotiation; you exploit the differ-

ences. *If I have something that you want very much and it's not important to me, and you have something I want very much and it's not important to you, and we trade that, boy, are we ahead!* . . . But if you explore only the things that everyone likes and don't explore the differences through a process of packaging, you don't get consensus. You don't even come close!"

Larry then distinguished negotiation *style* (competitive or co-operative) from questions of *effectiveness*. The key issue, he argued, was not style, but strategy. Either style could be effective, or be ineffective: "If your strategy is rotten, it won't matter if you're competitive or cooperative; and if your strategy's good, it's irrelevant if you're cooperative or competitive—you'll still be effective."

The lecture concluded with a discussion of integrative and distributive bargaining, ways of expanding the possibilities for realizing joint gains rather than simply splitting fixed sums. At the end of the session, Larry proposed a strategy of "principled negotiation" and compared it to either "hard" or "soft" bargaining. "Principled negotiation," he explained, involves four strategies: (1) separating the people involved from the problem at hand; (2) focusing on parties' interests rather than their positions; (3) inventing options for mutual gain; and (4) insisting on the use of objective criteria (Fisher and Ury 1983).

John Ruston presented the next lecture, on broader issues and models of environmental regulation and planning. Beginning with a slide show, John went on to discuss four ways of thinking about environmental behavior: via regulation, market incentives, mediation, or a view of resource flows. John characterized their strengths and weaknesses and put mediation strategies into a broader context of environmental planning, policy, and regulation.

After another scoreable game—a mediated dispute about fishing rights derived from a Lake Michigan case—Larry's last lecture shifted in part to a discussion of the planning process as well as planning strategy. The students had already worked through the Radwaste negotiation, and Larry said to them, "Well, you tried [another negotiation], and now I want to ask you: What worked, what didn't, and what did you learn?"

Once again the role players were debriefed. Had the first exercise mattered? The possibilities were suggested by the following exchange. Larry asked one student during the second debriefing,

"Why didn't you disclose what you really wanted?" The student replied, "Well, because of what you said last time about not telling everything right away."

When another student said, "I didn't do better because I didn't think I was important [to the outcome]," Larry presented a brief analysis of coalition formation: A third party with apparently little to gain may nevertheless be able to exert enormous influence on the strength of major actors.

This lecture focused finally on two sets of issues: a "principled negotiation" strategy and its advantages with respect to a strategy of hard bargaining; and a design for a process of planning understood as a mediation activity. Why was it important to analyze such strategies?

Larry argued, "Once someone goes through a mediation experience, they never negotiate the same way again. The point here has been to encourage you not just to be mediators, but to be principled negotiators as well."

Problematic Issues for Future Courses and Future Research

We will now consider several issues that these cases raised but hardly resolved. Then, in the final section, we will sketch a model of planning practice (and of the *teaching* of planning practice) that might account for these problematic issues in a systematic way.

Shoppers' Heaven: Representation, Institutional Context, and Criteria of Success

First, in the Shoppers' Heaven case, we saw a participatory planning process enthusiastically managed and orchestrated by Phil Herr. He posed problems rather than solved them for students. He subtly shaped the agenda and the actual composition of the groups' brainstorming results. Asked how participants were chosen ("whose images" these were), Phil had replied, with a humor that betrayed the sensitivity of the issue, "manipulated recruitment. . . . But I have a pure heart." If this planning process sought legitimacy through its participatory character—rather than through an appeal to expertise, for example—but actual participation and presumed representativeness were "manipulated," then certainly practical and ethical questions of the planner's political judgment remain. These questions are, of course, difficult ones, but they need explicit answers—answers or arguments that are available to students no less than to members of the affected communities.

Second, when the "results" of the brainstorming session were presented to the local and regional planners, a significant shift in conversation occurred. Before then, the students' attention had been focused wholly on the proposed project, the site, the encompassing region, and the potential geographic and socioeconomic impacts. In this session, though, students tried to talk for the first time about the legal, political, and economic institutional context within which any project-focused actions could or would be taken. Only then, one student exclaimed, "did we find out about the single most important issue—*taxes!*" The merit of that point aside, the students were not prepared to discuss the practical meanings of their lists of problems because they knew so little about the laws, regulations, political and administrative bodies, and procedural machinery through which any intervention would be carried out. The students were site-focused, but institutionally blind. Within the time constraints, could students learn about both the site *and* its institutional context?

Third, the Shoppers' Heaven case raises interesting questions about the intended outcomes of a planner's intervention. Is planning a success when coherent images of future development are produced by the participatory group? Or does success depend on someone else's learning from the planning exercise—perhaps the town council, or the planning board, or simply another group of concerned citizens? How do we know when a planning effort has succeeded? Consider one discussion from class. Concerned about Farmingdale, Phil asked the visiting planners, "Is anybody minding the store?" Referring then to Ashville (although he seemed less than pleased professionally with the conscious promotion of strip development there), Phil said, "They looked at the possibilities, and they got what they wanted." This raises the tension between politics and design that Gary Hack had pinpointed. Regulation, stopping the "bads," Gary had argued, would not necessarily produce the goods of good design. So, too, might political legitimacy (still requiring definition and discussion) fail to produce good design from the perspective of an urban designer or, more broadly, a professional planner.

In Farmingdale the planning board and the town meeting were indeed getting what they wanted: a game of private initiative weakly monitored by public officials playing catch-up. But the results, from a public-serving planning point of view, threatened to be disastrous, despite the apparently legitimate roles and functions played by elected officials and administrative bodies. (That the planning board had a history of corruption was not discussed, but was relevant here.) What is "legitimate" cannot simply be equated with what is "good"—and students should be aware, first, of the difference and, second, of the ways they might respond.

We are asking planning students as prospective professionals to lead, or perhaps more democratically to encourage, citizen participation, but we are also asking them to follow legitimate opinion. Such advice risks being directly contradictory. Just what are we encouraging students to do? We undoubtedly need to discuss both the practical decisions planners must make and the difficulties of having "pure hearts."

Note what the first case accomplished. The simulation required students to take community planning roles, and the brainstorming sessions demonstrated the scope of "comprehensive planning" approaches to the project. The brainstorming sessions also demonstrated a group-process technique designed to generate creative ideas, excite and stimulate participation, and encourage feelings of "ownership" (however tenuous) of the process. Meeting with the planning staff, the students could appreciate the concrete and constrained character of planning practice, despite the best or most ambitious intentions. The students had not only listened to a description of a planning process; they had also to some extent carried one out. So they learned not only "about" mixtures of comprehensive and incremental planning, but they learned "how to do it" in a preliminary way as well.

The South Bronx:
Strategy, Racism, and Hope

Three issues grew out of the examination of Logue's plan for the South Bronx. The first was the problem of planners cast as "development czars." Leave aside for the moment the normative questions of legitimacy raised above (surely the very mention of a "czar" in a democratic political culture raises issues concerning representation, accountability, and concentrated power). Yet the reference to a development czar also involves strategic questions of comprehensiveness. "Comprehensiveness" here includes, of course, not just traditional land-use or physical planning, but equally complex issues of community development, too.

Frank Jones's position on the strategic question might be paraphrased: "Comprehensive problems call for comprehensive solutions. Big problems call for big solutions." What that means for a planning document is relatively clear: Be wide-ranging, inclusive, and broadly yet specifically focused. But what that means for implementation and intervention is less clear, and it was less clear in the case. How can such plans best be carried out? A student put this question to Logue, and Logue finessed it (more than once, as several students later remarked): "Where to start on all these problems?" Logue had restated the question. "On all of them at once!"

The incrementalists were skeptical. The issue was management and administration: where strategically to focus attention; whom to involve; how to negotiate the enormously complex intergovernmental system of agencies, officials, elections, and public-private relations; which working agreements to pursue; how to manage and leverage resources; and so on. A systematic treatment of these questions (i.e., what are the alternatives?) did not occur, but it might have been possible in the session following the enormously rich, if rambling, discussion with Logue.

Second, the South Bronx case provided occasions for ambitious but anguished discussions of race and racism. The dis-ease and tension that surrounded these discussions provide us with perhaps the clearest indication possible that planners—students, practitioners, and professors alike—do not yet know how to *think* about, much less deal with, these sensitive issues. Questioning the relevance of racism in the face of its burning centrality to others risks signaling not so much a request for information as a deep misunderstanding of the character of the issue. The issue is precisely not one about data, information, or argument, but first and foremost one about respect for the real suffering involved in being racially victimized and marginalized.

But racism is still more complex morally, because it inevitably raises questions about the complicity of the silent. We hardly seem to know, in this highly individualistic political culture, how to think about being responsible, and perhaps culpable, for silence. Planners, of course, remain silent at even greater moral risk than others, because many of them feel called by their vocation to speak, and to speak practically, to such issues of suffering. What seems staggering intellectually is not our ignorance, but the apparent collective poverty of our moral vocabulary: We are unable to speak—which reflects our inability to think—about racism. Will issues of gender be thought through, spoken about and practiced, any more competently or compassionately?

Racism is "relevant" not to the question of *how* to plan but rather to the questions of *with* and *for whom* any planning at all is to take place. When issues of racism in the context of planning are raised, not only are questions of effectiveness or utility at stake, but so, too, are questions of integrity and identity. With *whom* should planners actually plan: stereotypically rational economic men? The fiction of the wholly rational, self-interested individual not only is a caricature, but it also warps our understanding when another's personal experience is dominated not by rich arrays of choices but by an institutional history of bigotry so far from any semblance of decency that it represents a continuing national disgrace—the Voting Rights Act, school busing, and affirmative action notwithstanding. (The Reagan strategy—avoid the news by killing the messenger—hardly improves the news. We should ask, "Are some facts too threatening for planners to hear?")

Victor Frankl (1985) wrote of the acute pain that concentration camp survivors experienced *after* their release as they found that *no one wanted to hear* about the beatings, the shootings, the mass graves, the fires, the stench, the selections, the gassings. No one wanted to listen—and this caused pain and anguish for the survivors that they compared to what they had endured emotionally in the camps. But why? Were they not now, as survivors, rational beings, faced with arrays of options from which they were free to choose, and were they not lucky to have survived at that? Yes, they were lucky, and they were rational, but these facts altogether miss the point of recognizing their specific identity, of recognizing an experience and a history that had profoundly and irrevocably shaped who they were, that could not but color everything they thought, felt, and could yet hope for. The pain these survivors felt was the pain of being typecast, being dehumanized, being ignored as people with a unique history, being obliterated as real people once again—now not by Nazis, the Gestapo, and the camp guards, but by those in the "free" and generally "liberal," even humanistic, communities in which they sought to live.

When the issue of racism arises, then, what is being raised is not an issue of planning technique, or process skills, or liberal sympathy. What is being raised at the very least is a prima facie claim for respect: the respect due *to* those affected and directly shaped by histories of institutional and personal racism and *from* those who are claiming to plan with, or for, them. This first-order claim for respect of a community's identity and history is not directly instrumental. When these issues were broached briefly during the South Bronx case, Phil Clay warned of the dangers of sentimentalizing the discussion. That danger exists. Sentimentality could subvert an effective planning process. Yet the fury and pain unleashed in the face of the utter disregard of racism also threatens effective planning processes. Before any institutionally powerful planning can be successful in pluralistic communities of color, planners are likely to have to find ways to come to terms with issues of race and racism.

But what does "coming to terms" mean? In part, it means having an articulated sense of the particular community's history. In the black South Bronx, for example, what proportion of families have roots in northward migrations from the rural South? Under what conditions did the families move? Articulating such histories can be as important as "knowing" them; respect is expressed *and* enacted, shown as well as thought. But how much history, how much analysis of cultural and institutional racism, how much discussion of the continuum between complicity and witness can one case contain? The South Bronx case hardly let us answer these questions, but it allowed us to pose them.

Planners, then, may face situations structured by and replete with the cruelties of history, and neither ignoring nor dwelling on that fact is likely to improve planning practice. Likewise, to maintain the fiction that the beneficiaries of planning are atomistic and autonomous calculators of self-interest has its costs. Until the presumption of such an asocial and hedonistic rationality is pushed aside, the boil of racism and long histories of pain, suffering, and hatred will continue to fester, be the victims black, Hispanic, Jewish, Asian—or women, as the sea change of gender relations should make abundantly clear.

A third, and still unresolved, issue was presented by the South Bronx case. At several points in the discussions, questions of "the spirit of the people" became entangled with, or even displaced by, issues of racism. Yet a review of the case suggests that matters of "spirit" could, and even should, have been treated as a wholly separate issue.

Recall the discussions seeking an evaluation of Logue's work. When pressed, Frank had looked back at what Logue had done, and he said, "I have to say, he got something done here. Somehow you've got to create a 'can-do' spirit." And later, regarding the plan of the SBDO, Frank had argued, "No, you can't control the context, but to my mind [the plan] is wonderful—I'll say it: It's a big problem, and it needs a big solution."

Logue had echoed these points in his careful attention to public image: He asked the reporter to photograph him in front of a South Bronx success story, Mr. Serra with his outboard motor boat, not in front of an abandoned building. Logue had recounted, and Frank had suggested, how important it was for planners not simply to solve problems but to shape impressions, public attention, the public's sense of possibilities and of *hope*. These last comments suggest a role for planners that is neither solely technical nor administrative. This role, curiously, is instead theatrical and rhetorical in the classical senses of these terms. Planners must shape the spirit and hopes of the people they work with; they must attend to the images they present, the faces they show to others; they must do *more than speak truth* (even to power), for they must excite imaginations. But how can planners address the "spirit of the people"? This case allowed us to pose this question squarely.

The World Bank: Constrained Definitions of Problems, Normative Learning, and Social Transformation

The World Bank case had, roughly, two parts. The first treated organizational diagnosis, and the second introduced organizational intervention, although the two parts are intimately related, even simultaneous, in practice. Upon review, each part raises pressing questions about the nature and scope of planning practice.

In the work of organizational diagnosis, first of all, consider which puzzles are being addressed. Puzzles, it should be remembered, are to lead us to build, test, and revise models of organizational behavior. These models then guide our subsequent interventions.

Puzzles are generated by the organization's staff as they review their experiences in a collaborative inquiry with the intervenor. Organizational intervention, as Don Schön had advocated it, encourages practitioners to examine, re-envision, and refine their own tacit theories of organizational behavior. If posing puzzles and refining models can lead to new, more explicit theories of organizational behavior, then organizational learning and improved practice might result.

How, though, are puzzles selected, grouped, and then evaluated? Are all puzzles fair game? Does group consensus "select"? On what intellectual and practical bases are puzzles selected? What initiative does the intervenor have to take at the diagnostic stage, and what analytic criteria may guide his or her judgments? Perhaps the group wishes to suppress certain puzzles and consider only "safer," less threatening ones. What then? The process of inquiry in such a case may be politically as well as psychologically constrained, it seems, but neither the fact nor, far more significantly, the *variability* of such constraints was discussed in this case. At best, collaboration promises collective criticism and inquiry, a conjunction of scientific wonder and democratic participation. At worst, of course, it threatens the most conservative muddling along—along, and perhaps not *through*. The political meaning of "collaborator" strongly suggests the *normative* conditions that must be satisfied in truly collaborative inquiry. If some members of a group are afraid to raise certain issues as puzzles, we can hardly assume those issues are unimportant to the organization's behavior or the staff's practice. Surely such fear might itself be important to work through. How could an astute diagnostician—and intervenor—work to address these puzzles?

Further, the puzzles considered in the World Bank case generally appear to be *behavioral:* What obstructed clear communications? What effects did the performance measures have? What internal differences, between economists and others, for example, affected performance? But what about *normative* puzzles—puzzles not about high turnover or poor information, but about what *ought* to be done? In a planning context, an organizational diagnosis that asks only about "how" the organization works avoids the question of what ends such knowledge will serve. Put differently, a behavioral organizational diagnosis requires another kind of diagnosis, a normative one, before its results can be used. Without a sense of an organization's mission, our understanding of how the organization works cannot be put to use. If planners reflect on how an organization works, they will also be led to parallel reflections—or to notice the lack of such—about how that organization *should* work.

Yet the scheme for diagnosis and improved understanding sketched in the World Bank case seems to stress the behavioral components. This problem can be raised polemically to emphasize its practical character. Could Don's model of organizational diagnosis be used to "improve the understanding" of staff working for altogether perverse ends—say, for banks illegally redlining neighborhoods, or for neighborhood planning agencies deliberately excluding concerned and directly affected residents?

Does such intervention create a collaborative and therefore normative learning process, or does it claim a technical neutrality so that it could be used to any ends? Behavioral problem-solving here threatens to displace important aspects of normative inquiry—a high price for planning practitioners, educators, or students to pay.

Another important problem involves testing the models that are constructed for resolving puzzles. How will such testing take place? How heuristic, and how rigorous, can it be? What actually does "testing" mean in such a context, compared, for example, with its more strictly scientific meaning?

More important, what is the outcome of building and testing models? Notice that the obvious answer, "better models," is at best ambiguous within a world sharply distinguishing between espoused and tacitly held theories of action and behavior. If we reply that building and testing models through collaborative inquiry produces better "accounts," better and more elegant explanations for widely perceived puzzles and problems, this may please social scientists. The practitioner must worry, however, whether an earlier mélange of stories had not now simply been displaced by a more elegant story called a "model"—but without a clear relationship to action. Improved intervention depends not only on more powerful accounts of the practical world but on will and interest as well. What else, besides better "accounts," does the collaborative process of building and testing models really produce? It produces a *shared* sense of staff identity and a renewed, *collective* sense of purpose and direction, helped along by a *commonly* revised story suggesting ways for the staff to proceed together. This emphasis on "shared," "collective," and "common" is not incidental: Successful collaborative inquiry produces cognitive or propositional results, just as it also *reproduces* (and transforms) important social relationships.

The model-building interventions obviously can produce revised models. Less obviously, such interventions can also produce an essential public forum in which organization members *transform themselves* as collaborative members of the same organization. Facilitated by the intervenor's presence and *questioning*, staff members may recognize in others what they themselves express: They express to one another in part their worries and their hopes, and their professional and personal senses of mission and frustration. In so doing, they publicly commit themselves, for they have reputations and senses of self not only to protect but to refine and even honor. If the intervenor has framed the collaboration as an attempt to foster organizational learning rather than complaint, the stage will have been set so that staff participation in the activity of probing puzzles and building models effectively co-opts the staff members and *reintegrates* them as a group of people with commonly held (and now commonly stated and respected) aspirations and purposes. Participation in the collaborative model-building activity may thus accomplish two things. It generates the tacit consent of the participants, first, to improve the group's practice and, second, to support the new directions for practice implied by the "account" being discussed, collectively created, and then ratified in the process. Collaborative inquiry can produce a new, more explicit "account" of a set of organizational puzzles (an account or belief now to be espoused), *and* it can also reproduce the *tacit* consent and practical commitments of the organization's members.

Collaboration can thus produce new ideas and reproduce evolving forms of cooperation as well.

Collaborative organizational diagnosis may accomplish far more, then, than Don Schön was prepared to claim for it—and far more than he had discussed explicitly with the students. The stakes in such interventions include the hearts as well as the minds of the host organization's members. Successful organizational diagnosis and intervention can thus encourage learning on several levels: explanatory accounts; practical, if tacit, consent; and senses of self (commitment and direction). With a simple experiment, we could test the hypothesis that group model-building produces significantly more than new explanations because of its public, collaborative, indeed ritually transformative character. This experiment would compare the result achieved by a collaborative group resolving a puzzle to that achieved by a parallel group, whose members were consulted *individually* about their puzzles (even if they were informed about one another's proposed models). My bet is that the whole would be more than the sum of the parts.

Environmental Planning and Regulation

We turn now to several pressing issues raised in the last case. How can mediation as a planning role fit routinely within the ongoing institutional processes of environmental planning and regulation? Even as a supplement to formal decision-making processes, can it nevertheless be institutionalized? What important work must take place in the pre-negotiation phases of potentially mediated disputes? Does the "*voluntary* participation" of parties have limits as a rationale that legitimates mediation as a planning strategy? We will consider each of these questions briefly below.

First, mediation is a compelling strategy with which planners can address isolated and discrete public disputes. What is not yet clear, however, is what the "mediator role" means for planners working not only *on* an array of public disputes but also *in* public-sector organizations that make diverse and often unpredictable demands on planners' time and attention. Several questions arise here: Can public agency staff be accepted by other parties as sufficiently disinterested mediators in disputes that fall within the jurisdictions (and thus the interests) of their agencies? Will the demands of their other roles, such as providing public information, conflict with their work as mediators? These questions assume, for the sake of argument, that planners should learn mediation skills to extend their repertoire of practical strategies. The issue that remains, however, is just how "ad hoc," supplementary, or, alternatively, institutionalized mediating roles can be.

Second, discussions of mediation and negotiation focus so much attention on the dispute at hand that the importance of pre-negotiation strategies may be neglected. But pre-negotiation work is crucial to dispute resolution; it affects both the practicality and the ethical desirability of negotiated settlements. The heart of the matter is this: The "best alternative to a negotiated agreement" by its very nature is an alternative that exists outside of a prospective negotiation. If the desirability of entering any negotiation depends in large part on a party's "best alternative," then the desirability of mediating any particular public dispute will depend on the capacity of the parties' pre-negotiation strategies to improve their alternatives. Take an urban land development situation in which large development firms compete with minimally organized neighborhood groups for rapidly appreciating properties. A local planner might seek either to mediate a given dispute—say, about the disposition of a number of parcels—or to assist either party instead to improve its "best alternative to a negotiated (or mediated) agreement." A planner's decision about when to mediate a potential dispute will depend in part on the pre-negotiation strategies available to all participants.

Parallel questions about power can be raised in this fashion. The power that participants bring to a dispute is complex: It is partially manifest in their alternatives to negotiation, and partially present in their abilities to negotiate effectively, too. If planners might well at times encourage parties not to join a negotiation prematurely but rather to "develop alternatives" or "build power," it is still not clear how such judgments should be made. Mediation and negotiation strategies need to be assessed in the context of available *pre-negotiation* strategies that disputants and planners might employ.

This attention to alternatives also suggests the possible limits of "voluntary" participation in mediated public disputes. A medical analogy may make the point best: We call a patient's decision to undergo a procedure "voluntary" when the patient has reasonable alternatives and gives his or her "informed consent." If no reasonable alternative exists, there is little sense in calling the patient's decision voluntary—he or she has only unreasonable alternatives. Similarly, if conditions of informed consent are not satisfied, the patient may be manipulated, or duped, or misled, and no decision made under such conditions could be called voluntary. Should not the same provisos govern the meaning of voluntary participation in public-sector mediation efforts? If a relatively powerless group has no reasonable alternative but to negotiate—*not because of the merits of the case but because of imbalances of power*—does it make sense to call its participation voluntary? Can we then say that the mediated outcome is "legitimate"? If planners have information that might help to redress such extreme inequalities of power and they withhold it, do they violate the conditions assuring informed consent?

These questions of power imbalances and the character of voluntary and informed participation have practical answers, to be sure. To qualify mediation as a planning strategy by discussing these questions will not weaken but rather will strengthen it as a new and powerful approach for planners to master.

Teaching and Research: The Anticipatory Character of Planning Practice

Notice the attention paid in the above cases to the *roles* of various actors. In each case, the practitioner did not simply present a problem and a method of solution; he set a stage upon which a variety of planning (and other) roles could be envisioned, characterized, enacted, and even actually practiced in the recitations. The faculty asked the students essentially *to enter* a virtual world, *an anticipated world of practice,* to imagine, or even at times to assume, others' identities, and then to try to move about, to try to learn to negotiate their way.

Whether in role-playing exercises or lecture sessions, the students were continually asked to anticipate acting in the world of the case. "What would *you* have done in this case?" was the paradigmatic question that faced the students. Notice how much more engaging this question is than the more objectifying and distanced "What is happening in this case?"

Asking the students to *anticipate* acting within the cases encourages them to become participants, actors who can try or propose various courses of action. Conversely, if students are simply asked for an account of a case, they will become spectators, not intervenors, observers rather than engaged and thus responsible, even culpable, actors hoping to make a difference in the case at hand.

How, then, can one explore the practical work of such *anticipation* in its own right? In *Modern English Usage* Fowler suggests that the meaning of "anticipate" in the phrase "to anticipate a crisis" is not simply to expect or to foresee the crisis, but "to take steps beforehand to meet it" (1965). So, too, were the students asked how they might have tried to meet the problems of the Shoppers' Heaven expansion, of the massive poverty in the South Bronx, and so on.

Consider a simple view of the structure of planning practice understood as fundamentally anticipatory. To anticipate a problematic situation, we must first *envision* that situation, then we must *prepare or manage good arguments* (testing ideas and learning) about that situation and possible courses of action, and finally we must use those arguments and resources to *negotiate strategically* a justifiable course of action. This may, of course, be an overly simple model of planning practice—*envision, prepare, negotiate*—but it may be instructive nevertheless.

The four cases illustrate these elements of practice in uneven ways. In the Shoppers' Heaven case, for example, Phil Herr helped students envision the site by using visuals and providing a history of the mall and its surroundings. The students then prepared arguments through the brainstorming sessions and presented them to the local and regional planners. In the South Bronx sessions, the students envisioned the neighborhood setting by reviewing Logue's plan and Frank Jones's political history. They devised arguments about problems and strategies in the recitation. In the World Bank case, Don Schön helped students to envision the setting of the Bank by describing relations between the Bank and the field and by providing written materials. The students prepared and managed arguments about possible intervention strategies as they generated puzzles, proposed and contrasted alternative explanations, and worked together to produce shared accounts that reflected a new working consensus. The environmental planning and regulation case provided a counterpoint to the first two cases; it focused less on envisioning the facts of a case and more on preparing arguments and negotiating strategically in the scoreable games.

In the sections that follow, we will briefly discuss two central problems that these cases call to our attention: that of argumentation, and that of learning.

The Centrality of Persuasive Argument

If a central part of planners' anticipatory work requires them to prepare and manage arguments, then planning education must provide the analytic tools—or better, the elements of a repertoire—that will *enable the students to argue, and thus to reflect on their judgments, about what ought to be done in a given case and why.* Such argument was broached in the four cases, but it was hardly developed in any substantial way. Explicitly normative arguments seemed undiscussable. Perhaps they were avoided because we do not yet recognize them as members of a family of persuasive arguments, as the recent literature on "informal (i.e., argumentative) logic" suggests. Surely practitioners should not be doomed to wonder silently about "should" questions, the appropriateness of what they are doing.

But how then can such practical, normative arguments actually be made, evaluated, and refined, in class sessions *and* in practice? The classroom can be a setting in which a virtual world of practice is created. That virtual world requires, as the actual world does, more than internal conversations about questions of goodness, beauty, rightness, and justice. That virtual world, like the ordinary world, requires participants *who wish to act together* to make persuasive arguments (political, aesthetic, and ethical) about what is to be done.

When planning students ask for practice in making presentations, they are making both a practical and a theoretically rich point. They are telling us that acting in the virtual worlds staged in class requires them to do something that their instructors have not paid attention to or assisted them with: *the practical need* not simply to make presentations but also, *in order to act competently, to be able to devise and present persuasive and valid arguments.*

This issue could be addressed pedagogically by encouraging student presentations of competing intervention strategies in a format of mutual questioning, challenging, persuasion, and analysis. (In only a few instances did presenting faculty encourage debate between students; in fact, the danger that a few students might dominate the class seemed to lead to a more central faculty role.) The point here is not simply to promote student interaction, but to enable students to *practice* debate and argumentation in *systematic* and powerful ways.

These considerations seem simple enough, but they are fundamental. They call into question the axiom of the nonneutrality of expertise, and they do so in a new way: not as a theoretical proposition but as a practical matter. When planners frame problems and recommend strategies, how should they justify, support, or even elaborate their inherent value commitments? The doctrine that facts can be rationally debated while values can only be emotionally expressed (the doctrine of emotivism) dies hard. This contentious and now discredited philosophical position persists in the planning profession—and in the planning academy, too—as a cultural truth, but it does so at enormous cost. Students work to address planning situations that call for normative, highly evaluative interventions, yet when the students consider *how to think* about what they *should* do, they are unlikely to find much good advice. They might be told to do cost-benefit analysis. They might be told to advance and defend their own value positions in the apparently pluralist political arena. Or they might face a barrage of pithy statements of worn-out positions: "Clarify your values," which is the contemporary version of the existentialist's "stand where you must"; "Be professional," which is the technician's credo; or "Challenge hegemonic class, race, and gender relations," which is the left's litany, leaving only the question "Yes, but how?"

Strangely enough, such pithiness helps, for in the land of the normatively silent, the laconic may be kings. But all this does not help much.

The daily requirements of planning practice present a real opportunity for planning schools to explore practical issues of persuasion, argumentation, and presentation that are theoretically crucial as well. What forms of argumentation are available and appropriate in various contexts (the South Bronx or the World Bank)? How are these forms contingent on institutional pressures that contra-dict (that literally speak against) the planner's arguments? A host of further research questions could easily be generated here (Forester 1987).

As Mandelbaum suggests, different forms of argumentation may affect and reflect the moral competence of the communities—and the classrooms—in which they occur (1984). If case analyses of planning practice are conducted so that normative arguments are dismissed as irrationally political or emotive, then students are likely to leave the university with one hand tied behind their backs. In planning practice, they would be a bit like a driver afraid to steer, with one hand on the gear shift but the other holding on to the seatbelt for dear life. Who would want to ride with such a driver?

We teach students the strategies and techniques of shifting gears, but do we teach them how to *think and then speak about where to go*? To ignore normative questions in planning—and the *skills of normative and aesthetic argument*—is to put planning students into impossible roles: Care but don't show it; think about justice, but don't talk to anyone about it; evaluate and recommend alternatives, but be "objective."

Professionals are called on to profess. However technical it is, planning is an inescapably normative enterprise. Planning schools, then, must learn how to help students construct, assess, and present normative arguments because planning *practice* will demand these abilities—not incidentally but fundamentally.

Consider now how planners might learn about future problems. We think of learning as tied to direct experience, but if that were correct, planners might not learn about problems they worked on until it was too late. How can planners learn through their work of anticipating future situations? Is such learning through anticipation possible?

Learning by Anticipating

Realists and pragmatists often seem to discount classroom discussions of practice as "unreal." If their skepticism were well founded, however, no learning could occur. So before asking how anticipatory learning can take place, consider first how "real" the classroom anticipation of practice settings can be.

Although the staged classroom setting is not the actual case setting, it is real in many other ways. The participants are hardly the fully rational actors posited by some theories of decision making; they are likely to be diverse, risk-averse, skeptical, and uncertain about their roles in a new setting. They may hear but not listen. They may offer opinions but back off, or suppress their thoughts and judgments altogether. They are, in fact, quite active and self-interested members of complex social organizations (professional degree programs) in which their performance will affect future opportunities, career moves, their autonomy, and their self-esteem.

But maybe the classroom situation is unreal because the identities, roles, and purposes of the students differ from those of the central actors in the imagined case? Not altogether, for in the short space of several months, every member of the class is likely to find himself or herself in just such a practice setting—in a part-time job, an internship, a job following graduation, and so on.

In fact, a strong argument exists for treating the classroom anticipation of case situations as quite real. In an actual case setting, on the job, the participants must routinely anticipate an enormous range of future settings in which they will act but in which they are not yet involved: a meeting tomorrow; a demand likely to come from a developer, a politician, or a community group a month hence; and so on. Thus the apparent unreality of the classroom can be in fact curiously real because at any moment in practice we are never really and fully "in" all the situations that make up a real case. Our abilities to envision situations that we are *not yet in,* our abilities to anticipate practice situations, are fundamental elements of planning practice, just as they are required and practiced in the classroom.

Discussion in the classroom is not so much unreal as it is *abstracted* from another (and perhaps projected) situation. As such, the conversation of the classroom produces less theory-in-action and more theory-in-play: Abstracted elements of arguments, behavioral and normative, can be joined, offered, considered, rejected, or played with until some closure is reached. The game comes to a tentative end, sometimes with winners and losers (like chess), sometimes with cooperation and harmony (like playing music to-gether). But how, then, is learning possible in such "real but still unreal" anticipatory situations?

To anticipate practice situations, the cases suggest, we must en-vision three dimensions of our practice: (1) a descriptive account of the "problem" or the "site" in question; (2) an account of the formal and informal rules of the encompassing institutions and traditions in which our planning and intervention are located; and (3) an account of the distinctive identities of the people inhabiting these sites and institutions, and their personal interests and institu-tional positions, loyalties, and ideologies. Each of these dimensions raises questions of subsequent inquiry, challenge, elaboration, criti-cism, and learning, but in profoundly different ways. To anticipate practice situations, *we can learn in each of three dimensions:* one *factual and behavioral,* one *normative,* and one *cultural* (Forester 1983b, 1987).

Learning About "Is": The Facts and Explanations. Some ways of presenting a case could discourage factual learning: Questions about data could seem "too complex" to answer, for example. Yet other ways of staging a case might deliberately enhance learning: Faculty could encourage active questioning of data and conse-quences, formally or informally, and could make the search for more powerful and elegant accounts a matter of direct public in-quiry. In the Shoppers' Heaven case, for example, the process of group comparison of "goods" and "bads" was also one of popular corroboration of the facts: Consistency with the conjectures of peers substituted for actual testing of any given proposition or hy-pothesis.[1] In the World Bank case, "puzzle-model-test" defined both organizational diagnosis and the agenda of the class. Here was a staged learning process: the public search for, and testing of, behavioral models that might explain organizational members' factual puzzles about their workplaces. When hypotheses about organizational facts or project consequences survive as plausible after a process of public review and criticism, we then witness the anticipatory learning process we call "scientific."

Learning About "Shoulds": What Is to Be Done? By anticipat-ing practice situations in each of the cases, how did the students learn, if they did at all, about what *should* have been done? In the Shoppers' Heaven case, recommendations about what should be done in the case were implicitly justified by the presumed *legitimacy* of the participatory process. This case structured the process of learning about questions of good and bad, should and should not, in a clear and culturally compelling way: via public participation.[2] In the South Bronx case, Frank appealed to the requirements not of a participatory process but of the problem itself. "A big problem," the argument went, "requires a big solution" (and a big stick, as the term "development czar" would suggest). This argument implied that learning about what should be done might depend directly on the *merits* of the case. Yet Frank and Phil also sought to root normative prescriptions in long-standing (therefore legitimate?) traditions or ideologies of social analysis. Thus the point of presenting conservative, liberal, socialist, or black radical perspectives depended on the explicit appeal to sets of values that might *justify* practical policy and interventionist positions. Whether such perspectives are irreconcilable remains to be discussed. When a liberal planner meets a conservative bureaucrat, or neighbor, can there be any agreement about what should be done? Does power alone dictate what should be done? If so, normative questions are pointless. If not, then how can questions of "what should be done" be explored?

In the World Bank case, inquiry into normative questions was muted. Yet organizational diagnosis immediately becomes normative when an organizational boundary is chosen: Should the boundary encompass Bank employees alone, or include staff-client relations as well?

The negotiation sessions refined the traditional participatory approaches to normative questions. The legitimacy of participation was only one criterion used to gauge a good outcome. The effective mediator, Susskind argued, would enable disputants to "exploit their differences," to make trades in order to achieve joint gains, to reach both-gain rather than zero-sum outcomes. In this instance, learning about "shoulds" was based partly on democratic theory (legitimacy derived from voice) and partly on welfare economics (elegance derived from maximizing joint gains).

Normative arguments can be offered, challenged, rejected, and refined in much the same way that arguments concerning behavioral model-building can (see, e.g., Johnson and Blair 1985). It would be a significant contribution to planning education, research, and practice to show how normative arguments can be systematically criticized and refined.

Evidently, even if a good deal is known about testing behavioral propositions, nearly as much still needs to be assessed (studied, practiced, taught) about normative inquiry, argumentation, and learning. Why hand these questions over to the lawyers? Why not study them, teach the repertoire of strategies available to address them, and respond insightfully and practically to the students' inevitable and justly abiding questions, "What should I do? How can I *think* better about what I should do?"

Learning About Cultural Identities: Who's Who?   Consider now the third dimension in which anticipatory learning takes place. In a world where personality, custom, personal and group history, ideology, and identity matter, practitioners need to learn not only about one another's roles or good intentions but also about their strong points and quirks, soft spots and peeves, loyalties and suspicions, friendships and feuds. Learning how to answer these questions is ordinarily difficult enough; but how are students entering an anticipated practice situation in class to learn about the unique identities of others in the planning process? On the job, we often hear, "It'll take you the first year to find out who's who and why they do the things they do." In the classroom we have not a year but a few hours. What can be done?

Certainly learning about the history of key actors can help: What have their commitments been? What fights have they waged? How have they been treated and how have they treated others? What reputations do they have? Still, getting to know others depends on our real listening, attentiveness, and sensitivity—on our ongoing judgment: What can we infer from *how* others say what they say and *how* they do what they do? Whom are we able to trust? Whom must we be wary of, be careful not to depend on? In the World Bank case, for example, Don's sense of Bailey's personality was integral to his decision to meet with him: Bailey was the boss, "extremely smart, confident, and feared within the Bank"; top officials were known to leave his office "red-faced." Bailey's persona was hardly the decisive criterion in Don's decision to meet with him, yet it was far from irrelevant, affecting how the meeting was anticipated and, no doubt, conducted.

In the Shoppers' Heaven case, Phil worked to establish rapport with the students: his tone enthusiastic, his jokes about flawed market studies congenial and reflective, his references to his own "introduction to reality" humble and disarming. Phil not only played the role of group facilitator, he *personified* it; he showed what it might be like, personally, stylistically, and affectively, to facilitate a participatory planning process.

The South Bronx case raised questions of identity the most directly. What role did race play in planning in the South Bronx? Were race and racism relevant at all? Why? These questions were posed but hardly answered. Yet to have them raised at all taught one hard lesson at least: In communities of color, the history of racism and racial relations will predefine the character of initial working relationships at least, if not those relationships from start to finish. *Could anyone really believe that Frank Jones's persistent posing of the problem of race would arise only in the classroom?* Or perhaps was it that the restrained grace with which he raised it would be found only in the classroom, that in community settings the question would not arise but explode, and not only once but continually? The very fact that it was raised so persistently made it relevant and promises to make it relevant in the Bronx as well as in many other communities; if planners cannot deal with the question of race, or the complexity of race, directly, other work is likely to be sidetracked or run off the rails.

Given a legacy of racism, north and south, east and west, a planner's good intentions will hardly provide "a new beginning," new and unblemished relations of trust, reciprocity, dialogue, or rational discussion. Trust and dialogue, reciprocity and rationality may be possible, but they will have to be earned, constructed together, built out of the ruins of past hatred, betrayal, and scorn. Planners, especially white planners, who work in communities of color will have to establish their own reputations, their own identities, their own credibility. To envision the possible tensions here, we need only imagine the prospect of any planner of color entering the white Philadelphia neighborhood where a biracial couple recently moved in—as hundreds of white "neighbors" shouted racial epithets—and then was driven out.

Similarly, the young woman planner who joins an all-male staff, who finds herself the only woman in meetings of "old boys" at the public works department, who is first asked to fetch coffee, faces a situation in which she must learn to sustain a professional identity no less than to resist others. In these situations, issues that reach beyond "is" and "should," facts and models and strategies and recommended alternatives, are at stake. How have planners managed here? Does anyone know? Shouldn't we find out? How can and do planners learn where relationships can be established and where not, how and how not? As ugly as racism and sexism are, their presence in planning processes cannot be wished away. Better then to anticipate such problems of practice in school, when we have the chance to learn about them more, and suffer their consequences a bit less.

The negotiation games also encouraged the students to "try on" roles and to explore one another's identities. In these exercises, learning about other participants took the form of gauging their interests and their styles of negotiating. These games raise a central question about social identity: How and when might public-sector disputants act collaboratively to achieve "joint gains," that is, how might social *differences* lead not simply to compromise but to far better, mutually beneficial, "both-gain" solutions? This question needs to be explored further.

Identities can be explored and interpreted (learned) in a rich variety of ways. Identities may be shown or role-played. They may be explored as constellations of interests, or via history and reputation. They may finally be linked to historical forms of domination as well; the "isms" of racism and sexism remain to be anticipated, and overcome.

These cases suggest that we can learn as we plan, as we work to anticipate future problems, about *factual behavior,* about *normative "should" questions,* and about *social identities,* in a wide variety of ways. Shouldn't these models of learning—anticipatory learning—be explored?

The model of anticipatory practice presented above suggests both a pedagogic and a research agenda.[3] If planning practice consists of the elements of *envisioning a problem situation, managing arguments concerning it,* and *negotiating strategically to intervene,* then case presentations can directly present, assess, and facilitate these three linked activities. Envisioning, preparing good arguments, and negotiating should receive attention in *each* case.

Finally, sets of research questions follow from this discussion. We know, for example, a little about technologies that help us to envision future behavior, but do we know how to envision the ambiguous demands of institutional contexts, or the identities of other participants in the planning process? We have much to learn, in the planning academy and profession, about the substantive aspects of practical argumentation, including the normative structure of collaboration and learning. What strategies have planners used, and which might they yet use, to prepare and manage arguments that are articulated in the planning process? Given a wide range of contexts and cases, how can planners then negotiate to intervene legitimately and effectively? If this analysis has been even half right, these questions about planning practice should be studied in further research, examined in the classroom, and considered in our practice as well.

Notes

Chapter One

1. The following chapters focus on issues of planning practice. Only Chapter Nine turns wholly to the problem of planning theory: to account empirically, interpretively, and critically for planning and administrative practice in a political world. That ninth chapter provides a synthetic and integrative framework for the book as a whole. Readers who wish first to assess that theoretical framework should review the ninth chapter early on; others can read it last for a summary analysis that integrates the arguments of the preceding chapters. With the partial exception of Chapter Six, each chapter of this book has been extensively reworked and revised from an earlier published version. Wherever possible, I have tried to strengthen, clarify, or develop further earlier arguments, in addition to integrating them into the larger argument of this book. Accordingly, Chapter Two presents a substantial adaptation of my article "What Do Planning Analysts Do? Planning and Policy Analysis as Organizing," *Policy Studies Journal* 9, no. 4 (Winter 1980–1981): 595–604. Chapter Three and the title of the book have been derived from an earlier incarnation in "Planning in the Face of Power," *Journal of the American Planning Association* 48 (Winter 1982): 67–80. Chapter Four has been developed from "Bounded Rationality and the Politics of Muddling Through," *Public Administration Review* 44, no. 1 (January–February 1984): 23–31. Chapter Five is an extension and substantial revision of "Know Your Organizations: Planning and the Reproduction of Social and Political Relations," *Plan Canada* 22 (March 1982): 3–13. Chapter Six has been adapted from "Planning in the Face of Conflict," *Journal of the American Planning Association* 53 (Summer 1987): 303–314. Chapter Seven reflects a substantial reworking of "Listening: The Social Policy of Everyday Life

(Critical Theory and Hermeneutics in Practice)," *Social Praxis* 7, no. 3–4 (1980): 219–232. Chapter Eight has been adapted from "Designing as Making Sense Together in Practical Conversation," *Journal of Architectural Education* 38 (Summer 1985): 14–20. Chapter Nine is an extension and substantial revision of "Critical Theory and Planning Practice," *Journal of the American Planning Association* 46 (July 1980): 275–286. Finally, the Supplement on Planning Education has been adapted from "On Practice: Teaching Planning and Institutional Processes at M.I.T.," *Journal of Planning Education and Research* 6, no. 2 (Winter 1987): 116–137.

Chapter Two

1. See Seeley (1963), Schön (1983), Tribe (1972, 1973), Vickers (1965), and Churchman (1968). For information-processing or more generally "cybernetic" views, see Etzioni (1968), Faludi (1973), and the related literature on "learning systems," e.g., Schön (1971). See also Dudley Burton (1981). Cf. van Gunsteren (1976).

2. The information-processing view of planning can be understood as an attempt to apply cybernetics to the management of complex social systems (see, e.g., Buckley 1967). The root of "cybernetics" is linked to the Greek words for steering and the role of the helmsman. For a recent example of an information-processing view of planning, see Kochen and Barr (1986).

3. We will see in Chapter Six how personal distance and detachment in the name of "professionalism" may be self-defeating, producing not professionalism but the impression of insensitivity, misunderstanding, callous neglect, and, as a result, not cooperation but anger directed at the planning analyst. For a related analysis, cf. Belenky et al. (1986). For a more abstract appeal to scientific criticism, but without a consideration of the necessarily political and ethical criteria that make such criticism possible and indeed desirable, see Landau (1973).

4. See, for example, Meltsner (1975, 1976), Benveniste (1977), and Marris and Rein (1984).

5. For the technical analysis of speech acts, see Searle (1969); for Jürgen Habermas's appropriation of Searle's work, see Habermas (1979, 1984). We apply this analysis in the chapters that follow; cf. the notes in Chapter Five and the extended discussion in Chapter Nine. For an accessible introduction, see Wardhaugh (1985).

6. Of course, when only token participation is being requested, attention is being directed, and responsibility is being shifted (or virtually re-

tained), in very particular, politically deceptive ways—thus the insidious uses of co-optation (Arnstein 1969).

7. This is not a hopelessly ahistorical description of what planners do. As we will see, this account of planning practice explains both what planners do when they serve narrow and special interests and what they do when they work to protect and serve broader, less well organized publics. In the latter case, planners may assist the organizing that promotes democratic voice; in the former case, they may disorganize the same voice, preempting some, excluding others, and so on, as we explore in later chapters.

8. See Sir Geoffrey Vicker's discussion of action as communication (1984, 93–96). See also Marris (1975, 1982) and Rohr (1978).

9. On the tensions and opportunities of "organizing" in local city planning departments, see Carolyn Needleman and Martin Needleman (1974).

10. In a striking paper, Howell Baum (1988) explores planning theorists' complicity in this denial of politics. Compare Hannah Arendt's (1958) powerful characterization of action and politics as fundamentally involving risk, new beginnings, and the ambiguities of speech.

11. Theoretically, we can move from the abstract rationalism of a means-ends view and the information-based pragmatism of cybernetic accounts to the critical pragmatism underlying the attention-organizing view. We treat these implications in detail in Chapter Nine.

12. Personal conversations, Stephen Blum, University of California, Berkeley, School of Public Health (1977). See Berry (1981).

13. See, e.g., Ben Barber (1984) on the richness of democratic talk and the vital importance of speech to democratic politics. On argument as communicative interaction, see Jürgen Habermas (1975, 159) and compare Habermas's response to Steven Lukes in Thompson and Held (1982); cf. Arendt (1958) and Pitkin (1972). This point, distinguishing needless from inevitable distortions, suggests the difficulties of Michel Foucault's account of power/knowledge in discourse, an account of the systemic organization of attention without organizers (agents). Cf. Foucault (1980), Fraser (1981), Walzer (1983).

14. See Hummel (1982). Cf. Edelman's (1977) discussion of the political language of the helping professions.

15. See Singer (1977). Also see the work of Donald Schön and Chris Argyris, who contrast what they find to be typical self-sealing, control-seeking actions (their Model I) with a relatively rare, though possible, model of action that promotes social learning (Model II); see especially Argyris and Schön (1974, 1978) and Schön (1983, 1987). See Baum

(1987) for another interpretation of Model I defensive behavior; also Diamond (1986).

16. See Freire (1979, 73). Cf. Misgeld (1985).

17. As a leading city-planning director for ten years and more recently as president of the American Planning Association, Norman Krumholz has repeatedly stressed this point to planning practitioners. Krumholz has argued not only that there is no escaping politics, but also that planning analysts can do far more in the service of redistribution and empowerment than they now do (Krumholz, e.g., 1982). The present analysis builds theoretically on Trent Schroyer's insight that Habermas has refined the conventional "critique of ideology" into a concretely specifiable "critique of systematically distorted communications"; see Schroyer (1973, 160ff.). Cf. Habermas (1973, 1–40); and McCarthy's "Translator's Introduction," in Habermas (1973, x–xxiv). See also Chapter Four, below, and the "Editor's Introduction" in Forester (1985).

18. This analysis seeks to move beyond both utilitarianism (e.g., cost-benefit analysis) and deontological ethics (e.g., appealing to universal maxims) by building on recent work exploring the project of "communicative ethics." In everyday life we typically undertake, and take for granted, ordinary responsibilities to keep from lying or deceiving, to speak accurately, to offer relevant or important information. We often anticipate that others will honor such responsibilities as well. This makes listening to one another possible and sensible, as difficult as it may sometimes be. If this were *not* the case, misunderstanding would be the rule; most ordinary and simple, even superficial, communication as we know it would not exist. We would not be able to ask for the time of day, nor would planning analysts, significantly, be able to *check* any information they doubt. To communicate with one another at all, even to disagree, we must presuppose such implicit norms of intersubjective communication, and in another sense, sustain and not deny them (Habermas 1973, 18; Dallmayr 1974; McCarthy 1978). But a communicative ethics does *not* simply lead to naïve and simple rules: "Always tell the truth!" for example. Judging how much to tell, whom to tell, and when are rarely simple matters—which is all the more reason to study such practical judgments carefully. On the "ethics of ordinary discourse," see Dallmayr (1974). Cf. Ben Habib (1986) and Simpson (1986). See Habermas's reference to Apel's work in Habermas (1975, 158–159).

19. See Brian Murphy (1976) on the pervasive political significance of "modern cynicism." On professional power and language, see Edelman (1977).

20. Planners have been concerned with the organization of participation in many ways, of course. It is instructive to compare the organiz-

ing strategies reflected in the work of Paul Davidoff, Chester Hartman, Frances Fox Piven and Richard Cloward, Norman Krumholz, David Korten, and Lawrence Susskind. See, e.g., Davidoff (1965), Hartman (1978, 1984), Piven and Cloward (1977, 1982), Korten (1980), Burton and Murphy (1980), Susskind and Ozawa (1983), and Susskind and Cruickshank (1987). Cf. Freire (1970) and Forester (1988).

Chapter Three

1. See Altshuler (1965), Balkas (1979), Baum (1980a, 1980b), Bradley (1979), Howe and Kaufman (1979), Page (1977), and Roche (1981).

2. Cf. Forester (1981b).

3. See, e.g., Marris and Rein (1984), Krumholz, Cogger, and Linner (1975), Benveniste (1977), Rabinowitz (1969), Kaufman (1974), and Needleman and Needleman (1974).

4. The term "progressive" is used because "radical" has been discredited as not pragmatic, "advocate" is overly narrow, "ethical" is conventionally misunderstood to be simply idealistic, and "professional" has been reduced, colloquially, from implying a "calling" to denoting merely the possession of expertise and socioeconomic status. Our use of "progressive" appropriates those elements of the Progressive Era that called into question the structural relations of nondemocratic control of capital and investment; this use rejects, however, those elements of the same era that sought instead to rationalize, objectify, manage, and quiet the conflicts and exploitation inherent in the political-economy. In sociological terms, the problem of this chapter, and the book as a whole, is to clarify the diverse possibilities of counter-hegemonic practices.

5. E.g., Rabin (1980).

6. E.g., Bradley (1979).

7. See, e.g., Altshuler (1965), Benveniste (1977), Bradley (1979), Jacobs (1978), Krumholz, Cogger, and Linner (1975), Meltsner (1976), and Roche (1981).

8. Cf. Benveniste (1977), Kravitz (1970), Lindblom (1959), Meltsner (1976), Nilson (1979), Thompson (1967), and Wildavsky (1979).

9. The classic analysis is Davidoff (1965).

10. Cf. Davidoff (1965) and Mazziotti (1974).

11. Cf. Harvey (1978), Piven and Cloward (1971), and Saunders (1979). Like that of the other perspectives, the brief description of the structuralist perspective here is ideal-typical. Structuralist perspectives have been both forcefully presented (Poulantzas 1973) and criticized (Thompson 1980). The intention here is not to delineate substantially a structuralist position but rather to characterize it briefly, if necessarily

too simply; a fuller treatment is a task for critical accounts of the way planning theory draws on the broader fields of social and political theory and political-economy. The structuralist position is sketched here to indicate that problems of local effectiveness versus system determinism (or the philosophical "problem" of voluntarism versus determinism) are always present in planning practice, as shown in the familiar question planners ask: "Am I really making a difference here, or is everything I'm doing getting washed out by the larger political and economic system?" Depending on how this question is asked, it may lead to paralysis or, alternatively, to sharper strategic thinking. In any case, the structuralist view of information as power is presented here not to represent Marxist structuralist work in general (nor to represent all work that simply takes into account social, political, or economic structures), but instead to indicate how a view of systems-determinism might be manifest, and have extremely undialectical consequences, in practice. There are, of course, other Marxist positions, in theory and in practice, besides that of the structuralist perspective briefly presented here (Tabb and Sawers 1978).

12. Necessary and unnecessary distortions, as well as structural and nonstructural distortions, are discussed and distinguished in the next section of this chapter. These distinctions are presented schematically in Table 1 (p. 34).

13. E.g., Burlage and Kennedy (1980), Burton and Murphy (1980), Bradley (1979), Forester (1981a), Freire (1970), Friedmann (1980), Gorz (1967), Hartman (1978), Kemp (1980), Kraushaar (1979), Needleman and Needleman (1974), and Schroyer (1973). Cf. Krumholz (1982).

14. Cf. Szanton (1981) and Meltsner (1976).

15. See Lindblom (1959).

16. Two fascinating discussions of the liberal attitude described so briefly here may be found in the work of John Schaar (1967) and Isaac Kramnick (1981); their essays discuss the inegalitarian ironies of traditional liberal arguments for equal opportunity. Kramnick's historical analysis suggests that the liberal doctrine of equal opportunity arose as an argument against the claims of eighteenth-century English aristocracy. Although the resulting promotion of meritocracy can be seen as an emancipatory movement in the context of aristocracy, the same doctrine of equal opportunity today, leading to the same results, meritocracy, can hardly be appreciated as emancipatory any longer.

17. See Saunders (1979).

18. It might be conjectured that planners holding such a view do not last long as planners or, alternatively, that this perspective provides an all-encompassing rationalization for planning inefficacy, if not also for finding cynical satisfaction in meeting lower expectations, Herbert Simon's "satisficing."

19. As we will see, *how* the misinformation confronting planners comes about is a matter of the specific institutional settings in which planners work. In a capitalist political-economy in which the state functions both productively, to protect and foster capital accumulation, and reproductively, to promote and gain legitimation, the actual content of the misinformation faced by planners and citizens generally will, of course, differ in specific ways from that faced by members of bureaucratic socialist or other political-economic systems. Nevertheless, misinformation and systematic distortions of communication may be anticipated in a variety of political-economies, and our analysis here attempts only to provide a framework for research that suggests the dimensions in which hegemonic misinformation and communicative distortion can be expected to occur. It remains for analysts of planning in capitalist, bureaucratic socialist, and other political-economies to specify the contents of expectable misinformation generated in those institutional settings.

20. For the purposes of this discussion, "systemic," "systematic," and "structural" will be used virtually synonymously. Further analyses of misinformation must distinguish between distortions of communication that are rooted in (Weberian) status structures and those distortions that are rooted in (Marxist) class structures. What substantive theory of social and political-economic structure planners assume or employ will determine what sorts of structural distortions they may be able to anticipate in practice. Social and political theory, thus, informs planners' abilities to anticipate problems of practice, problems calling for preemptive response on the one hand, and threatening failure on the other (Forester 1987). See Clegg's work (1975, 1979), for example, for a critical discussion of power and structure; see also Stone (1980).

21. E.g., Bolan and Nuttal (1975), Burlage (1979), Burlage and Kennedy (1980), Checkoway (1981), Lancourt (1979), and Roche (1981).

22. See Brownstein (1981).

23. Cf. Lukes (1974), Gaventa (1980), and Forester (1982a, 1982b).

24. The next chapter develops this analysis at length. Table 1 (p. 34) presents a reformulation of the meaning of the "boundedness" of rational action. These categories (necessary versus unnecessary, ad hoc versus systematic) may provide an initial, graphic representation of the meaning of Richard Bernstein's claim that Habermas's critical communications theory of society is essentially an attempt to reformulate a comprehensive social and political theory of rationality (Bernstein 1976). See also McCarthy (1978) and note 47, below. The task of any critical social and political theory is to be able to distinguish carefully the necessary from the unnecessary, and the ad hoc from the systematic constraints on social action (whether involving planners, citizens, decision-makers, or others) so that appropriate responses (enabling what social and political rationality

there may be) will be possible. The analysis of misinformation and communicative distortion provides the basis for an ethically and politically refined assessment of both (i) the problematic rationality of social and political action; and (ii) the practical responses and actions possible to counteract the threats to—and especially the systematic distortions of—socially and politically rational interaction. The paradigmatic types of systematic distortions of social action are social-psychological neurosis and political-economic ideology. In each case systematic distortions produce domination rather than emancipation (Held 1980). By providing an analysis of communicative distortions that allows actors to anticipate and then respond practically to misinforming or distorting communicative influences, a critical social theory joins an account of power relations to an account of emancipatory, politically informed and guided practice. This analysis thus suggests research to clarify, first, those bounds or constraints on rationality (types of communicative distortions) and, second, those actions and practices required to counteract or avoid those distortions mapped schematically in Table 1.

25. Table 2 (p. 38) arrays the effects of misinformation against the various levels of the exercise of power through which such misinformation may be communicated. These dimensions of Table 2 are based on recent analyses of political power (Lukes 1974; Gaventa 1980) and of the pragmatic structure of communicative interaction (Habermas 1979; Held 1980; Shapiro 1976; McCarthy 1978; and Forester 1981c); cf. Chapter Nine. The problem of political misinformation might be approached in two ways: either by cataloguing the types of "symbolic" power that political acts may manifest (Edelman 1964, 1971, 1977) or by assessing the vulnerability of political action to distorted communications (Habermas 1970a, 1975, 1979; Bernstein 1976; Shapiro 1976). The former approach illuminates the functions of "symbolic politics," but it fails to ground those functions in an account of practical interaction, a theory of social action. Thus, the argument of this chapter complements the analysis of communicative action in planning practice (Chapters Five and Nine, for example) to consider problems of practice and relations of power directly. On parallels to Foucault's analysis of power and discourse, see Ingram (1986).

26. Habermas (1979), Forester (1981c). See Chapter Nine for a more detailed exposition.

27. In the field of transportation planning, Yale Rabin, for example, writes: "Some believe that central city decline, minority isolation, and gasoline dependent dispersal have merely evolved from the incremental effects of millions of free choices and independent transactions in the metropolitan marketplace and that these conditions therefore simply re-

flect the mainstream values of a pluralistic society. The evidence, however, strongly suggests that these choices and transactions and the values which motivated them have been profoundly influenced by the systematic withholding by public officials of essential information about the fundamental nature and foreseeable impacts of highway policies and projects" (1980, 35).

28. Again, we can expect vulnerabilities of social action (to the structural management of attention, trust, consent, and knowledge) to be present whether that action (negotiating, bargaining, covering up, arguing, appealing, promising, threatening, and so on) is situated historically in capitalist or noncapitalist political-economies. But *how* actors actually face particular structural influences managing their knowledge, consent, trust, and framing of problems will vary, and must therefore be specified concretely (and strategic and practical anticipation and resistance must therefore also vary and likewise be specified) across differing political-economic systems. The analysis of misinformation and response, then, may provide a framework for comparative analysis of planning practices. For work in this direction, cf. Adler (1986).

29. E.g., Checkoway (1981), Needleman and Needleman (1974), and Forester (1982b).

30. See Benveniste (1977), Jacobs (1978), Krumholz, Cogger, and Linner (1975), Lancourt (1979), Meltsner (1976), Needleman and Needleman (1974), and Roche (1981).

31. See, e.g., Goffman (1981), Lyman and Scott (1970), Needleman and Needleman (1974), Susskind and Cruickshank (1987), and Wilensky (1967).

32. See Needleman and Needleman (1974), Fainstein and Fainstein (1972), and Gondim (1986).

33. See Krumholz, Cogger, and Linner (1975); also Hoch and Cibulskis (1987).

34. Answering this question analytically will prevent unjustified acts in planning no more than distinguishing perjury from truth-telling will prevent perjury. Still, without the analytical distinctions, confusion and mystification are guaranteed, for one could never then distinguish perjury from truth-telling or outright lies from honest claims.

35. See Rohr (1978), Bok (1978), Howe and Kaufman (1979), Marcuse (1976), Euben (1981), Fleischman and Payne (1980), Forester (1980, 1981b), and Wachs (1985).

36. This analysis reflects the help of Stephen Blum. For a related analysis, see Anderson (1985).

37. See, e.g., Bok (1978).

38. See Lukes (1974), Gaventa (1980), and Roche (1981).

39. See, e.g., Meltsner (1976), Benveniste (1977), Kemp (1980), Rabinowitz (1969), Needleman and Needleman (1974), Marris and Rein (1984), and Checkoway (1986).

40. See Lukes (1974).

41. See, e.g., Clark (1977) and Checkoway (1981).

42. I.e., sociologists refer to such power as "hegemony." Cf. Thompson (1984).

43. To argue that power works as communication, in several dimensions, is not to argue that power and force are unrelated. Even dictatorial power may work far more often through the communication of the threat of force than through the application of force itself. Legitimate power, while retaining its potential use of force, appeals to and depends on consent rather than on the threat of violence. See, for example, Habermas's (1977a) discussion of Arendt's concept of power, and Pitkin's (1972) discussion of the distinction between legitimate power (authority) and illegitimate power (domination); cf. Forester (1986). As applied here, and presented schematically in Chapter Nine, critical theory is an analysis of contingent, hegemonic power (cf. Giroux 1983; Marris 1982 [discussion of metaphors of power]).

44. Forester (1982b) argues that these dimensions of misinformation provide a powerful reformulation of the notions of agenda setting and mobilization of bias in discussions of political power. That essay emphasizes variations in the content of agenda setting and needs shaping; the present chapter emphasizes the types of misinformation (necessary or avoidable, ad hoc or systematic) that may be anticipated and counteracted by progressive planning practitioners. See also Chapter Five below.

45. Thus, further research should identify in detail the appropriate strategies to respond to the particular types of misinformation (see Tables 2 and 3).

46. See, e.g., Fisher and Foster (1978), Forester (1981b), Gaventa (1980), Hartman (1978), Kraushaar (1979), Lancourt (1979), Needleman and Needleman (1974), Roche (1981), and Scott (1985).

47. Table 1 (p. 34) also allows us to locate the differences in outlook that separate several conventional planning perspectives and political sensibilities more generally. For example, incrementalists and pragmatists seem to assume a world where the significant distortions are inevitable; their typical question, then, is "What can we do, given that distortions will always haunt whatever planning we attempt?" Incrementalists, pragmatists, and technicians seem to spend little time separating socially unnecessary distortions from apparently necessary ones. While technicians hope that more powerful methods will mitigate the effects of distortion, incrementalists and pragmatists retreat to a "satisficing" position. Liber-

als, in contrast, find inequalities of access, knowledge, expertise, and information to be socially unnecessary and hardly inevitable, so they work to provide compensatory or remedial programs designed to overcome and eliminate those socially unnecessary distortions of human action. The liberal, though, seems generally unconcerned with distinguishing ad hoc distortions from socially systematic or structural ones. Here is the crux of the difference between the liberal and the progressive: the progressive seeks to isolate the ad hoc from the more structurally rooted distortions and then respond to each accordingly.

In terms of Table 1, technicians may treat all information problems as if they are located in quadrant 1; incrementalists and pragmatists treat distortions as if they are located in quadrant 1 or 2. Liberals, in contrast, worry less about inevitable distortions than about politically contingent ones; thus, lacking a theory of the reproduction of social structures, they concentrate their attention in quadrant 3. Progressives, in contrast, distinguish the four quadrants and concentrate their attention on those avoidable distortions they can anticipate regularly (because these are structurally rooted) and then work to counteract, i.e., those in quadrant 4. If planners fail to distinguish the distortions in quadrant 4 from those in the other quadrants, they risk either mistaking recurring and expectable distortions for ad hoc and transient ones, or accepting avoidable distortions as if they were inevitable. In the former case, the error produces recurring surprise and avoidable distortion; in the latter case, the error produces fatalism while opportunities to improve the quality of practical work in the planning process remain unappreciated. The next chapter develops these arguments at length.

Chapter Four

1. See, for example, Friedmann (1973).

2. For an excellent summary, see March (1982); cf. March and Simon (1958).

3. This characterization of actual decision-making situations is a composite derived from discussions of bounded rationality in March and Simon (1958) and Perrow (1972).

4. Perrow (1972, 149).

5. See Lindblom (1959, 1965) and Etzioni (1968).

6. See Simon (1957).

7. Compare here the closely related work of Ray Kemp (1980, 1982, 1985).

8. Note that this account of rational action is richer than a simple means-ends or instrumental model of action. For a related argument de-

veloping this point at length, see Forester (1984). For an empirical study of contingent planning strategies, see Bryson and Delbecq (1979).

9. See Schattschneider (1960) and Lukes's treatment of these issues (1974).

10. See Lindblom (1965).

11. See Lindblom (1959).

12. Ibid.

13. See the strong conclusions in Lindblom (1977).

14. See Lukes (1974) and Dyckman (1969), for example.

15. See, e.g., Gorz (1967). For a recent discussion of progressive public administration in cities across the United States, see Clavel (1986).

16. Important reform legislation often extends service delivery to those in need without altering relations of power concerning accountability, investment, control of information, and so on. For example, Medicare and Medicaid extended medical coverage without altering those political relations holding the medical profession accountable, directing hospital capital investments, or making information regarding environmental and industrial causes of illness more readily accessible (Burlage 1979; Burlage and Kennedy 1980).

17. For a fascinating discussion and an evolution of analytical thinking, see Piven and Cloward (1982), and compare their earlier work taking a less nuanced view of the state (1971).

18. See, e.g., the differing approaches reflected in Castells (1979) and Katznelson (1981); cf. Piven and Cloward (1977).

19. See Forester (1981b, 1986).

20. Cf. Susskind's argument for a model of activist mediation in recognition of the limits of a pluralist bargaining model, in Susskind and Ozawa (1983, 277).

21. Note that Tables 1 and 4 raise an important practical and political question for the analysis of decision-making situations: "Do decision-makers face structural constraints, systematic distortions of information, e.g., or not?" Pluralists seem to deny the existence of such constraints; they prefer instead an imagery of rather fluid, ever-shifting, and realigning social and institutional relations reflecting equally fluid constellations of group interests. Marxists answer this question in the strong affirmative: class (i.e., productive) relations define the practical conditions of decision making. The practical point is that expected and anticipated obstacles, opportunities, and thus practical strategies vary according to one's operative political theory.

22. Tables 1 and 4 suggest a research agenda addressing the following sorts of questions: How do various public administrators and planners actually perceive their own decision-making situations? Do these per-

ceptions vary by policy area? Do these perceptions vary culturally? Ideologically?

23. Cf. Baum (1987, 1988).

24. For a more technical discussion, cf. notes 10 and 11 in Chapter Five.

25. William Torbert suggests that some types of bounds on decision making are desirable—when they represent the resistance of others who help the decision-maker to learn. Beyond the analysis of constrained decision making, then, further research might illuminate which structures and forms of organization and learning might foster human growth, community well-being, and political freedom (personal conversation, 1983).

26. See note 47, Chapter Three.

Chapter Five

1. See Baum (1983) for a study building on in-depth interviews with planners drawn from "a random sample of 50 members of the Maryland Chapter of the American Institute of Planners." Baum's study finds "that *a majority of planners do not see bureaucratic structures or the ways in which organizational decisions are made.* As a result, they have little chance of influencing these decisions" (italics in original; xiii).

2. This result is reported in a study that surveyed "a random sample of 616 planners who belonged to the American Institute of Planners and who worked for public planning agencies." See Howe and Kaufman (1979).

3. Theoretical arguments have been placed in the endnotes to make the general argument most accessible but yet to provide relatively technical points as well. For further theoretical work, see, for example, Morgan (1983) and Harmon and Mayer (1986).

4. I sketch the social and instrumental positions not to describe particular schools of thought in the history of organization theory, but rather to point to significant differences of emphasis reflected in such schools and in ordinary thinking about organizations as well. Following Perrow (1972), "human relations" and "institutional" schools would fall under the "social view" as I present it here, while the "neo-Weberian" schools would be included within the domain of "instrumental views." The point of this chapter, in part, is to contribute to the synthesis of these views and schools that Perrow calls for at the close of his study. Cf. Harmon and Mayer (1986).

5. For an intriguing study of these issues, see Dutton and Kraemer (1985).

6. For an instructive comparison of public-sector and private-sector

organizations and the increasing difficulties of making a viable public-private distinction at all, see Yates (1985). See also Lax and Sebenius (1986).

7. Silverman (1970) presents such a phenomenological view of organizational relations, and Weick (1969) stresses the ongoing role-recreation or "enactment" of organizational actors. In these views, actors continually elaborate, negotiate, and socially construct the organizations of which they are members; the organizations are the evolving interactions of their members.

8. We now extend and apply the previous chapters to analyze the organizational settings in which planners work. Chapter Two introduced the notion of planning *practice* as communicative action; Chapter Three assessed the planner's and others' *control of information* as sources of power. In this chapter we focus on *organizations* as structures of ever contingent communicative action. Thus, for our purposes here, it is important that organizations be recognized as structures of ongoing argument, of practical communicative interactions in which actors make claims on one another's formulation of problems, beliefs, trust, and sense of legitimacy (speaking properly in context). This analysis extends political analyses of organizations that follow Schattschneider (1960) by focusing on the discrete, pragmatic performance of communicative, argumentative claims-making: we explore the microsociological strategies and dimensions of the organization of bias. Habermas (1979) takes a more restricted formulation of communicative action (as that oriented to reaching understanding) so that he may assess both the ordinary claims made in speech and the ways that those claims, and the understanding of those claims by other actors, may be shaped by (and be vulnerable to) the social and political structures in which they occur. Habermas has not addressed questions of organizational behavior at any length. See also Forester (1981b, 1981c, 1983a, 1986) for discussion of the political-organizational implications of Habermas's analysis of communicative action.

9. See, e.g., Giddens (1979). Cf. notes 13, 20 below. See also Giroux (1983).

10. We see that these processes are conventional and rule-structured because (i) they are matters of application and not automation, and (ii) we know that mistakes (rule violations) can be made. Were these processes not conventionally rule-structured, the notions of mistakes, oversights, misinterpretations, errors, and faults might have no socially shared, rule-structured, conventional sense. Technical work is fallible and socially constructed.

11. For those readers with a particular interest in Habermas's "critical

theory of society," this point should be taken as an attempt to clarify a central ambiguity in his work: the problematic distinction between the realm of the purposive-rational, the "technical," on the one hand, and the realm of communicative action, the "practical," on the other. Habermas (1970a) differentiates these as if they were ontologically distinct, yet in other passages he points more clearly, though never at length, to the derivative character of the technical from the practical. This last position is compatible with Wittgenstein's later and Heidegger's early rooting of technical languages in socially shared, ordinary language (how else could prospective scientists or technicians learn or debate? Cf. Krieger 1981), and is also compatible with neo-Marxist and other socially constructivist theories of political socialization as well. For example, Habermas (1975, 10) writes, "The structures of intersubjectivity are just as constitutive for experiences and instrumental action as they are for attitudes and communicative action." Or Habermas (1979, 118): "Strategic actions must be institutionalized, that is, embedded in intersubjectively binding norms that guarantee the fulfillment of the motivational conditions" of action. For example, a speaker's strategic lie depends on the listener's trust. The instrumental or strategic act depends on the sociopolitical institutional structure in which it makes any sense at all. Cf. Giddens's contribution in Thompson and Held (1982).

12. For a revealing analysis, see Dutton and Kraemer (1985).

13. Cf. note 8 above. In Chapter Three, the reproduction of social relations of knowledge, consent, trust, and problem formulation was developed more narrowly as central to the ongoing production of information and misinformation. In this analysis, the reproduction of those social relations is presented as an intrinsic, structural aspect of the communicative interaction that constitutes *any* social organization. Chapter Three focused on the phenomenon of power; this analysis describes the ongoing productive character of human organization as well as its reconstituting, reproductive character.

Here we explore the organizational implications of the analysis of communicative action broached in Chapter Three and to be developed in more detail in Chapter Nine. In a nutshell, all communicative interaction involves the making and acceptance or rejection (by the listener, reader, etc.) of four precarious pragmatic claims: that the utterance's representation is true, that it is properly "in context," that it sincerely expresses intentions, and that it is clearly put forward. As these claims become problematic, communicative interaction will fail. The paradigm case, here, is the promise no more than the report, question, or challenge; for the success of each depends on the extent to which the listener accepts the speaker's claims to truth, propriety, sincerity, and clarity.

Consider how we may face and seek to criticize such claims in every-day life: The newspaper reporter may be sincere, but wrong. The advisor might be an expert in the context, but be incomprehensible. The salesper-son may be clear, but not sincere. Angry community residents may speak the truth, and be clear and sincere, but they may be in no position to speak legitimately for the whole community. In these ways, when any of the claims to truth, legitimacy (in context), sincerity, and clarity are re-jected, action may fail. Yet as these claims are accepted in ongoing orga-nizational interaction, not only may a given communicative action suc-ceed (a challenge made, a question asked, a report presented, etc.), but *so then are social relations of belief, consent, trust, and problem formula-tion reproduced.* See Habermas (1979), Forester (1981c, 1982a), and cf. Chapters Three and Nine. What is the practical point for each of us as actors? In an earlier work (Forester 1988) I argue that these pragmatic claims can add up into practical arguments, which in turn may form ele-ments of planning and political strategies.

14. The work of Anthony Giddens may be distinguished from that of Habermas by the attention each gives to the question, "How does the reproduction of social relations reproduce or subvert illegitimate 'au-thority'?" Giddens assesses the reproduction of social action but neglects this question. In contrast, the issue of legitimate authority and its repro-duction lies at the heart of Habermas's entire project of assessing "sys-tematically distorted communication." See Giddens (1979) and Haber-mas (1979), for example; cf. Giddens (1984) and Bernstein (1986).

15. This analysis represents a Habermasian account of hegemony, an account assessing hegemonic power as a continually practical, commu-nicative, and performative accomplishment. Power may be understood not as a possession of an actor working mysteriously on another actor, but rather as a normative relationship binding the two together, a rela-tionship that structures one agent's *dependency* on the other's informa-tion, *deference* to the other's supposed authority, *trust* in the other's in-tentions, or *consideration* of the other's claims to attention. See Forester (1981c, 1982b) and Giddens (1979). Cf. Gondim (1986), contrasting two regimes in Brazil, for a study that explores the significance of intra-organizational relations of power and, in the face of political pressure from outside the planning agency, the potential shielding of lower-level planning staff by their supervisors.

16. See Forester (1982b). Trent Schroyer writes, "Ideologies are those belief systems which can maintain their legitimacy despite the fact that they could not be validated if subjected to rational discourse. . . . Ideolo-gies remove whole aggregates of social norms from public questioning and discourse" (1974, 163). The nondemocratic reproduction of social

relations appears as blocked access to those theoretical and practical discourses in which the claims of citizens could be most freely debated. Where citizens have no recourse to such discourses with those influencing their lives, those citizens are subject to domination and the illegitimate exercise of power. Only through democratic political discourse, Habermas suggests, is the true legitimation of power, the rational creation and mandate of authority, possible (cf. Habermas 1979, 186). Cf. note 20, below.

17. See, e.g., Gaventa (1980) and the extensive literature related to participation, pluralism, and agenda setting cited there.

18. Cf. the acute and compelling work of Richard Titmuss (1968), for example. For a brilliant analysis of technology, see Winner (1986, ch. 1).

19. See Peter Marris's argument that planning and policy-making lead to change, that change often disrupts integrative systems of meaning and so produces feelings of loss, and that the experience of loss calls in turn for the reintegration of meaning by those affected, whether the change is "all for the good" or not, whether the change is happenstance or systemically and structurally rooted (1975; cf. Marris 1982).

20. How the reproduction of social and political relations takes place in any given organization is an empirical question to which this chapter points. This chapter suggests the dangers, the risks, and the political and social costs that planners and citizens can anticipate where the processes of organizational and institutional reproduction are nondemocratic, where they deny affected citizens or their representatives the possibility of genuine participation free from domination due to class, race, religion, or sex. Cf. Habermas (1979, 186), on the distinguishing feature of democratic forms as "a rational principle of legitimation," and Burton and Murphy (1980).

21. Again, Gaventa provides a vivid historical account of economic and political power as it may shape participation and self-consciousness (1980). Our argument here, to sum up the potential Habermasian contribution to a critical organization theory, is that the contemporary analysis of hegemony must take the form of the concrete analysis of distorted pragmatic communications (cf. Table 1, Chapter Three).

22. In this chapter, the relationship of these claims to the Marxist concept of alienation can only be suggested. Nevertheless, this analysis seeks to broaden the conventional Marxist account of capitalist exploitation (the private appropriation and control of surplus, and the corresponding appropriation of the consent of labor). Here we assess the appropriation of consent regarding the control of accumulation in addition to the appropriation and management (through the reproductive, communicative behavior of organizations) of citizens' trust, knowledge, and

senses of problems and needs. The strong claim here is that the exploitation of labor is not simply located on the productive side of the social relations of production but is rooted in—and is only one aspect of the political-economic exploitation tied to—the reproduction of those social relations.

By recasting the social relations of production as systematically distorted but nevertheless practically communicative relations, Habermas makes it possible to recognize exploitation, appropriation, and domination in four integrally related dimensions of those social relations of production: social beings' knowledge and belief, consent and control, trust and cooperation, attention and sensibility. Because this analysis suggests types of exploitation and domination that operate not only in the workplace but throughout the reproduction of social relations (e.g., in the school or at home), such an analysis can refine and extend Marxist analyses of exploitation and suggest a systematic basis for integration with feminist analyses and with those of political alienation that already call attention to the importance of the more general reproduction of social relations. See, e.g., Giddens (1984), Thompson (1984), Giroux (1983), Markusen (1980), and Wolfe (1974). For more traditionally political-economic analyses of "reproduction," see Castells (1977, 1979), Feldman (1978), and Roweis (1979); and compare Markusen (1980).

23. Such reproduction of social relations exemplifies the "systematically distorted communications" that Habermas has attempted to analyze and expose. Habermas's notion of systematically distorted communication may be developed concretely, in organizationally and politically practical ways, by locating its effects within the basic communicative processes of the reproduction of social relations that constitute any real social organization. Habermas's analysis of the structure of ordinary communicative action and speech, his so-called universal pragmatics, suggests the dimensions of that reproduction (relations of knowledge, consent, trust, and comprehension). See Habermas (1979, ch. 1), Habermas in Thompson and Held (1982), Forester (1986), and Chapter Nine here. Cf. note 13, above.

24. See, e.g., Krumholz (1982) and Clavel (1986).

25. For information about a national network of planners working toward such ends, see the *Planners Network Newsletter,* Planners Network, 1601 Connecticut Ave. N.W., 5th floor, Washington, D.C. 20009.

Chapter Six

1. For illuminating and contradictory views regarding power and neutrality, see Colosi (1983) and Susskind and Ozawa (1983). The possibility and desirability of mediator neutrality are controversial issues in the

mediation community. Colosi argues the traditional position: Mediators' effectiveness depends on the perception of their neutrality. Susskind and Ozawa argue, to the contrary, for a more substantive conception of activist mediation: Mediators of public disputes can and should bring representatives of affected but weakly organized parties to the negotiating table. For an assessment of the limits of the traditional conception, see, e.g., Amy (1987) and Schoenbrud (1983). For a review of recent work in environmental mediation, see Bingham (1986), and for analysis, see Bacow and Wheeler (1984). For a deceptively simple introduction to negotiation theory and technique, see Fisher and Ury (1983). For extensive applications to planning issues, see Susskind and Ozawa (1983, 1984) and Susskind and Cruickshank (1987). Two recent studies of planning practice indicate the centrality of these issues for the profession: Knack (1986, 10) estimates that more than 40 percent of the American Planning Association membership concentrates on zoning and subdivision issues; Dalton (1987) suggests that planners in a statewide California sample spend a majority of their time administering regulations in permit-granting processes. Cf. Zartman and Touval (1985).

2. Formal permit decisions are often debated in the specialized language of zoning regulations, and speaking this language is often easier for developers than for ad hoc neighborhood groups. If neighbors then turn to planning staff for help, the planners may feel awkwardly cast in the ambiguous role of zoning lawyer for the neighborhood. If neighborhoods have no planners assigned to serve as their advocates, local planners are likely to find that the problem of a "common language" subtly aligns them with development interests. Knowledge and power are closely linked here.

3. Indeed, face-to-face mediation might be avoided by planners who expect shuttle diplomacy to protect their own influence or leverage. In one community, for example, a developer proposed a 150-unit apartment complex; neighbors, although concerned about scale, were generally supportive, and the planning staff hoped to have a fraction of the units designated as "affordable." Several days before the decision-making board was to review the project, the planning staff and the developer negotiated an agreement: 15 percent of the units would be offered at below-market rates; design alterations would be made; and planning staff would strongly recommend project approval without delay. One of the planners justified the exclusion of the neighborhood from the negotiations in this way: "What we got that we didn't think we'd get was the '15 percent affordable' agreement. But if we'd had the neighborhood involved in that meeting, we might not have been able to give so much on the height and bulk. . . . Each faction values these things differently; the neighbors, abuttors, weigh design and aesthetics much more—I'm guessing—than

affordability, so [even though we're trying to make more housing available to people] we might not have gotten the 15 percent."

Should advocates of affordable housing have participated along with abutting neighbors concerned about scale? The negotiated outcome might have been better, but coming just days before the board meeting, the negotiating meeting might also have been unmanageable, disrupted by personality, or simply inconclusive. These risks—the apparent unpredictability of face-to-face mediation under severe time constraints, the threat of disruption, and potential failure to reach agreement—appear to make shuttle diplomacy (and other strategies discussed here) more attractive to planners than more traditional face-to-face mediation (cf. Susskind and Ozawa 1984).

4. For an analysis of the complexity of planners' practical anticipation, see Forester (1987).

5. Consider here the elemental promise of mediated negotiations: If disputing parties value issues at hand differently—one cares more about design, the other cares more about use—then the disputants can achieve more than grudging compromises, ways of settling for less. Instead, they can make valuable trades, giving on issues they do not feel strongly about in order to gain on issues that they value greatly. Consider a rezoning proposal in which scale and design-review authority are key issues. If local property owners value scale more than they are threatened by the prospect of design review, and if neighbors are much more concerned about design review than about scale, then an outcome far better than compromise may be possible: strong design-review provisions for the neighborhood, and scale allowances for the owners. Both may gain—relative to likely compromises reached without mediation.

When planning disputes involve multiple issues, trades between the disputing parties can be possible because the parties value different things differently. If planners can identify these differences, they might enable trades across issues (design and scale, for example) and thus transform conflicts from what appear to be purely "win-lose" into "both-gain" situations—in which the parties may not simply compromise, but actually gain. By helping conflicting parties to "exploit their differences" (Susskind and Cruickshank 1987), the planner-mediator works to achieve mutually beneficial results, "both-gain" outcomes, outcomes realizing "joint gains" (Raiffa 1982). The more differences between parties, the greater the potential for "joint gains."

6. Deborah Kolb notes that business managers may often call on "free-floating mediators" in their organizations for help. In every organization, she suggests, such ad hoc mediators might be effective not because

of their substantive knowledge, but rather because of their communication and conflict-management skills (personal communication, March 1986). Cf. Kolb (1986, 1988).

7. Such agreements could then be reviewed and perhaps refined during and after the formal hearings. Howard Raiffa's (1985) idea of post-settlement settlements could then be explored. To paraphrase, "Okay, you've both agreed to this; now let's see if we can devise a package that's even better for each of you!"

8. This entire discussion assumes no statutory changes in local permit-granting regulations. In general, local planners have the discretion to adopt mediated negotiation strategies without risk of violating existing zoning statutes and ordinances. Although a discussion of revised statutes that might encourage mediated negotiation is beyond the scope of this chapter, note, for example, that local ordinances might be modified: (i) to enable a specified authority (e.g., building commissioner or planning director) to determine on a case-by-case basis which projects should be considered candidates for mediated negotiations; (ii) to require those projects to be reviewed in a multiparty forum, whose meeting dates would fall well before mandated public hearings; (iii) to encourage, as a matter of public policy, all participants in local land-use permit processes to seek mediated, collaborative agreements as a *supplement* to existing formal processes; and (iv) to require local building departments to refer project proposals for review (see item [i]) before allowing proponents to file for permits and "start the clock."

9. Lax and Sebenius (1986) provide an excellent summary of the analytic issues involved. See also Susskind and Cruickshank (1987). Planners must address, too, dilemmas of mediated negotiations, e.g., premature definition of problems and representation of affected parties, reviewed in Amy (1987). They must be equally sensitive to the politics of litigation, and local organizing, about which Amy (1987) is too silent. Cf. note 1, above.

10. This point is crucial. Planning strategies are always context-dependent, and, thus, if we are to recognize possibilities within the micro-politics of planning practice, we must assess the character of planners' discretion. See, e.g., Needleman and Needleman (1974) and Forester (1982b).

11. See Susskind and Ozawa (1983, 1984) and Zartman and Touval (1985).

12. For an interesting analysis, see Fisher (1983) and compare to Lukes (1974).

13. See, e.g., Bailey (1983) and Freire (1970).

Chapter Seven

1. To listen well as planners or citizens, we must be able to employ what Mills has called "the sociological imagination" (1959). For a discussion of the significance of listening as part of "democratic talk"—the character of our talk as citizens when we are living democratically—see Barber (1984). On the intersection of the personal and the political, see, e.g., the title essay in Rich (1979).

2. For a discussion of "care" and a reformulation of moral development and the psychology of decision making, see Gilligan (1982). For extensive discussion of Gilligan's work, see Kittay and Meyers (1987). As we will show below, the practices of listening and questioning are intimately related. On the "hermeneutical priority of the question," see Gadamer (1975, 325–341). Recent feminist research powerfully extends the political and developmental implications of questioning and listening practices (Belenky et al. 1986). Belenky et al. argue that "question posing . . . is central to maternal practice in its most evolved form. Question posing is at the heart of connected knowing. We argue that women's mode of talk, rather than being denigrated, should become a model for all who are interested in promoting human development" (1986, 189). For parallel political arguments about the centrality of questioning in practice, see Freire (1970), Forester (1981b), and Misgeld (1985).

3. When we listen, we can do far more than hear words. Listening includes but should not be reduced to hearing. On the political character of speech, see Pitkin (1972).

4. For a stunning analysis exploring these issues, see Seeley (1963). Compare the comment in the last chapter from the planning director who argued that he needed staff members who were able to listen critically to the interests, positions, *and* passions of neighbors and developers alike. Albrecht Wellmer makes a closely related theoretical point when he refers to the anticipation by critical social theory of the "total social subject," an anticipation expressing the emancipatory interest in cognition (1974, 135). Paulo Freire (1970) shows what this means in practice, as do Belenky et al. (1986; quoted in note 2, above). See O'Neill (1974, 1985).

5. Cf. Susskind's stress on "exploiting differences" discussed in the last chapter. A cardinal rule for negotiation and mediation is to expect and explore the ambiguities of the interests of all parties to a negotiation. Because what is most important to one party may not be what is most important to another, the careful assessment of ambiguity may lead to areas of potential trades and joint gains. See Chapter Six, note 5; and cf. Chapter Nine, note 25. Feminist theories of power and practice

and recent work on mediation promise to inform each other in fascinating ways.

6. See Friedmann (1979, 138). For Buber's emphasis on concreteness and practice, see Buber (1977). Cf. Friedmann (1972).

7. The encouragement of "voice" is important in two related senses—the broadly political and democratic sense of "the voice of the people," and the more specific experiential sense conveyed by Belenky et al. in their study of women's epistemological and ethical development: "What we had not anticipated was that 'voice' was more than an academic shorthand for a person's point of view. Well after we were into our interviews with women, we became aware that it is a metaphor that can apply to many aspects of women's experience and development. In describing their lives, women commonly talked about voice and silence: 'speaking up,' 'speaking out,' 'being silenced,' 'not being heard,' 'really listening,' 'really talking,' 'words as weapons,' 'feeling deaf and dumb,' 'having no words,' 'saying what you mean,' 'listening to be heard,' and so on in an endless variety of connotations all having to do with sense of mind, self-worth, and feelings of isolation from or connection to others. We found that women repeatedly used the metaphor of voice to depict their intellectual and ethical development; and that the development of a sense of voice, mind, and self were intricately intertwined" (1986, 18). Throughout this book, we have argued that by organizing attention selectively, planners can encourage (or obstruct) the development of the voices of men and women alike, especially those who may be vulnerable politically for reasons of class, race, or gender.

8. See Ricoeur (1960) and Thompson (1984). For a related argument concerning historiography, see LaCapra (1982).

9. Peter Marris (1975) argues that ambiguity is fundamental to processes of change and the rebuilding of meaning, value, and identity. Listening is our mode of address in such situations of disruption, loss, growth, or change.

10. This is not to confuse friendship with emancipatory political organizing, even if the emancipatory and ideology-critical aspects of friendship are rarely discussed. See Pitkin (1972, 290, 336) for an analysis of the political character of language and speech and for the problematic implications of Wittgenstein's work in particular. Throughout, we address the problem of which Alvin Gouldner writes: "It remains a central task of critical theory to focus on face-to-face communication" (1976, 150).

11. To listen critically, planners must bring to bear the analyses of Chapters Three and Four. If relevant data are missing from a neighbor's

account of a project, is that because of an oversight, an essentially ad hoc error, or does it result from a strategy to misrepresent the case at hand? When a developer argues that design changes will make a proposed project no longer economically viable, is that simply a project-specific bargaining claim, or is it an element of a broader, structurally based strategy (threatening localities with the power of mobile capital) to extract concessions from the city? If the developer is making the former, case-specific argument, then the city, organized neighbors, or the developer might link concessions on this project to gains on another site. But if the threat is structurally based, the planners and community residents alike should recognize that the claim may actually have little to do with the case at hand. They should also expect a similarly general threat to be made about future projects.

Depending on how the planners listen, then, the same apparent threat may provide the basis for a strong negotiated development agreement in the former case, but it could be recognized to undermine such an agreement in the latter case. If planners do not anticipate, and do the necessary analysis to counteract, structurally based threats, they are likely to give away the store in development negotiations and project development more generally. Cf. note 47, Chapter Three. For accounts of planners' anticipatory use of theory, see Forester (1987, 1988).

12. On the practical problems of realizing reform, Peter Marris writes: "The reformers must listen as well as explain, continually accommodating their design to other purposes. . . . If they impatiently cut this process short, their reforms are likely to be abortive" (1975, 167). Radicals and conservatives both begin from the truism that Peter Berger states as he seeks to justify morally and pragmatically his principle of "cognitive respect" and its requisite listening: "Policies that ignore the indigenous definition of a situation are prone to fail" (1976, 201). See also the discussion of the "negotiator's dilemma" in Lax and Sebenius (1986).

13. Politically put: If there is no listening, then there is no criticism of ideology, no criticism of the needlessly false claims of the powerful or of others' internalized senses of powerlessness and oppression (cf. Freire 1970). In a seminal work that assessed recent critical social theory, Trent Schroyer boldly argued that today the "critique of ideology," the ongoing struggle for emancipatory knowledge, takes the form of a more pointed "critique of systematically distorted communications" (1973, 163). Schroyer's point is crucial. Although the presence of ideology writ large may often be difficult to identify in the minutiae of everyday life, systematically distorted claims (owing to structures of power and constrained processes of inquiry) can be identified and counteracted. We may de-

construct meaning, but we need to reconstruct social and political action. Cf. note 17 in Chapter Two.

14. These might be called "resistance" or "counter- hegemonic" strategies of everyday life (cf. Scott 1985; Giroux 1983).

15. See Ricoeur (1974), Dallmayr and McCarthy (1977), Thompson (1984), and Fay (1987).

16. Compare the discussion in Chapter Three (Table 1), and see especially note 47. The theoretical issues are suggested by Habermas (1977b) and Mendelson (1979).

17. See Kochman (1981). Robert Mier, former commissioner of economic development for the City of Chicago, brought this book to my attention while speaking of the necessity for his staff to be not only technically competent but also competent to speak clearly and persuasively in several different neighborhoods, each with distinctly differing styles of interaction. He has written: "Seventy-five of the 110 people who work in Chicago's Department of Economic Development occupy positions for which, given my conception of planning, I believe planners ought to be the best qualified. As a practical matter, I find that today's graduates of planning schools probably qualify for only a quarter of those positions. Their primary weaknesses, I believe, are their perception and communications skills" (Mier 1986, 69).

18. The trained concertgoer hears the same notes but a different performance than the untrained initiate sitting nearby hears. Education, training, and preparation make appreciation possible, and appreciation makes subsequent discriminating judgments possible, too (Schön 1983; Vickers 1984). Neighbors who say of a developer's proposal only "I like it" or "I don't like it" give the planner far less to work with than if they explained that "I like it because it respects surrounding buildings" or "I don't like it because the scale is all wrong, the density is too great, and the traffic impacts will be substantial."

19. We may, of course, resist such conventional role prescriptions.

20. See Kochman (1981), Gilligan (1982), and Forester (1987).

21. See Mills (1959, 8).

22. From Beck (1962, 18); in McLane (1977).

23. So we must attend to both part and whole, countering individualism on the one hand and historicism on the other. See Ryan (1976).

24. See Freire (1970).

25. See Freire (1970) and Pitkin (1972).

26. John O'Neill writes: "The ultimate feature of the phenomenological institution of reflexivity is that it grounds critique in membership and tradition. Thus the critic's auspices are the same as those of anyone work-

ing in a community of language, work, and politics. In the critical act there is a simultaneity of authorship and authenticity which is the declaration of membership in a continuing philosophical, literary, or scientific community" (1972, 234); see also O'Neill (1974).

27. In the next chapter these arguments are developed and extended with regard to political and professional design practice. Since this chapter was originally drafted, several "how-to" books have appeared on the subject of listening, and one major U.S. corporation has launched a massive advertising campaign to point out the pragmatic and organizational virtues of "listening." We should not allow a narrow corporate interpretation, however, to displace an understanding of the praxis of listening that questions ideology, relations of domination, and the possibilities of progressive and emancipatory action.

Chapter Eight

1. See Cuff (1982).

2. The metaphor of "making sense together" is drawn from the compelling work of John O'Neill; see, e.g., O'Neill (1974). By "sense-making," this chapter refers to the ordinary rather than any technical, linguistic meaning of that phrase; the fuller significance of the metaphor is explored in detail in the second part of this chapter.

3. For a recent review of the literature on design practices and the fundamental place of design activity (as the formulation of alternatives) in policy making and decision making as well as in architecture, see the work of architect and planner Ernest Alexander, especially Alexander (1982).

4. For recent treatments of the social psychology and political-economy of design practices respectively, see Schön (1983), Mayo (1978, 1985), and Mayo, Burgess, and Littman (1981).

5. For the purposes of this chapter, the notion of "search" as a metaphor for design activity is taken from Simon (1969). Martin Krieger (1981, 195–196) has pointed out that the "search" metaphor may have further, richly existential qualities as characterized in Walker Percy's *The Moviegoer*. This chapter suggests the limits of understanding design practice as a *formal* search process. Yet, in its *existential* variation, the designer's "search" for sense, meaning, coherence, and wholeness is a process wholly compatible with the conversational, sense-making conception proposed here.

6. The notion of design as making sense in practical conversation runs parallel to contemporary work in the social sciences and humanities that concerns itself with issues of interpretation, language use, communicative

action, and conversation as a model of political interaction. See, e.g., Bellah et al. (1985), Rabinow and Sullivan (1979), and Beiner (1983).

7. Performance standards could be considered; this might reduce, but hardly eliminate, the ambiguities here.

8. Simon Neustein puts the point more sharply by suggesting that "search" is founded on a model of an individual who looks for some optimal outcome, whereas "sense" is founded on a model of people who try to create durable relationships (personal correspondence, November 1983).

9. For a related argument, see Donald Schön's discussion of design as a conversation with the materials of the situation (1983). A designer's conversation with the materials derives in part, of course, from his or her socialization, education, and training, as well as from immediate social influences ("no benches!"). Schön seeks to demonstrate the importance of the designer's own theorizing in action—and the possibilities of improved reflection in action (cf. Schön 1987).

10. For a useful discussion of the work of problem-setting that must precede problem-solving, see Rein and Schön (1977).

11. James March is a brilliant, friendly critic of decision-making models patterned on the logic of optimal search behavior. For a review of related arguments that suggest that solutions in hand often dictate which problems are to be solved, and that play and passion have important problem-solving roles, see March (1978, 1982).

12. This was, of course, a central argument of the last chapter. See Wiggins (1978) for the centrality of assessing the particulars of the context, as a requirement for practical judgment and action, and as an in-principle argument against reducing practical judgment to optimization (however constrained) and calculation.

13. See Vickers (1984) and Schön (1983). See LaCapra (1982, 47–85) regarding contexts of interpretation; and Rabinow and Sullivan (1979).

14. See March (1978, 1982), and Chapter Nine, below, especially note 25.

15. Cf. Bailey (1983).

16. See Goodman (1978), Whiteman (1983), Krieger (1981), Burton (1975), and Dekema (1981).

17. Recall the discussion in Chapter Two that criticized instrumental and information-processing views of planning practice and argued that we should understand such practice as the work of selectively shaping attention. We apply that argument here in analytic detail to the work of designing.

18. See Forester (1982b, 1987).

19. For a disturbing suggestion that architects may be self-defeatingly

inattentive to such issues, see Bolman (1981). For similar findings about the organizational and political blindness of planners, see Baum (1983). By focusing on the interactive character of design processes, this chapter seeks to open up avenues of inquiry to prevent such problems and thus to prepare designers for the vicissitudes and nuances of the complex processes in which they will most often inevitably be participants rather than sole authorities. Compare Chapters Three, Four, and Five, above.

20. See Cuff's research on architectural practice (1981). For further discussion of the boundedness of professional practices, see Forester (1984).

21. See Chapter Nine. For a discussion of political dimensions of role ambiguity and implicit role reproduction, see Mayo, Burgess, and Littman (1981).

22. See the provocative exploration and analysis of the social constitution of design in Hayden (1984). On the related systematic distortions of communication, see Chapters Three, Four, and Five, above.

23. For a discussion of generalizable interests and their suppression, a discussion of legitimacy and its vulnerabilities, see Habermas (1975), especially Part III. Cf. note 18 in Chapter Two, above. The paradigm of design practice as a sense-making activity makes the rationality of design depend on conditions of practical discourse in which neither instrumentality, political interest, nor aesthetic judgment dominates the other members of their tripartite family. For a clear and accessible discussion of the rationality of value judgments and practical discourses in which questions of "ought" are at stake, see Fischer (1980).

Chapter Nine

1. This chapter draws on several strands of modern social theory, particularly a critical communications theory of social *action,* to assess the practical and political character of planning practice. "Critical theory" here refers predominantly to the work of Jürgen Habermas and the interpreters of his recent work (1970a, 1971, 1973, 1975, 1979, and 1984). Excellent interpreters of Habermas's critical theory are Richard Bernstein (1976, 1983), Thomas McCarthy (1978), and Trent Schroyer (1973). See also Thompson and Held (1982) and, for a range of applications, Forester (1985). Note, however, that we are using "strategy" in its ordinary, rather than in Habermas's restricted, sense; cf. notes 8 and 11 in Chapter Five.

2. Chapter Three drew from the same field research. Other relevant field research, including that reported in Chapter Six, assessed the com-

municative behavior of planning staff in the face of local land-use conflicts and planning strategies in health planning processes.

3. For one distinction between instrumental and communicative action, see Habermas (1970a, 91f.). Weber's concept of "meaningful social action" is a precursor to communicative action, as Habermas argues (1984). For one approach to the systematic structuring of attention (rooted in the sociology of knowledge), see Berger and Luckmann (1966). For a lucid analysis of the important noninstrumental aspects of ordinary meetings, see Bailey (1983).

4. See Lukes (1974) for the treatment of the structural distortions of communications and information considered by E. E. Schattschneider, Peter Bachrach, and Morton Baratz; Murray Edelman's work (1971, 1977) provides another view of distorted communications. Schroyer (1973) and Claus Mueller (1973) attempt to bridge Habermas's analysis of communicative action (and its distortions) and more traditional treatments of power and political structure. See also, for example, the lengthy introductory essay in Habermas (1973). Cf. Alvin Gouldner's misleading reading of systematic distortions of communication as "censorship" (1976). Cf. also Paulo Freire's powerful and moving *Pedagogy of the Oppressed* (1970), which provides many fascinating parallels with Habermas's work, as suggested by Misgeld (1985) and O'Neill (1985) and in Chapter One, above. See also the striking work of Michel Foucault, as discussed cogently in Hoch (1987); Foucault's broader claims about power are in part belied by his own political agency, a contingent, staged agency that this book attempts to reveal for planning analysts.

5. See note 1, above. For a related, though less critical and normatively systematic, account, see Giddens's account of "structuration" (1984). Cf. Bernstein (1986).

6. Thus, in the language of modern social theory, the critical theory articulated here is a theory of hegemonic power and counter-hegemonic action. Chapter Five has presented an extended analysis.

7. Anyone who doubts that systematically yet unnecessarily distorted communications might have enormous influence should consider the problems of achieving "informed consent" in medical-care settings. A striking contribution to the understanding of power could be made by the researcher who assessed the obstacles to informed consent in medical care and assessed the parallel obstacles and their contingencies in a variety of planning and policy-making processes.

8. Such distorted communications mediate, in Marxist terms, the contradictions between working and ruling classes, between the means of production and the social relations of production, between labor and

capital. In more ordinary terms, these distortions hide from citizens the end results of their labor, the possibilities of collective improvement that now exist in modern cooperative organization and technology, and the social costs of the private control of investment and labor. For a parallel analysis, but one that lacks the analysis of the pragmatics of speech and interaction that we present below, see Giroux (1983).

9. Critical theorists are devoting increasing attention to empirical research into these systematic distortions of communications. See, e.g., Misgeld (1985). As Chapter Two suggested, the empirical "micropolitical" promise of critical theory is to carry forward the classical Marxian "critique of ideology" into a subtle and refined analysis of the structurally, systematically distorted pragmatic communication and language use, the concrete social actions, that constitute, mediate, and find expression in the social relations of production, politics, and culture. Habermas and Foucault thus have related projects, however much they differ in their strategies of execution. Cf. Fraser (1981), Ingram (1986), and Roweis (1988).

10. This question is especially important to the extent that the listener has no opportunity to engage the speaker and question the given description—thus enabling a richer account to be given. But when the listener is uninformed and trusting, even the recourse to conversation and interaction may not change matters. The offered account, selective as it must be, will effectively stand. (The planner, for example, may say to the community organization member or developer, "There's nothing much you can do." It's helpful to remember, of course, that planners are not omniscient and that such statements, like others, may or may not actually be true; they may nevertheless have real effects, real influence.)

11. The classic analysis of "speech acts" appears in the work of John Austin (1965) and John Searle (1969). For an accessible introduction, see Wardhaugh (1985).

12. Nonverbal communication counts, too, but this idea must be developed further elsewhere. In face-to-face interaction, nonverbal communication can take the form, for example, of tone, gesture, or deadpan or lively facial expressions. At the organizational level, nonverbal communication is effective in the structuring of agendas, meetings, work programs, and the character (e.g., more or less formal, comprehensible, or encouraging) of the planning or policy-formulation process. At both levels, what remains unsaid may be as important, and effective, as what is said. See, e.g., Watzlawick, Beavin, and Jackson (1967).

13. Habermas calls the theory of these speech acts "the theory of universal pragmatics": universal because all social communication seems to depend on the structure and possibility of such acts, and pragmatic be-

cause these acts are contingently performed and concretely practical—
they make a difference in our lives. See the chapter "What Is Universal
Pragmatics?" in Habermas (1979). See also note 10, above.

14. See, for example, Karl-Otto Apel's "The A Priori of Communication and the Foundation of the Humanities" (1977). Consider Hannah
Arendt: "There may be truths beyond speech, and they may be of great
relevance to man. . . in so far as he is not a political being, whatever else
he may be. Men in the plural, that is, men in so far as they live and move
and act in this world, can experience meaningfulness only because they
can talk with and make sense to each other and to themselves"; "Speech
is what makes man a political being . . . wherever the relevance of speech
is at stake, matters become political by definition"; quoted in Pitkin
(1972, 330–331).

15. Watzlawick shows that even a threat depends on effective communication; the minimal conditions for a threat to be successful are that it
must "get through" and be believable (1976, 197ff.).

16. See, for example, Cavell (1969), especially the essay "Must We
Mean What We Say?" Cf. Pitkin (1972).

17. See Searle (1969) for the difference between regulative and constitutive rules. Charles Taylor develops some of the political implications
of this difference for politics and the study of politics in his "Interpretation and the Sciences of Man" (1971).

18. "Please check out the proposal" may have many nonliteral practical meanings, too. It may mean, "This proposal isn't documented properly," for example. But our understanding of such nonliteral meanings
presupposes that we know how to apply the ordinary rules of language
use. Otherwise, we would not, at the first level, be able to recognize the
literal meaning, its possible implications, and then, at the second level, its
fit or possible misfit with the context of its use (i.e., whether or not we
should take it literally).

19. Extended analysis of such presuppositions and anticipation of
the "universal pragmatic" norms of speech can be found in McCarthy
(1978). Cf. Shapiro (1976). See also Ben Habib (1986) and Fay (1987).

20. See "What Is Universal Pragmatics?" in Habermas (1979, 50–
68). Cf. Chappell (1964).

21. To gauge another's sincerity differs significantly from assessing the
truth of what that speaker says. Sincerity refers to the more general expression of the speaker's inner dispositions; truth refers to the fit or misfit
of statements, references, or representations of reality with the reality
supposedly represented. A speaker may be sincere or insincere; a statement may be true or false. (One might say, though, that an expression, as
an indication of a speaker's intentions, is sincere or insincere.) The differ-

ence here is quite practical: a physician may be utterly *sincere* in prescribing a medication to alleviate certain symptoms, but the medication may nevertheless not *truly* alleviate the symptoms. A planner may be wholly sincere in saying that a street widening will draw twice the existing traffic flow, but the widening may not, in fact, have those consequences. In each case, the speaker is sincere, but what is said is not true. Insincerity threatens and subverts trust; inaccuracy weakens and subverts knowledge. Part of our competence as listeners depends on our abilities to make these distinctions: for example, "He really did (not) mean well, but we should check his figures anyway." Note that the force of a lie depends on the listener's failure to gauge the speaker's sincerity and accuracy.

22. "Since our ability to cope with life depends upon our making sense of what happens to us, anything which threatens to invalidate our conceptual structures of interpretation is profoundly disruptive" (Marris 1975, 13).

23. Fred Dallmayr argues that the violation and the respect of these universal pragmatic criteria for communication may be taken to ground a "communicative ethics" and a normative political vision (1974). Compare Chapter Two, above. For debate here, see Lukes's criticism and Habermas's reply in Thompson and Held (1982), and Simpson (1986). See also, as noted, Trent Schroyer (1973, 162–163) for the argument that Habermas's critique of systematically distorted communications is a refined form of the classical critique of ideology.

24. To date, unfortunately, no one has studied how planners make such judgments.

25. This analysis suggests how issues of pressing normative *ambiguity* can mistakenly be reduced to questions of cognitive certainty or *uncertainty*. I draw here from Forester (1983b). Whether we use the language of economy and society or productive forces and productive relations, efficiency and equity or accumulation and legitimation, the environment of planning nevertheless structurally presents planners not just with uncertainties that call for more information, but also with ambiguities that call for more explicit value judgments. Faced with uncertainties, planners look for clues and evidence. Faced with ambiguities about rules, obligations, promises, mandates, duties, and so on, planners must look for precedent, tradition, a source of legitimacy, a consensually based interpretation, or more generally, an appropriate, fitting response (Moch and Pondy 1977).

Ambiguity and uncertainty are just not the same, and they require planners to act differently in response. That an event will take place may be uncertain but not ambiguous; a pun is ambiguous but not uncertain. Questions of purpose and intent, of ethical and political choice, of obligation and responsibility, of the proper interpretation of meaning—these are issues of ambiguity; planners must look not for certainty in response, but for justification (March and Olsen 1976). Questions of scientific and technical results, of systems performance or the prediction of consequences—these are primarily issues of certainty and uncertainty; planners need to look for evidence, not for interpretations of precedent.

If practical problems of ambiguity and uncertainty are confused, then necessarily ambiguous political, normative, and "value" problems are likely to be reduced to matters of supposed scientific certainty and uncertainty. Practical, "should we?" problems, ethical and normative problems will be rendered technical and apolitical. Planners' and the broader public's attention, too, will then continue to be distracted from the constructive moral, legal, and political processes that exist to address these issues of ambiguous and conflicting needs, desires, interests, precedents, and obligations. Overly attentive to "scientific" questions about certainty, planners will fail to work skillfully in political and social processes (consultation, bargaining, consensus-building, structured argument, and so on) that might actually foster an effectively democratic, not technocratic, planning process. Facing uncertainty, planners hope to *discover* solutions; recognizing ambiguity, planners hope to *construct* solutions. Problems of uncertainty might be solved technically; problems of ambiguity need to be managed politically.

Planners cannot avoid these problems, for they are a systematic part of all practical action. When questions of content are raised, issues of uncertainty (at least) appear. When questions of context or planners' institutional relationships are raised, issues of ambiguity arise (Bolan 1980). Uncertainty and ambiguity are not incidental, then; they are, rather, systematic elements present in the very *structure* of practical social action. On the "double structure" of speech, see Habermas (1979, 41–44).

26. Cavell distinguishes the semantic meaning of an uttered sentence from the pragmatic meaning of the same utterance, and he argues that as speakers and actors we are responsible for both. Good intentions are not enough; pragmatics count (1969).

27. From the journal of a young planner in California: "Sitting in Environmental Review Committee meetings, I notice how the applicants interact with the Committee—the 'slickies' know the genre. They speak with professional language, e.g., 'that's correct' for 'that's right.' Others come in and get bounced around by the strange terminology and the unfamiliar process. What a humiliating experience for them" (personal correspondence, S. Bok, Autumn 1978).

28. Cf. a Public Health Department director, facing a planning commissioner's proposal of additional formal interagency meetings: "What

you're proposing is a formal structure that'll look great on paper but won't be operational. What we need is ongoing informal consultation and communication so we know what each other's doing—that's what works!" (Tompkins County Comprehensive Health Planning Subarea Council, March 1979).

29. "The normative foundation of a critical theory is implicit in the very structure of social action that it analyzes" (Bernstein 1976, 213); for critical discussion of this idea, see Ben Habib (1986), Simpson (1986), and Fay (1987).

30. A central question for the empirical study of planning ethics arises immediately: When planners do not meet the ordinary criteria that we use to gauge mutual understanding, what justifications do they use (or abuse, or fail to give)? The double structure of speech and the associated criteria above provide the basis for the more general analysis of action and social reproduction, e.g., as argued in Chapter Five.

31. When citizens have no actual means of checking the claims of planners, developers, politicians, or even one another, they are particularly vulnerable. They may then accept claims as true, legitimate, genuine, or meaningful when what is claimed is instead inaccurate, improper, deceptive, or confused. For a parallel argument assessing the ways that policy making shapes citizens' abilities to check such claims, see Forester (1982b). Cf. R. R. McGuire: "Insofar as systems of rules and norms contribute to systematically distorted communication, insofar as they exist as systematic barriers to discursive will formation, they are irrational. . . . And insofar as [communication structures] create a fiction of reciprocal accountability, concomitantly creating ideologies by sustaining the 'legitimacy' of these very structures they are irrational . . . and hence illegitimate—involving no moral obligation" (1977, 44). Cf. Lukes (1974).

32. It is important to make clear, even while presuming that conflict is ever-present in social and political life, that the proposition, P, that all interactions are so conflictual as to be untrustworthy sources of misrepresentation, is untenable, not only because it renders the checking of any one position impossible but also because it would be impossible for the proposition P itself to be credible, for there to be any consensus that P was trustworthy or true.

33. See Sissela Bok (1978) for an extended discussion; cf. Chapter Three, above.

34. Assessing the distorted communications prevalent in modern bureaucracies, Ralph Hummel argues that bureaucratic organizations are characterized not by two-way communication, but by one-way information. "The 'language' through which a bureaucracy speaks to us is not a language designed for problem-solving [together]. Bureaucratic language is a language for passing on solutions" (1977, 158–159).

35. See, e.g., Mueller (1973); cf. note 4, above, and Chapters Three and Five.

36. On responses to distortions in face-to-face interactions, see Chapter Seven. On responses dealing with organizational interactions, see Chapter Five. To correct structural distortions is to challenge the ideological obscuring of citizens' real possibilities and to call for political organizing and the continual democratization of public policy. To politicize planning in this way does *not* mean to encourage a war of all against all, to grind planning to a halt. This misreading of politics encourages an overly rationalistic, organizationally blind planning practice. To politicize planning means instead to diversify alternatives, to strengthen participation and include previously excluded groups, to support progressive social movements, to balance the reliance on technique with attention to regular political debate, negotiation, and criticism (Pitkin 1972; Barber 1984). Recall this chapter's epigraph (Wolfe 1977, 314).

37. The normative goal or ideal of organizing and opening communications should not be dismissed as romantic or utopian, a call for absolute trust or listening forever—for it requires us practically to prevent noise, misinformation, needless ambiguity, and the misleading elevation or lowering of citizens' expectations. See Chapters Three and Four, above.

38. Organizing does not simply mean "getting more citizen input," getting more bodies to meetings. This is precisely how "input" misleads us, for it is not input, but political responsibility, participation, and mobilization that are at issue. For three suggestive approaches, see the work of Krumholz, Cogger, and Linner (1975), and Krumholz (1982); Hartman (e.g., 1978, 1984); and Susskind and Ozawa (1983), and Susskind and Cruickshank (1987).

39. See, for example, on complexity and uncertainty, Benveniste (1977) and our arguments above in Chapter Four for matching solution strategies to contingent contextual constraints.

40. When the context of a planner's description or evaluation is political, that description or evaluation may have a pragmatic political effect in addition to reporting its technical message. Watzlawick, Beavin, and Jackson write, "The paramount communicational significance of context is all too easily overlooked in the analysis of human communication, and yet anyone who brushed his teeth in a busy street rather than in his bathroom might be quickly carted off to a police station or a lunatic asylum—to give just one example of the pragmatic effects of nonverbal communication" (1967, 62).

41. Let me emphasize that this is not to argue against technical work; it is simply to call attention to its inescapably political character. Cf. Ivan Illich's argument: "Paradoxically, the more attention is focused

on the technical mastery of disease, the larger becomes the symbolic and non-technical function performed by medical technology" (1977, 106). For a lucid and compelling analysis of the profoundly political character of technological systems, see the work of Langdon Winner (1977, 1986).

42. Such a "clarity criterion" falls under only the first of the four universal pragmatic criteria discussed above: comprehensibility, sincerity, legitimacy, and truth.

43. For a useful review, see "Theories of Ideology and Methods of Discourse Analysis," Chapter Three in Thompson (1984). Thompson's work is particularly interesting because it, too, moves in the direction of linking the particulars of practical actors' speech to the reproduction of, or resistance to, encompassing social and political ideologies.

44. This point can be derived from two quite different sources: philosophers and social theorists such as Karl Mannheim (1949) and John Dewey (1927), and the recent literature on mediation and collaborative problem-solving applications to planning processes (Susskind and Cruickshank 1987). Like political critics, planners must worry about getting affected people in the door of decision-making arenas affecting them; like mediators and facilitators, planners also have to worry about what to do once deeply interested, angry, and often fearful people get in that door. Mediation skills offer promise not only for managers and organizers but also for planners, who find that part of their job is to make democracy, writ small, work—not just to get results, but to enhance relationships and nurture public virtue, a sense of a political "we."

45. Compare an argument from another professional setting. Jeffry Galper writes of professional social work practices: "In every interaction in which we engage, we encourage certain responses in others and discourage other responses. Workers who are themselves politicized . . . will offer suggestions and interpretations from this perspective. . . . [These interpretations] must clearly be offered in service to the client and not in service of political ends that are somehow separate from the situation and well-being of the client" (1975, 212).

46. A co-worker looks you in the eye and says in a quick and agitated voice, "Me? I'm not nervous. I'm not nervous." The tone and the style contradict the literal message; they meta-communicate meaning over, above, and beyond that of the literal words. The detachment of the apparently neutral professional meta-communicates in the same way. Think of the importance of dress, here, and other small but hardly unimportant social rituals (e.g., sharing meals, "social drinking"). The style of performance of rituals communicates even more significant meaning than does their literal content. For a brief analysis in planning, see Forester (1983b) and, more generally, Bailey (1983).

47. See especially Szanton (1981), Wilensky (1967), and Baum (1983). See also Meltsner (1976) and Krumholz, Cogger, and Linner (1975). Cf. Needleman and Needleman (1974) and Alinsky (1971).

48. See, on argument, Toulmin (1964), Churchman (1971), Fischer (1980), Mason and Mitroff (1980–1981), and Webber and Rittel (1973); on political discourse, Pitkin (1972) and Barber (1984); on dialogue, Freire (1970); on mediated negotiation, Susskind and Ozawa (1983, 1984), Susskind and Cruickshank (1987), Forester (1988), and Amy (1987); on policy or design criticism, Krieger (1981); on democratization, Habermas (1975), Dewey (1927); and, on organizing, Hartman (1975, 1984) and Clavel (1986).

49. See McGuire (1977), Fay (1987), Dallmayr (1974), Apel (1977), and Chapter One, above. The shift from the treatment of "information" to "attention" is a shift from a Cartesian, rationalistic, and idealistic philosophical tradition to a critical, historical, and phenomenological one, to a critical pragmatism (Bernstein 1976, 1983; Hoch 1987). The deeper roots of such an alternative view (Krieger 1974, 1981) are in the traditions of English language philosophy (Pitkin 1972), German phenomenology (Gadamer 1975; Bauman 1978; Schutz 1970; Bolan 1980), American pragmatism (Bernstein 1971; Hoch 1984), Sir Karl Popper's "critical rationalism" (Popper 1963; Lakatos and Musgrave 1972; Friedmann 1978; Faludi 1986), and Habermas's "critical communications theory of society" (Habermas 1970a, 1971, 1973, 1975, 1979, 1984; McCarthy 1978; Held 1980; and Hemmens and Stiftel 1980).

50. This argument has not presented a specific account of class or social structure. Class analysis will often be appropriate when workplace issues are at stake; yet when workplace issues of race and gender arise, class alone will not suffice to explain—and, more significantly, to anticipate—possible strategies and outcomes.

51. This analysis provides the relatively macrosociological account of O'Connor (1973) with a microsociological foundation informed by Habermas's theory of communicative action; cf. Forester (1982a).

52. Cf. Lukes (1974), Gaventa (1980), and Chapters Three and Four, above.

53. For one analysis, see Forester (1988).

54. For the developed argument, see Adler (1986).

55. To argue "always contingent" here is not to appeal to pluralism or voluntarism, but to argue that structural, i.e., structurally reproduced, patterns of social interaction depend dialectically at any given time on a balance of forces that work to sustain and to change those structures. Social structures can be altered through the work of social movements, not single agents.

56. See Lukes (1974).

57. Keyed to planners' and citizens' understandings and interpretations, the analysis of communicative action is both empirical (for it specifies a domain of observable speech acts and of nonverbal acts as well) and interpretive, tied to the meaning-giving capacities, strategies, and predispositions of diverse social and political actors; cf. Forester (1988).

58. This was the central argument developed in Chapters Three and Four.

59. Further research should investigate planners' strategies in the dimensions delineated here and at face-to-face, organizational, and structural levels of analysis.

Chapter Ten: Supplement

1. This "substitution for testing" is crucial here. Support from the "community of inquirers" served to establish (or reject) hypotheses about consequences that could not actually be tested without building the whole project. Phil's participatory planning process was thus directly a learning process of sorts, if one operating within definite limits.

2. If participation was indeed demonstrated, the conceptual question neglected here concerned its first cousin, the question of *representation*.

3. Note, of course, that the anticipation discussed centrally in this supplement depends wholly on the analysis of this book as a whole. Without attention to necessary and unnecessary, ad hoc and systematic constraints, for example, the "envisioning" necessary for powerful anticipation will be blinded. Without attention to the structure of communicative action and the distinct problems of shaping belief, consent, trust, and focus of problems, the preparation of arguments and negotiations will be impoverished. Thus, the anticipatory model presented here depends in large part on the analysis of the entire book, just as those chapters are linked and extended by the integrating model of anticipatory practice. For an analysis of the possibilities of planners playing negotiated mediation roles, for example, see Chapter Six. Cf. Forester (1987).

Bibliography

Adler, Seymour
    1986   "A Comparative Analysis of Planning Domains." Paper
                prepared for the National Conference of the Association of
                Collegiate Schools of Planning, Milwaukee, Wisconsin,
                10–12 October.
Alexander, Christopher
    1968   *Notes Toward a Synthesis of Form.* Cambridge, Mass.:
                Harvard University Press.
Alexander, Ernest
    1981   "Design in the Planning Process: Theory, Education and
                Practice." Paper prepared for the National Conference of
                the Association of Collegiate Schools of Planning, Wash-
                ington, D.C., 23–25 October.
    1982   "Design in the Decision-Making Process." *Policy Sciences*
                14:279–292.
Alford, Robert
    1975   *Health Care Politics: Ideological and Interest Group Bar-
                riers to Reform.* Chicago: University of Chicago Press.
Alinsky, Saul
    1971   *Rules for Radicals.* New York: Random House.
Altshuler, Alan
    1965   *The City Planning Process: A Political Analysis.* Ithaca,
                N.Y.: Cornell University Press.
Amy, Douglas
    1987   *The Politics of Environmental Mediation.* New York: Co-
                lumbia University Press.
Anderson, Charles W.
    1985   "The Place of Principles in Policy Analysis." In *Ethics in*

Planning, edited by Martin Wachs, 193–215. New Brunswick, N.J.: Center for Urban Policy Research, Rutgers University.

Apel, Karl-Otto

1972 "Communication and the Foundations of the Humanities." *Acta Sociologica* 15:7–26.

1977 "The A Priori of Communication and the Foundation of the Humanities." In *Understanding and Social Inquiry,* edited by Fred Dallmayr and Thomas McCarthy, 292–315. Notre Dame, Ind.: University of Notre Dame Press.

Arendt, Hannah

1958 *The Human Condition.* Chicago: University of Chicago Press.

Argyris, Chris, and Donald Schön

1974 *Theory in Practice: Increasing Professional Effectiveness.* San Francisco: Jossey-Bass.

1978 *Organizational Learning: A Theory of Action Perspective.* Reading, Mass.: Addison-Wesley.

Arnstein, Sherry

1969 "Ladder of Citizen Participation." *Journal of the American Institute of Planners* 35:216–224.

Austin, John

1965 *How to Do Things with Words.* New York: Oxford University Press.

Bachrach, Peter

1967 *The Theory of Democratic Elitism: A Critique.* Boston: Little, Brown.

Bachrach, Peter, and Morton Baratz

1962 "The Two Faces of Power." *American Political Science Review* 56:947–952.

1963 "Decisions and Non-Decisions: An Analytical Framework." *American Political Science Review* 57:641–651.

Bacow, Lawrence

1980 "The Technical and Judgmental Dimensions of Impact Assessment." *Environmental Impact Assessment Review* 1(2): 109–124.

Bacow, Lawrence, and Michael Wheeler

1984 *Environmental Dispute Resolution.* New York: Plenum.

Baer, William

1977 "Urban Planners: Doctors or Midwives?" *Public Administration Review* 35(6): 671–678.

Bailey, F. G.
  1983   *The Tactical Uses of Passion: An Essay on Power, Reason, and Reality.* Ithaca, N.Y.: Cornell University Press.
Balkas, Denise M.
  1979   "An Investigation into the Professional Status of City Planning." Master's thesis, Department of City and Regional Planning, Cornell University.
Barber, Benjamin
  1984   *Strong Democracy: Participatory Politics for a New Age.* Berkeley and Los Angeles: University of California Press.
Bateson, Gregory
  1975   *Steps to an Ecology of Mind.* New York: Ballantine.
Baum, Howell
  1980a   "Analysts and Planners Must Think Organizationally." *Policy Analysis* 6(4): 480–494.
  1980b   "Sensitizing Planners to Organization." In *Urban and Regional Planning in an Age of Austerity,* edited by Pierre Clavel, John Forester, and William Goldsmith, 279–307. New York: Pergamon.
  1982a   "Policy Analysis: Special Cognitive Style Needed." *Administration and Society* 14:213–236.
  1982b   "What Is to Be Learned? Alternative Views of Theory-in-Use." Paper prepared for the National Conference of the Association of Collegiate Schools of Planning, Chicago, Illinois, 22–24 October.
  1983   *Planners and Public Expectations.* Cambridge, Mass.: Schenkman.
  1987   *The Invisible Bureaucracy: The Unconscious in Organizational Problem-Solving.* New York: Oxford University Press.
  1988   "Planning Theory as Political Practice." In *Planning Theory in the 1990's: New Directions,* edited by Robert Burchell and George Sternlieb. New Brunswick, N.J.: Center for Urban Policy Research, Rutgers University.
Bauman, Zygmunt
  1978   *Hermeneutics and Social Science: Approaches to Understanding.* London: Hutchinson.
Beauregard, Robert
  1980   "Thinking About Practicing Planning." In *Urban and Regional Planning in an Age of Austerity,* edited by Pierre Clavel, John Forester, and William Goldsmith, 308–325. New York: Pergamon.

Beck, Dorothy
    1962   *Patterns in the Use of Family Agency Service.* New York:
                Family Association of America.
Beiner, Ronald
    1983   *Political Judgment.* Chicago: University of Chicago Press.
Belenky, Mary F., B. M. Clinchy, N. R. Goldberger, and J. M. Tarule
    1986   *Women's Ways of Knowing: The Development of Self,
                Voice, and Mind.* New York: Basic Books.
Bellah, Robert N., Richard Madsen, William M. Sullivan, Ann Swidler,
    and Steven Tipton
    1985   *Habits of the Heart: Individualism and Commitment in
                American Life.* Berkeley and Los Angeles: University of
                California Press.
Bendix, Selina
    1979   "A Short Introduction to the California Environmental
                Quality Act." *Santa Clara Law Review* 19(3): 521–539.
Ben Habib, Seyla
    1986   *Critique, Norm and Utopia: A Study of the Foundations of
                Critical Theory.* New York: Columbia University Press.
Benveniste, Guy
    1977   *The Politics of Expertise.* 2d ed. San Francisco: Boyd and
                Frazier.
Berger, Peter
    1976   *Pyramids of Sacrifice: Political Ethics and Social Change.*
                New York: Anchor.
Berger, Peter, and Thomas T. Luckmann
    1966   *The Social Construction of Reality.* New York: Anchor.
Bernstein, Richard
    1971   *Praxis and Action: Contemporary Philosophies of Human
                Activity.* Philadelphia: University of Pennsylvania Press.
    1976   *The Restructuring of Social and Political Theory.* Philadel-
                phia: University of Pennsylvania Press.
    1983   *Beyond Objectivism and Relativism: Science, Hermeneu-
                tics, and Praxis.* Philadelphia: University of Pennsylvania
                Press.
    1986   "Structuration as Critical Theory." *Praxis International* 6:
                235–249.
Berry, Wendell
    1981   "Discipline and Hope." In *Recollected Essays 1965–1980.*
                San Francisco: North Point Press.
Bingham, Gail
    1986   *Resolving Environmental Disputes: A Decade of Experi-
                ence.* Washington, D.C.: Conservation Foundation.

Blum, Alan
    1974   *Theorizing.* London: Heinemann.
Bok, Sissela
    1978   *Lying: Moral Choice in Public and Private Life.* New York:
                Vintage.
Bolan, Richard S., and Ronald L. Nuttal
    1975   *Urban Planning and Politics.* Lexington, Mass.: Lexington
                Books.
    1980   "The Practitioner as Theorist: The Phenomenology of the
                Professional Episode." *Journal of the American Planning
                Association* 46:261–274.
Bolman, Lee
    1981   "Education and Practice in Architecture." Project report
                sponsored by the Consortium of East Coast Schools of
                Architecture. Cambridge, Mass.: Department of Architec-
                ture, M.I.T.
Bourdieu, Pierre
    1977   *Outline of Theory of Practice.* Cambridge: Cambridge Uni-
                versity Press.
Boyte, Harry
    1980   *The Backyard Revolution: Understanding the New Citizen
                Movement.* Philadelphia: Temple University Press.
Bradley, John
    1979   "Volunteer Education: Key to Building an Effective Plan-
                ning Process." *Health Law Project Library Bulletin*
                4(May): 164–172.
Braybrooke, David, and Charles Lindblom
    1970   *A Strategy of Decision.* New York: Free Press.
Brownstein, Ronald
    1981   "Making the Worker Safe for the Workplace." *The Nation,*
                6 June, 692–694.
Bryson, John
    1981   "The Role of Forums, Arenas, and Courts in Organiza-
                tional Design and Change." Typescript.
    1982   "Strategic Planning as the Design of Forums, Arenas, and
                Courts." Paper prepared for the National Conference of
                the Association of Collegiate Schools of Planning, Chicago,
                Illinois, 22–24 October.
Bryson, John, and André Delbecq
    1979   "A Contingent Approach to Strategy and Tactics in Project
                Planning." *Journal of the American Planning Association*
                45:167–179.

Buber, Martin
    1977   *On Judaism.* Edited by Nahum Glatzer. New York:
                Schocken Books.
Buckley, Walter
    1967   *Sociology and Modern Systems Theory.* Englewood Cliffs,
                N.J.: Prentice-Hall.
Burlage, Robb
    1979   "New Health Care Alliance Could Build New System."
                Democratic Left (June): 9–11.
Burlage, Robb, and Louanne Kennedy
    1980   "Repressive vs. Reconstructive Forces in Austerity Plan-
                ning Domains: The Case of Health." In *Urban and Re-
                gional Planning in an Age of Austerity,* edited by Pierre
                Clavel, John Forester, and William Goldsmith, 117–139.
                New York: Pergamon.
Burton, Dudley
    1975   "A Constitutional Theory of Planning." Ph.D. diss., Uni-
                versity of California, Berkeley.
    1981   "Methodology for Second Order Cybernetics." *Nature and
                System* 3 : 13–27.
Burton, Dudley, and Brian Murphy
    1980   "Democratic Planning in Austerity: Practice and Theory."
                In *Urban and Regional Planning in an Age of Austerity,*
                edited by Pierre Clavel, John Forester, and William Gold-
                smith, 177–205. New York: Pergamon.
Castells, Manuel
    1977   *The Urban Question: A Marxist Approach.* London: Ed-
                ward Arnold.
    1979   *City, Class and Power.* London: Macmillan.
Catron, Bayard
    1977   "Intuition and Rationality in Decision Making." Paper
                presented at the annual meeting of the American Society
                for Public Administration, Atlanta, Georgia, 30 March–
                2 April.
Cavell, Stanley
    1969   *Must We Mean What We Say?* New York: Charles Scrib-
                ner's Sons.
Champaign County Health Care Consumers Newsletter
    1979   Urbana, Illinois.
Chappell, V. C.
    1964   *Ordinary Language.* Englewood Cliffs, N.J.: Prentice-Hall.
Checkoway, Barry
    1979   "Citizens on Local Health Planning Boards: What Are the

Obstacles?" *Journal of the Community Development Society* 10: 101–116.

Checkoway, Barry, ed.

1981   *Citizens and Health Care: Participation and Planning for Social Change.* New York: Pergamon.

1986   *Strategic Perspectives on Planning Practice.* Lexington, Mass.: Lexington Books.

Checkoway, Barry, and Michael Doyle

1980   "Community Organizing Lessons for Health Care Consumers." *Journal of Health Politics, Policy and Law* 5 (Summer): 213–226.

Christensen, Karen

1982   "Planning and Uncertainty." Paper prepared for the National Conference of the Association of Collegiate Schools of Planning, Chicago, Illinois, 22–24 October.

Churchman, C. West

1968   *The Systems Approach.* New York: Delta.

1971   *The Design of Inquiring Systems.* New York: Basic Books.

Claiborne, R.

1979   "A Penny of Prevention: The Cure for America's Health Care System." *Health Law Project Library Bulletin* 5(7): 237–241.

Clark, Wayne

1977   "Placebo or Cure? State and Local Health Planning Agencies in the South." Atlanta: Southern Regional Council.

Clavel, Pierre

1986   *The Progressive City: Planning and Participation, 1969– 1984.* New Brunswick, N.J.: Rutgers University Press.

Clavel, Pierre, John Forester, and William Goldsmith, eds.

1980   *Urban and Regional Planning in an Age of Austerity.* New York: Pergamon.

Clegg, Stewart

1975   *Power, Rule and Domination.* London: Routledge & Kegan Paul.

1979   *The Theory of Power and Organization.* London: Routledge & Kegan Paul.

Colosi, Thomas

1983   "Negotiation in the Public and Private Sectors." *American Behavioral Scientist* 27(2): 229–253.

Connerton, Paul

1976   *Critical Sociology: Selected Readings.* London: Penguin.

Cuff, Dana

1981   "Negotiating Architecture." In *Design Research Interac-*

tions, edited by Arvid Osterberg, C. Tiernan, and N. Findlay. 12th Proceedings of the Environmental Design Research Association (EDRA).

1982   "The Context for Design: Six Characteristics." In *Knowledge for Design,* edited by P. Bart, A. Chen, and G. Francescato. 13th Proceedings of the Environmental Design Research Association (EDRA).

Dahl, Robert

1961   *Who Governs? Democracy and Power in an American City.* New Haven: Yale University Press.

Dallmayr, Fred

1974   "Toward a Critical Reconstruction of Ethics and Politics." *Journal of Politics* 36:926–957.

1981   *Beyond Dogma and Despair.* Notre Dame, Ind.: University of Notre Dame Press.

Dallmayr, Fred, and Thomas McCarthy

1977   *Understanding and Social Inquiry.* Notre Dame, Ind.: University of Notre Dame Press.

Dalton, Linda

1987   "Local Plan Implementation in California: Planning as Development Control." Department of City and Regional Planning, California Polytechnic State University, San Luis Obispo. Typescript.

Davidoff, Paul

1965   "Advocacy and Pluralism in Planning." *Journal of the American Institute of Planners* 31:596–615.

Dekema, Jan D.

1981   "Incommensurability and Judgment." *Theory and Society* 10:521–546.

DeNeufville, Judith

1982   "Planning Theory and Practice: Bridging the Gap." Paper prepared for the National Conference of the Association of Collegiate Schools of Planning, Chicago, Illinois, 22–24 October.

Denhardt, Robert

1977   "Praxis as Enlightened Action." Paper presented at a meeting of the Southern Political Science Association, New Orleans, Louisiana, November.

1981   *In the Shadow of Organization.* Lawrence: Regents' Press of Kansas.

Descartes, René

1964   *Discourse on Method.* Baltimore: Penguin.

Dewey, John
1927   *The Public and Its Problems.* Denver: Holt.

Diamond, Michael
1986   "Resistance to Change: A Psychoanalytic Critique of Argyris and Schön's Contributions to Organization Theory and Intervention." *Journal of Management Studies* 23(5): 542–562.

Dreitzel, Hans-Peter, ed.
1970   *Recent Sociology #2: Patterns of Communicative Behavior.* New York: Macmillan.

Dutton, William, and K. Kraemer
1985   *Modelling as Negotiating: The Political Dynamics of Computer Models in the Policy Process.* Norwood, N.J.: Ablex.

Dyckman, John
1969   "The Practical Uses of Planning Theory." *Journal of the American Institute of Planners* 35:298–301.

1978   "Three Crises of American Planning." In *Planning Theory in the 1980's,* edited by Robert Burchell and George Sternlieb. New Brunswick, N.J.: Center for Urban Policy Research, Rutgers University.

Edelman, Murray
1964   *The Symbolic Uses of Politics.* Urbana: University of Illinois Press.

1971   *Politics as Symbolic Action.* New York: Academic Press.

1977   *Political Language: Words That Succeed and Policies That Fail.* New York: Academic Press.

Etzioni, Amitai
1968   *The Active Society.* New York: Free Press.

Euben, J. Peter
1981   "Philosophy and the Professions." *democracy* 1(2): 112–127.

Fainstein, Norman, and Susan Fainstein
1972   "Innovation in Urban Bureaucracies: Clients and Change." *American Behavioral Scientist* 15(4): 511–530.

1982   *Urban Policy Under Capitalism.* Beverly Hills, Calif.: Sage.

Faludi, Andreas
1973   *Planning Theory.* New York: Pergamon.

1986   *Critical Rationalism and Planning Methodology.* London: Pion.

Fay, Brian
1987   *Critical Social Science.* Ithaca, N.Y.: Cornell University Press.

Feldman, Marshall
  1978   "Manuel Castells' *The Urban Question:* A Review Essay."
              Review of Radical Political Economics 10(3): 136–144.
Ferguson, Kathy E.
  1984   *The Feminist Case Against Bureaucracy.* Philadelphia:
              Temple University Press.
Feshbach, Dan, and Takuya Nakamoto
  1981   "Political Strategies for Health Systems Agencies." In *Citi-*
              zens and Health Care: Participation and Planning for
              Social Change, edited by Barry Checkoway. New York:
              Pergamon.
Fischer, Frank
  1980   *Politics, Values and Public Policy.* Boulder, Colo.: West-
              view.
Fischer, Frank, and C. Sirianni, eds.
  1984   *Critical Studies in Organization and Bureaucracy.* Phila-
              delphia: Temple University Press.
Fisher, Roger
  1983   "Negotiating Power." *American Behavioral Scientist* 27(2):
              149–166.
Fisher, Roger, and William Ury
  1983   *Getting to Yes: Negotiating Agreement Without Giving In.*
              New York: Penguin.
Fisher, Steve, and Jim Foster
  1978   "Class, Political Consciousness, and Destructive Power:
              Strategy for Change in Appalachia." *Appalachian Journal*
              5(3): 290–311.
Fleischman, Joel L., and Bruce L. Payne
  1980   *Ethical Dilemmas and the Education of Policy Makers.*
              Vol. 8, Monographs on the Teaching of Ethics. Hastings-
              on-Hudson, N.Y.: Hastings Center.
Forester, John
  1977   "Questioning and Shaping Attention as Planning Strategy:
              Toward a Critical Theory of Planning." Ph.D. diss., Univer-
              sity of California, Berkeley.
  1980   "How Much Does the Environmental Review Planner Do?"
              Environmental Impact Assessment Review 1: 104–107.
  1981a   "Hannah Arendt and Critical Theory: A Critical Re-
              sponse." *Journal of Politics* 43(February): 196–202.
  1981b   "Questioning and Organizing Attention as Planning Strat-
              egy: Toward a Critical Theory of Planning."*Administration*
              and Society 13(2): 161–205.

1981c   "Selling You the Brooklyn Bridge and Ideology (A Review of Habermas's *Communication and the Evolution of Society*)." *Theory and Society* 10:745–750.

1982a   "A Critical Empirical Framework for the Analysis of Public Policy." *New Political Science* 2:145–164.

1982b   "Critical Reason and Political Power in Project Review Activity." *Policy and Politics* 10(1): 65–83.

1983a   "Critical Theory and Organizational Analysis." In *Beyond Method: Strategies for Social Research,* edited by Gareth Morgan, 234–246. Beverly Hills, Calif.: Sage.

1983b   "The Geography of Planning Practice." *Environment and Planning D: Society and Space* 1:163–180.

1984   "Practical Rationality in Planning." In *Rationality in Plan-Making,* edited by Michael Breheny and Alan Hooper, 48–59. London: Pion.

1985   *Critical Theory and Public Life.* Cambridge, Mass.: MIT Press.

1986   "Critical Theory and Public Life: Only Connect." *International Journal of Urban and Regional Research* 10(2): 185–206.

1987   "Anticipating Implementation: Normative Practices in Planning and Policy Analysis." In *Confronting Values in Policy Analysis: The Politics of Criteria,* edited by Frank Fischer and John Forester, 153–173. Beverly Hills, Calif.: Sage.

1988   "How Planners Argue: Rhetorical Strategies and Problems of Substance, Power, and Passion in Planning Practice." In *Planning Theory in the 1990's: New Directions,* edited by Robert Burchell and George Sternlieb. New Brunswick, N.J.: Center for Urban Policy Research, Rutgers University.

Foster, Howard, A. Abramson, and M. Parella

1982   "Planners' Skills and Planning Schools: A Comparative Study of Alumni." Paper prepared for the National Conference of the Association of Collegiate Schools of Planning, Chicago, Illinois, 22–24 October.

Foucault, Michel

1979   *Discipline and Punish: The Birth of the Prison.* New York: Vintage.

1980   *Power/Knowledge: Selected Interviews and Other Writings.* Edited by Colin Gordon. New York: Pantheon.

Frankl, Victor

1985   *Man's Search for Meaning.* New York: Washington Square Press.

Fraser, Nancy

1981   "Foucault on Modern Power: Empirical Insights and Nor-
        mative Confusions." *Praxis International* 1 : 272–287.

Freire, Paulo

1970   *Pedagogy of the Oppressed.* New York: Seabury.
1973   *Education for Critical Consciousness.* New York: Seabury.

Friedland, Roger, F. F. Piven, and R. Alford

1977   "Political Conflict, Urban Structure, and the Fiscal Crisis."
        International Journal of Urban and Regional Research 1 :
        447–471.

Friedman, Maurice

1972   *Touchstones of Reality: Existential Trust and the Commu-
        nity of Peace.* New York: E. P. Dutton.

Friedmann, John

1973   *Retracking America.* New York: Anchor.
1978   "The Epistemology of Social Practice." *Theory and Society*
        6 : 75–92.
1979   *The Good Society.* Cambridge, Mass.: MIT Press.
1980   "On the Theory of Social Construction: An Introduction."
        DP 138, School of Architecture and Urban Planning, Uni-
        versity of California, Los Angeles.
1987   *Knowledge and Action: Mapping the Planning Theory Do-
        main.* Princeton, N.J.: Princeton University Press.

Gadamer, Hans-Georg

1975   *Truth and Method.* New York: Seabury.
1979   "The Problem of Historical Consciousness." In *Interpretive
        Social Science: A Reader,* edited by Paul Rabinow and
        William Sullivan, 103–160. Berkeley and Los Angeles:
        University of California Press.

Galper, Jeffry

1975   *The Politics of Social Services.* Englewood Cliffs, N.J.:
        Prentice-Hall.

Gaventa, John

1980   *Power and Powerlessness: Quiescence and Rebellion in an
        Appalachian Valley.* Urbana: University of Illinois Press.

Giddens, Anthony

1977   *New Rules of Sociological Method: A Positive Critique of
        Interpretive Sociologies.* London: Hutchinson.
1979   *Central Problems in Social Theory: Action, Structure, and
        Contradiction in Social Analysis.* Berkeley and Los An-
        geles: University of California Press.
1981   *A Contemporary Critique of Historical Materialism.* Berke-
        ley and Los Angeles: University of California Press.

1984   *The Constitution of Society: Outline of a Theory of Structuration*. Berkeley and Los Angeles: University of California Press.

Gilligan, Carol
1982   *In a Different Voice: Psychological Theory and Women's Development*. Cambridge, Mass.: Harvard University Press.

Giroux, Henry
1983   *Theory and Resistance in Education*. South Hadley, Mass.: Bergin and Garvey.

Goffman, Erving
1959   *The Presentation of Self in Everyday Life*. Garden City, N.Y.: Doubleday.
1981   *Forms of Talk*. Philadelphia: University of Pennsylvania Press.

Gondim, Linda
1986   "Planners in the Face of Power." Ph.D. diss., Cornell University.

Goodman, Nelson
1978   *Ways of Worldmaking*. Cambridge, Mass.: Hackett.

Gorz, André
1967   *Strategy for Labor*. Boston: Beacon.

Gouldner, Alvin
1976   *The Dialectic of Ideology and Technology*. New York: Seabury.

Grossman, Randolph M.
1978   "Voting Behavior of HSA Interest Groups: A Case Study." *American Journal of Public Health* 68(December): 1191–1194.

Habermas, Jürgen
1970a   *Toward a Rational Society*. Boston: Beacon.
1970b   "Toward a Theory of Communicative Competence." In *Recent Sociology #2: Patterns of Communicative Behavior*, edited by Hans-Peter Dreitzel. New York: Macmillan.
1971   *Knowledge and Human Interests*. Boston: Beacon.
1973   *Theory and Practice*. Boston: Beacon.
1975   *Legitimation Crisis*. Boston: Beacon.
1977a   "Hannah Arendt's Communications Concept of Power." *Social Research* 44(1): 3–24.
1977b   "A Review of Gadamer's *Truth and Method*." In *Understanding and Social Inquiry*, edited by Fred Dallmayr and Thomas McCarthy, 335–363. Notre Dame, Ind.: Notre Dame University Press.

1979   *Communication and the Evolution of Society.* Boston:
         Beacon.
1984   *The Theory of Communicative Action: Reason and the Ra-
         tionalization of Society.* Boston: Beacon.
Harmon, Michael, and Richard Mayer, eds.
1986   *Organization Theory for Public Administration.* New York:
         Little, Brown.
Hartman, Chester
1975   "The Advocate Planner: From Hired Gun to Political Par-
         tisan." In *The Politics of Turmoil,* edited by Richard A.
         Cloward and Frances Fox Piven. New York: Vintage.
1978   "Social Planning and the Political Planner." In *Planning
         Theory in the 1980's,* edited by Robert Burchell and George
         Sternlieb. New Brunswick, N.J.: Center for Urban Policy
         Research, Rutgers University.
1984   *The Transformation of San Francisco.* Totowa, N.J.: Row-
         man and Allanheld.
Harvey, David
1978   "Planning the Ideology of Planning." In *Planning Theory
         in the 1980's,* edited by Robert Burchell and George Stern-
         lieb. New Brunswick, N.J.: Center for Urban Policy Re-
         search, Rutgers University.
Hayden, Delores
1984   *Redesigning the American Dream: The Future of Housing,
         Work, and Family Life.* New York: W. W. Norton.
Heidegger, Martin
1962   *Being and Time.* New York: Harper & Row.
1968   *What Is Called Thinking?* New York: Harper & Row.
Held, David
1980   *Introduction to Critical Theory.* Berkeley and Los Angeles:
         University of California Press.
Hemmens, George C., Edward Bergman, and Robert M. Moroney
1978   "The Practitioner's View of Social Planning." *Journal of
         the American Institute of Planners* 44:181–192.
Hemmens, George C., and Bruce Stiftel
1980   "Sources for the Renewal of Planning Theory." *Journal of
         the American Planning Association* 46:341–345.
Heschel, Abraham
1965   *Who Is Man?* Stanford, Calif.: Stanford University Press.
Hirschman, Albert
1970   *Exit, Voice, and Loyalty.* Cambridge, Mass.: Harvard Uni-
         versity Press.

Hoch, Charles

1984   "Pragmatism, Planning, and Power." *Journal of Planning Education and Research* 4(2): 86–95.

1987   "A Pragmatic Inquiry About Planning and Power." Paper presented at the Conference on Planning Theory in the 1990's, Center for Urban Policy Research, Rutgers University, New Brunswick, N.J., 31 March–1 April.

Hoch, Charles, and A. Cibulskis

1987   "Planners Threatened: A Preliminary Report on Planners and Political Conflict." *Journal of Planning Education and Research* 6(2): 99–107.

Howe, Elizabeth, and Jerome Kaufman

1979   "The Ethics of Contemporary American Planners." *Journal of the American Planning Association* 45:243–255.

Hummel, Ralph

1977   *The Bureaucratic Experience.* 1st ed. New York: St. Martin's Press.

1982   *The Bureaucratic Experience.* 2d ed. New York: St. Martin's Press.

Illich, Ivan

1977   *Medical Nemesis: The Expropriation of Health.* New York: Bantam.

Ingram, David

1986   "Foucault and the Frankfurt School." *Praxis International* 6:311–327.

Jacobs, Allan B.

1978   *Making City Planning Work.* Chicago: American Society of Planning Officials.

Johnson, Ralph, and J. A. Blair

1985   "Informal Logic: The Past Five Years, 1978–1983." *American Philosophical Quarterly* 22(3):181–196.

Katznelson, Ira

1981   *City Trenches: Urban Politics and the Patterning of Class in the United States.* New York: Pantheon.

Kaufman, Jerome

1974   "Contemporary Planning Practice: State of the Art." In *Planning in America: Learning from Turbulence,* edited by David Godschalk. Washington, D.C.: American Institute of Planners.

1987   "Teaching Planning Students About Strategizing, Boundary Spanning and Ethics: Part of the New Planning Theory." *Journal of Planning Education and Research* 6(2): 108–115.

Kelman, Sander
    1980   "Laying on the Invisible Hand: Ideology in Health Eco-
                nomics." *International Journal of Health Services* 10(4):
                703–709.
Kelman, Sander, Pierre Clavel, John Forester, and William Goldsmith
    1981   "Planning the Planners." *Social Policy* 11(January–Febru-
                ary): 46–51.
Kemp, Ray
    1980   "Planning, Legitimation, and the Development of Nuclear
                Energy." *International Journal of Urban and Regional Re-
                search* 4:350–371.
    1982   "Critical Planning Theory: Review and Critique." In *Plan-
                ning Theory: Prospects for the 1980s,* edited by Patsy Hea-
                ley, Glen McDougal, and Michael J. Thomas, 59–67. New
                York: Pergamon.
    1985   "Planning, Public Hearings, and the Politics of Discourse."
                In *Critical Theory and Public Life,* edited by John Forester,
                177–201. Cambridge, Mass.: MIT Press.
Killingsworth, James
    1978   "System Hypocrisy: The Boundary Spanning Case." Paper
                prepared for the National Conference of the American So-
                ciety for Public Administration, Phoenix, Arizona, 9–12
                April.
Kittay, Eva, and Diana Meyers, eds.
    1987   *Women and Moral Theory.* Philadelphia: Temple Univer-
                sity Press.
Klosterman, Richard
    1978   "Foundations of Normative Planning." *Journal of the Ameri-
                can Institute of Planners* 44:37–46.
Knack, Ruth Eckdish
    1986   "Here's Looking at You." *Planning* 50(2): 9–15.
Kochen, Manfred, and Charles Barr
    1986   "How Rational Can Planning Be? Toward an Information-
                Processing Model of Planning." In *Interdisciplinary Plan-
                ning: A Perspective for the Future,* edited by Milan J.
                Dluhy and Kan Chen, 29–47. New Brunswick, N.J.: Cen-
                ter for Urban Policy Research, Rutgers University.
Kochman, Robert
    1981   *Black and White Styles in Conflict.* Chicago: University of
                Chicago Press.
Kolb, Deborah
    1986   "Who Are Organizational Third Parties and What Do
                They Do?" *In Research on Negotiations in Organizations,*

edited by Roy Lewicki, Blair Sheppard, and Max Bazerman. Greenwich, Conn.: JAI Press.

1988   "Out of Sight: Observations on Mediation in Organizations." In *Research in Mediation,* edited by Ken Kressel and Dean Pruitt. San Francisco: Jossey-Bass.

Korten, David

1980   "Community Organization and Rural Development: A Learning Process Approach." *Public Administration Review* 40(5): 480–512.

Kramnick, Isaac

1981   "Equal Opportunity and 'the Race of Life': Reflections on Liberal Ideology." *Dissent* (Spring): 178–187.

Kraushaar, Robert

1979   "Pragmatic Radicalism." *International Journal of Urban and Regional Research* 3(1): 61–79.

1980   "Policy Without Protest: The Dilemma of Organizing for Change in Britain." In *Urban Change and Conflict,* edited by Michael Harloe. London: Heinemann.

Kravitz, Alan

1970   "Mandarinism: Planning as Handmaiden to Conservative Politics." In *Planning and Politics,* edited by T. Beyle and G. Lathrop. New York: Odyssey.

Krieger, Martin

1973   "Lectures on Design." Department of City and Regional Planning, University of California, Berkeley. Mimeo.

1974   "Some New Directions for Planning Theories." *Journal of the American Institute of Planners* 40: 156–163.

1981   *Advice and Planning.* Philadelphia: Temple University Press.

Krumholz, Norman

1978   "Cut-Back Planning in Cleveland." Mimeo.

1982   "A Retrospective View of Equity Planning: Cleveland, 1969–1979." *Journal of the American Planning Association* 48: 163–174.

Krumholz, Norman, Janice Cogger, and John Linner

1975   "The Cleveland Policy Planning Report." *Journal of the American Institute of Planners* 41: 298–304.

LaCapra, Dominick

1982   "Rethinking Intellectual History and Reading Texts." In *Modern European Intellectual History: Reappraisals and New Perspectives,* edited by Dominick LaCapra and S. Kaplan. Ithaca, N.Y: Cornell University Press.

Lakatos, Imre, and A. Musgrave
    1972   *Criticism and the Growth of Knowledge.* Cambridge: Cam-
              bridge University Press.
Lancourt, Joan
    1979   *Developing Implementation Strategies: Community Orga-
              nization, Not Public Relations.* Boston: Health Policy Cen-
              ter, Boston University.
Landau, Martin
    1973   "On the Concept of a Self-Correcting Organization." *Pub-
              lic Administration Review* 33(6): 533–542.
Lax, David, and J. Sebenius
    1986   *The Manager as Negotiator.* New York: Free Press.
Lindblom, Charles
    1959   "The Science of Muddling Through." *Public Administra-
              tion Review* 19(Spring): 79–88.
    1965   *The Intelligence of Democracy: Decision Making Through
              Mutual Adjustment.* New York: Free Press.
    1977   *Politics and Markets.* New York: Basic Books.
    1979   *Usable Knowledge.* New Haven: Yale University Press.
Lukes, Steven
    1974   *Power: A Radical View.* London: Macmillan.
Lyman, Stanford M., and Marvin B. Scott
    1970   *A Sociology of the Absurd.* New York: Meredith.
McCarthy, Thomas
    1978   *The Critical Theory of Jürgen Habermas.* Cambridge,
              Mass.: MIT Press.
McGuire, R. R.
    1977   "Speech Acts, Communicative Competence, and the Para-
              dox of Authority." *Philosophy and Rhetoric* 10:30–45.
McLane, Stephen
    1977   "Outcomes as a Measure of Social Casework Effectiveness:
              Problems and Trends." Health, Arts and Sciences Program,
              University of California, Berkeley. Typescript.
Mandelbaum, Seymour
    1979   "A Complete General Theory of Planning Is Impossible."
              Policy Sciences 11:59–71.
    1984   "What Is Philadelphia? The City as Polity." *Cities* 4:274–
              285.
Mannheim, Karl
    1949   *Man and Society in an Age of Reconstruction.* New York:
              Harcourt Brace.

March, James
   1978   "Bounded Rationality, Ambiguity, and the Engineering of Choice." *Bell Journal of Economics* 9 : 587–610.
   1982   "Theories of Choice and Making Decisions." *Society* 20 (November–December): 29–39.

March, James, and Johann Olsen
   1976   *Ambiguity and Choice in Organizations*. Oslo, Norway: Universitetsforlaget.

March, James, and Herbert Simon
   1958   *Organizations*. New York: Wiley & Sons.

Marcuse, Peter
   1976   "Professional Ethics and Beyond: Values in Planning." *Journal of the American Institute of Planners* 42 : 264–294.

Markusen, Ann
   1980   "City Spatial Structure, Women's Household Work, and National Urban Policy." *Signs* 5(3): 20–41.

Marris, Peter
   1975   *Loss and Change*. New York: Anchor. Reprinted 1986, London: Routledge & Kegan Paul.
   1982   *Community Planning and Conceptions of Change*. London: Routledge & Kegan Paul. Republished 1987 as *Meaning and Action*.

Marris, Peter, and Martin Rein
   1984   *Dilemmas of Social Reform*. 2d ed. Chicago: University of Chicago Press.

Maruyama, Magoroh
   1963   "Basic Elements in Misunderstandings I." *Dialectica* 17 : 78–109.

Mason, Richard, and I. Mitroff
   1980–   "Policy Analysis as Argument." *Policy Studies Journal*
   1981   9 : 579–585.

Mayo, James
   1978   "Propaganda with Design: Environmental Dramaturgy in the Political Rally." *Journal of Architectural Education* (Special Issue: Politics and Design Symbolism) 32(2): 24–27.
   1985   "Political Avoidance in Architecture." *Journal of Architectural Education* 38(2): 18–25.

Mayo, James, Peter Burgess, and Elliott Littman
   1981   "Political Knowledge and the Architectural Studio." *Journal of Architectural Education* 34(3): 24–27.

Mazziotti, David F.
    1974   "The Underlying Assumptions of Advocacy Planning."
                Journal of the American Institute of Planners 40:38–46.
Meltsner, Arnold
    1975   "Bureaucratic Policy Analysts." *Policy Sciences* 1:115–131.
    1976   *Policy Analysts in the Bureaucracy.* Berkeley and Los An-
                geles: University of California Press.
    1979   "Don't Slight Communication: Some Problems of Ana-
                lytical Practice." *Policy Analysis* 5(3): 367–392.
Mendelson, Jack
    1979   "The Habermas-Gadamer Debate." *New German Critique*
                18:44–73.
Merleau-Ponty, Maurice
    1964   "The Philosopher and Sociology." In *Signs,* edited by Mau-
                rice Merleau-Ponty, 98–113. Evanston, Ill.: Northwestern
                University Press.
Mier, Robert
    1986   "Academe and the Community: Some Impediments to Pro-
                fessional Practice." *Journal of Planning Education and Re-
                search* 6(1): 66–70.
Mills, C. Wright
    1959   *The Sociological Imagination.* New York: Grove Press.
Misgeld, Dieter
    1985   "Education and Cultural Invasion: Critical Social Theory,
                Education as Instruction, and the 'Pedagogy of the Op-
                pressed.'" In *Critical Theory and Public Life,* edited by
                John Forester, 77–118. Cambridge, Mass.: MIT Press.
Moch, Michael, and L. Pondy
    1977   "The Structure of Chaos: Organized Anarchy as a Re-
                sponse to Ambiguity." *Administrative Science Quarterly*
                22:351–362.
Morgan, Gareth
    1983   *Beyond Method.* Beverly Hills, Calif.: Sage.
Mueller, Claus
    1973   *The Politics of Communications.* New York: Oxford Uni-
                versity Press.
Murphy, Brian
    1976   "Modern Cynicism." Ph.D. diss., University of California,
                Berkeley.
Murphy, Brian M., and Alan Wolfe
    1980   "Democracy in Disarray." *Kapitalistate* 8:9–25.

Needleman, Carolyn, and Martin Needleman
    1974   *Guerrillas in the Bureaucracy.* New York: Wiley Inter-
            science.
Nilson, Linda B.
    1979   "An Application of the Occupational 'Uncertainty Prin-
            ciple' to the Professions." *Social Problems* 26(5): 570–581.
Oakeshott, Michael
    1962   *Rationalism in Politics.* London: Methuen.
O'Connor, James
    1973   *The Fiscal Crisis of the State.* New York: St. Martin's Press.
Ogilvy, James
    1978   "Understanding Power." *Philosophy and Social Criticism*
            5(2): 129–144.
O'Neill, John
    1972   *Sociology as a Skin Trade.* New York: Harper & Row.
    1974   *Making Sense Together.* New York: Harper & Row.
    1985   "Decolonization and the Ideal Speech Community: Some
            Issues in the Theory and Practice of Communicative Com-
            petence." In *Critical Theory and Public Life,* edited by
            John Forester, 57–76. Cambridge, Mass.: MIT Press.
Page, John
    1977   *Environmental Planning in Canada.* Toronto: Faculty of
            Environmental Studies, York University.
Pateman, Carole
    1970   *Participation and Democratic Theory.* Cambridge: Cam-
            bridge University Press.
Perin, Constance
    1970   *With Man in Mind.* Cambridge, Mass.: MIT Press.
Perrow, Charles
    1972   *Complex Organizations: A Critical Essay.* New York:
            Scott, Foresman.
Pitkin, Hanna
    1972   *Wittgenstein and Justice.* Berkeley and Los Angeles: Uni-
            versity of California Press.
    1973   "The Roots of Conservatism: Michael Oakeshott and the
            Denial of Politics." In *The New Conservatives,* edited by
            Lewis Coser and Irving Howe. New York: Meridian.
Pitkin, Hanna, and Sara Shumer
    1982   "On Participation." *democracy* 2:43–54.
Piven, Frances Fox, and Richard A. Cloward
    1971   *Regulating the Poor: The Functions of Public Welfare.*
            New York: Pantheon.

1975   *Politics of Turmoil: Poverty, Race, and the Urban Crisis.*
         New York: Vintage.
1977   *Poor People's Movements: Why They Succeed, How They
         Fail.* New York: Pantheon.
1982   *The New Class War: Reagan's Attack on the Welfare State
         and Its Consequences.* New York: Pantheon.

Popper, Sir Karl
1963   *Conjectures and Refutations.* London: Routledge & Kegan
         Paul.

Poulantzas, Nicos
1973   *Political Power and Social Classes.* London: New Left
         Books.

Pred, Allan
1981   "Power, Everyday Practice, and the Discipline of Human
         Geography." In *Space and Time in Geography,* edited by
         Allan Pred. Ser. 3, Human Geography #48. Lund, Sweden:
         Lund Studies in Geography.

Rabin, Yale
1980   "Federal Urban Transportation Policy and the Highway
         Planning Process in Metropolitan Areas." *Annals of the
         American Academy of Political and Social Science* 451
         (September): 421–435.

Rabinow, Paul, and William Sullivan, eds.
1979   *Interpretive Social Science: A Reader.* Berkeley and Los
         Angeles: University of California Press.

Rabinowitz, Francine
1969   *City Politics and Planning.* New York: Atherton Press.

Raiffa, Howard
1982   *The Art and Science of Negotiation.* Cambridge, Mass.:
         Harvard University Press.
1985   "Post-Settlement Settlements." *Negotiation Journal* 1:9–
         12.

Rein, Martin, and Donald Schön
1977   "Problem Setting in Policy Research." In *Using Social Re-
         search in Public Policy Making,* edited by Carol Weiss.
         Lexington, Mass.: Lexington Books.

Rich, Adrienne
1979   *On Lies, Secrets, and Silence: Selected Prose 1966–1978.*
         New York: W. W. Norton.

Ricoeur, Paul
1960   *Freud and Philosophy.* New Haven: Yale University Press.

1974   "Ethics and Culture: Habermas and Gadamer in Dialogue." In *Political and Social Essays*, edited by David Stewart and Joseph Bien. Athens: Ohio University Press.

Rieff, Robert
1974   "The Power of the Helping Professions." *Journal of Applied Behavioral Sciences* 10(3): 451–461.

Roche, Joseph
1981   "Plan Implementation: A Community Organization Approach to Health Planning." In *Citizens and Health Care: Participation and Planning for Social Change*, edited by Barry Checkoway. New York: Pergamon.

Rohr, John Anthony
1978   *Ethics for Bureaucrats*. New York: Marcel Dekker.

Rorty, Richard
1979   *Philosophy and the Mirror of Nature*. Princeton, N.J.: Princeton University Press.

Rothman, David, W. Gaylin, I. Glasser, and S. Marcus
1979   *Doing Good*. New York: Pantheon.

Roweis, Shoukry
1979   "Review of Manuel Castells' *City, Class and Power*." *International Journal of Urban and Regional Research* 3(4): 572–579.
1983   "Urban Planning as Professional Mediation of Territorial Politics." *Environment and Planning D: Society and Space* 1:139–162.
1988   "Knowledge-Power and Professional Practice." In *The Design Professions and the Built Environment*, edited by Paul Knox. London: Croom Helm.

Ryan, William
1976   *Blaming the Victim*. 2d ed. New York: Vintage.

Saunders, Peter
1979   *Urban Politics*. London: Hutchinson.

Schaar, John
1967   "Equality of Opportunity and Beyond." In *Nomos IX: Equality*, edited by J. R. Pennock and J. Chapman. New York: Atherton Press.
1981   *Legitimacy in the Modern State*. New Brunswick, N.J.: Transaction Books.

Schattschneider, E. E.
1960   *The Semi-Sovereign People: A Realist's View of Democracy in America*. New York: Holt, Rinehart & Winston.

Schoenbrud, David

1983   "Limits and Dangers of Environmental Mediation: A Review Essay." *New York University Law Review* 58:1453–1476.

Schön, Donald

1963   *The Displacement of Concepts.* London: Tavistock.

1971   *Beyond the Stable State.* New York: Random House.

1978   "Generative Metaphor." Typescript.

1982   "Some of What a Planner Knows." *Journal of the American Planning Association* 48:351–364.

1983   *The Reflective Practitioner: How Professionals Think in Action.* New York: Basic Books.

1987   *Educating the Reflective Practitioner.* San Francisco: Jossey-Bass.

Schroyer, Trent

1973   *The Critique of Domination.* Boston: Beacon.

Schutz, Alfred

1970   *Phenomenology and Social Relations.* Edited by H. Wagner. Chicago: University of Chicago Press.

Scott, James

1985   *Weapons of the Weak: Everyday Forms of Peasant Resistance.* New Haven: Yale University Press.

Searle, J.

1969   *Speech Acts: An Essay in the Philosophy of Language.* Cambridge: Cambridge University Press.

Seeley, J.

1963   "Social Science? Some Probative Problems." In *Sociology on Trial,* edited by M. Stein and A. Vidich. Englewood Cliffs, N.J.: Prentice-Hall.

Shapiro, Jeremy J.

1976   "Reply to Miller's Review of Habermas's *Legitimation Crisis.*" *Telos* 27 (Spring):170–176.

Siembieda, William J.

1979   "Environmental Appeals Boards: A Case Study of the Influence of Citizen Expertise on Local Environmental Decisions." *Journal of Architectural Research* 7:21–30.

Silverman, David

1970   *The Theory of Organizations.* London: Heinemann.

Simon, Herbert

1957   *Models of Man.* New York: Wiley & Sons.

1969   *The Sciences of the Artificial.* Cambridge, Mass.: MIT Press.

Simpson, Lorenzo C.
1986   "On Habermas and Particularity: Is There Room for Race and Gender on the Grassy Plains of Ideal Discourse?" *Praxis International* 6 : 328–340.
Singer, Benjamin
1977   "Incommunicado Social Machines." *Social Policy* 8 (November–December): 88–93.
Spurling, Laurie
1977   *Phenomenology and the Social World.* London: Routledge & Kegan Paul.
Steckler, Allan B., and William T. Herzog
1979   "How to Keep Your Mandated Citizen Board Out of Your Hair and Off Your Back: A Guide for Executive Directors." *American Journal of Public Health* 69(8) : 809–812.
Stone, Clarence
1980   "Systemic Power in Community Decision Making: A Restatement of Stratification Theory." *American Political Science Review* 74(4) : 978–990.
Susskind, Lawrence
1981   "Environmental Mediation and the Accountability Problem." *Vermont Law Review* 6 : 147.
Susskind, Lawrence, and J. Cruickshank
1987   *Breaking the Impasse.* New York: Basic Books.
Susskind, Lawrence, and Louise Dunlap
1981   "The Importance of Non-Objective Judgments in Environmental Impact Assessments." *Environmental Impact Assessment Review* 2 : 335–366.
Susskind, Lawrence, and Connie Ozawa
1983   "Mediated Negotiation in the Public Sector: Mediator Accountability and the Public Interest Problem." *American Behavioral Scientist* 27(2) : 255–279.
1984   "Mediated Negotiation in the Public Sector." *Journal of Planning Education and Research* 4(1) : 5–15.
Szanton, Peter
1981   *Not Well Advised.* New York: Russell Sage Foundation.
Tabb, William, and Larry Sawers, eds.
1978   *Marxism and the Metropolis: New Perspectives in Urban Political Economy.* New York: Oxford University Press.
Taylor, Charles
1971   "Interpretation and the Sciences of Man." *Review of Metaphysics* 25 : 3–51.

Teitz, Michael

1974 "Toward a Responsive Planning Methodology." In *Planning in America: Learning from Turbulence,* edited by David Godschalk. Washington, D.C.: American Institute of Planners.

Thompson, Edward P.

1980 *The Poverty of Theory.* London: Monthly Review Press.

Thompson, James D.

1967 *Organizations in Action.* New York: McGraw-Hill.

Thompson, James D., and A. Tuden

1959 "Strategies, Structures, and Processes of Organizational Decision." In *Comparative Studies in Administration,* edited by James D. Thompson. Pittsburgh: University of Pittsburgh Press.

Thompson, John B.

1984 *Studies in the Theory of Ideology.* Berkeley and Los Angeles: University of California Press.

Thompson, John B., and David Held, eds.

1982 *Habermas: Critical Debates.* Cambridge, Mass.: MIT Press.

Thrift, Nigel J.

1983 "On the Determination of Social Action in Space and Time." *Environment and Planning D: Society and Space* 2:23−58.

Titmuss, Richard

1968 *Commitment to Welfare.* London: George Allen & Unwin.

Toulmin, Stephen

1964 *The Uses of Argument.* Cambridge: Cambridge University Press.

Tribe, Laurence

1972 "Policy Science: Analysis or Ideology?" *Philosophy and Public Affairs* 2(1): 66−110.

1973 "Technology Assessment and the Fourth Discontinuity: The Limits of Instrumental Rationality." *Southern California Law Review* 46:617−660.

van Gunsteren, Herman

1976 "Constructing a City in Speech: Planning as Political Theory." In *Power and Political Theory,* edited by B. Barry. New York: Wiley & Sons.

Van Hooft, Stanley

1976 "Habermas's Communicative Ethics." *Social Praxis* 4: 147−175.

Vickers, Sir Geoffrey

1970   *Value Systems and Social Processes.* London: Pelican.

1973   "Communication and Ethical Judgment." In *Communication: Ethical and Moral Issues,* edited by L. Thayer. London: Gordon and Breach.

1984   *The Art of Judgment.* New York: Harper & Row.

1987   *Policy-Making, Communication, and Social Learning.* Edited by Guy Adams, John Forester, and Bayard Catron. New Brunswick, N.J.: Transaction Books.

Wachs, Martin, ed.

1985   *Ethics in Planning.* New Brunswick, N.J.: Center for Urban Policy Research, Rutgers University.

Walzer, Michael

1980   *Radical Principles.* New York: Basic Books.

1983   "The Politics of Michel Foucault." *Dissent* (Fall): 481–490.

Wardhaugh, Ronald

1985   *How Conversation Works.* New York: Basil Blackwell.

Watzlawick, Paul

1976   *How Real Is Real?* New York: Vintage.

Watzlawick, Paul, Janet Beavin, and Don Jackson

1967   *Pragmatics of Human Communication.* New York: W. W. Norton.

Webber, Melvin M.

1963   "Comprehensive Planning and Social Responsibility: Toward an AIP Consensus on the Profession's Roles and Purposes." *Journal of the American Institute of Planners* 29: 232–241.

Webber, Melvin, and H. Rittel

1973   "Dilemmas in a General Theory of Planning." *Policy Sciences* 4:155–169.

Weick, Karl

1969   *The Social Psychology of Organizing.* Reading, Mass.: Addison-Wesley.

Wellmer, Albrecht

1974   *Critical Theory of Society.* New York: Seabury.

Whiteman, John

1983   "Dramatic Decisions: An Essay on Design and Decision Theory in Planning." Prepared for the National Conference of the Association of Collegiate Schools of Planning, San Francisco, 20–22 October.

Wiggins, D.

1978   "Deliberation and Practical Reason." In *Practical Reason-*

ing, edited by Joseph Raz. New York: Oxford University Press.

Wildavsky, Aaron

1972   "The Self-Evaluating Organization." *Public Administration Review* 32(5): 509–520.

1979   *Speaking Truth to Power: The Art and Craft of Policy Analysis.* New York: Little, Brown.

Wilensky, Harold

1967   *Organizational Intelligence.* New York: Basic Books.

Winner, Langdon

1977   *Autonomous Technology.* Cambridge, Mass.: MIT Press.

1986   *The Whale and the Reactor: A Search for Limits in an Age of High Technology.* Chicago: University of Chicago Press.

Wolfe, Alan

1974   "New Directions in the Marxist Theory of Politics." *Politics and Society* 4(2):131–159.

1977   *The Limits of Legitimacy.* New York: Free Press.

Yates, Douglas

1985   *The Politics of Management.* San Francisco: Jossey-Bass.

Zartman, I. William, and S. Touval

1985   "International Mediation: Conflict Resolution and Power Politics." *Journal of Social Issues* 41:27–45.

Index

Action, communicative: and anticipation, 246n.3; and attention-shaping, 141–143, 211n.8, 237n.3; and communicative ethics, 239n.19, 240n.23, 242n.30; as essential to identify conflict, 143; and interpretation of roles, 180; meta-communication in, 244n.46; and mutual understanding, 144; nonverbal, 238n.12, 243n.40, 244n.46; structure of, 143–147, 238n.13; and technology, 243n.41; testing, 180; theory of, in practice, 169; threats in, 239n.15; as vulnerable to structural distortion, 140. *See also* Organizational diagnosis; Reproduction; Speech
—content and context as dimensions of, 145–147; and expressive claims, 146, 223n.13, 239n.21; and factual claims, 145, 223n.13, 239n.21; and legitimacy claims, 146, 223n.13, 239n.21; and rhetorical claims, 145, 223n.13, 239n.21
Advocacy planning. *See* Planners Network; Planning
Alexander, Christopher, 166
Alexander, Ernest, 237n.3
Ambiguity: and appreciation, 233n.18; avoidance of, 110, 240n.25; in decision making, 53; in design, 124, 125–126; of goals, errors, success, 15; and ideology, 63; as inescapable in politics and speech, 211n.10; of interests, 230n.5; interpreted in listening, 109–110, 111; necessitating theory for decision making, 63; systematic presence of, in social action, 240n.25; and uncertainty, distinguished, 240n.25

Anticipation: of citizens' interests, 87; of constraints on decision making, 63; and context, 116, 126; of different skills in developers and residents, 86–87; and entering a virtual world, 197–198; as essential to counter distorted communications, 23, 145, 220n.21; and expectation, distinguished, 198; and failure to anticipate power, 27; institutional, in classroom, 186; learning in, 164, 201–208; of manipulation, ideology, bias, 113; of misinformation, 43–47, 220n.21, 232n.11; of misinformation, in progressive view of planning, 31, 33; of modes of power, 46; research to inform, 158; structure of, 164, 198–199, 207–208, 246n.3; of technical and practical requirements, 80; and theory of context, 63–64. *See also* Judgment; Learning; Listening; Practice; Strategies, mediated negotiation
—of power, 46; constraining design, 120, 130–132; in organizations, 76–78, 80–81; and rational action, 59–62. *See also* Hegemony; Power
Appreciative skills, 126. *See also* Judgment; Listening
Arendt, Hannah, 218n.43, 239n.14
Argumentation: and account of planning practice, 13; and action, 18–22, 199–201; in anticipation in practice, 164, 198; as communicative, attention-organizing, 11, 138–139; and democratic talk, 211n.13; as essential in planning practice, 5, 199–201; and ethics, 22–24; and focus of research,

Compositor: G&S Typesetters, Inc.
Printer: Maple-Vail Book Mfg. Group
Binder: Maple-Vail Book Mfg. Group
Text: 11/13 Sabon
Display: Sabon